REX HARRISON

REX HARRISON

by

Allen Eyles

W.H. ALLEN · LONDON
1985

Typeset by Phoenix Photosetting, Chatham
Printed and bound in Great Britain by
Mackays of Chatham Ltd, Kent
for the Publishers, W.H. Allen & Co. PLC
44 Hill Street, London W1X 8LB

ISBN 0 491 03901 8

4031

Contents

Acknowledgments   vii
1   Light Comedy's Master   1
2   A Lancashire Lad   11
3   A Contract with Korda   21
4   The War Years   37
5   Five for Fox   55
6   Escape from Hollywood   77
7   Enter Henry Higgins   91
8   From Sloane Square to Cinecittà   109
9   The Film of *My Fair Lady*   117
10 The Movie Star   129
11 Going with the Times   143
12 Full Circle   161
Theatre   171
Cinema and Television   193
Bibliography   231
Index   233

Acknowledgments

Particular thanks to Bernard Hrusa-Marlow, Tom Vallance, Alvin H. Marill, Mr and Mrs Gatt of Hokushin Video (distributors of *Shalimar*, for the kind loan of a cassette), Gillian Hartnoll and the British Film Institute's Library Services (for access to its far recesses), Jackie Morris and the National Film Archive (for viewings of rare Harrison films), and to my wife Lesley. The Mander and Mitchenson Theatre Collection provided the illustration from *French Without Tears*; other illustrations came from the National Film Archive or private collections and all were originally issued for publicity purposes.

1
Light Comedy's Master

'If you weren't the best light comedian in the country, all you'd be fit for is selling cars in Great Portland Street.'

Noel Coward to Rex Harrison, circa 1950

'THE MASTER OF LIGHT COMEDY' – THAT IS BOUND TO BE THE final snap summation of Rex Harrison, the actor. And it is certainly true, although the words carry their own in-built qualification: is that all? It still seems wrong to take light comedy as seriously as heavy drama, if only because it tends to be enjoyed more readily and is less demanding intellectually. We know really that comedy is at least as difficult to perform as heavy drama – but the problem is that nothing spoils comedy more than taking that into account while watching it. Even more than tragic drama, the obtrusive artifice of the musical encourages appreciation of performing skill while it is being watched – which is one reason why, for the vast majority of the world audience, Harrison is remembered first and foremost for his stage and screen portrayals of Henry Higgins in *My Fair Lady*, in which, fortunately, his comic gifts were to the fore as well as his unique way with a song.

Another complication is that Harrison's career is hard to digest. It is inconsistent. His stage work is split between Broadway and the West End, so that he hasn't

1

registered as a steady fixture in either country. His screen career has been divided between Hollywood and London in the same way, and he hasn't worked regularly with many important directors. He has spent long periods working exclusively or primarily for one medium or the other, but not (since the war) in one place.

However, there are some constants in his career. There is his acting style, which hasn't changed. It involves underplaying – giving an impression of being relaxed and natural. He has rarely put on heavy character make-up or played historical characters, and he has hardly ever varied his accent or manner of speech.

'When you do what I usually do – act in my own suit, so to speak – you are much more *exposed*,' says Harrison. 'Audiences seldom understand that. They think if a performance looks "natural" it can't involve much effort. If they can see how terribly hard an actor is working, they feel it must be a great performance.' And: 'It still annoys me that because I go in for a kind of inner energy instead of ranting and raving, people think it's just me, drifting along and not really working at it.' There are numerous testimonials to the hard work that Harrison actually puts in, such as the comments of John Van Druten, after directing him in *Bell, Book and Candle*: 'I think Harrison is probably the most brilliant actor I've ever worked with. He is fantastically meticulous. He will pause to think out every suggestion, and then try it over and over again until he's satisfied. He will even try out whether to put his weight on his toes, heel or ball of foot when he is turning and delivering a line.'

Harrison learned his craft in the era of gentleman actors, and was influenced by the relaxed naturalism of stage stars like Sir Gerald du Maurier (1873–1934), Sir Charles Hawtrey (1858–1923), Sir Seymour Hicks (1871–1949), Ralph Lynn (1881–1962) and Ronald Squire

2

(1886–1958). They were the popular figures of the time, remembered by Harrison as 'these rather elegant men who acted not like actors, but like drawing-room types – they made you believe they had just popped into the theatre for a spot of acting on the way to the club'. Rex picked up the knack of looking at ease in a dinner jacket, opening and closing the inevitable French windows, and manipulating a cigarette case in the best du Maurier manner. He learned to speak well and to throw away his lines with the best of them, because that was necessary to succeed.

So he became typecast in the sort of play that, as a fellow actor put it, called on him to balance a cup of tea in one hand and a Duchess in the other. His great natural gift was timing – 'so superb it hurts' (to quote Deborah Kerr). But he has been stuck with this over-riding impression of urbanity and affluence. As Irma Kutz has observed, 'The single thing which it is difficult to imagine Harrison being, or pretending to be, is poor.'

His difficulty as regards his stage career was that he came in at the tail end of the drawing-room comedies. According to Harrison, they had appealed 'because the audiences themselves were living the same sort of lives as the actors were depicting – they had butlers, they had servants and they dressed for dinner. They had little intrigues amongst themselves which were blown up into enormous dramas.' Certainly, by the 1960s authors and audiences had completely changed and were no longer interested in the lives of Dukes and Duchesses except perhaps as targets for savage ridicule, and Harrison has had problems locating worthwhile and suitable contemporary material – hence his penchant for revivals. In old age, his patrician style has also been of limited usefulness to the cinema. Despite John Gielgud's Oscar for *Arthur*, Harrison says (a little tartly, one imagines), 'I have no especial desire to play butlers in films.'

A second constant in Harrison's work is the use of humour. 'I've always tried to infuse comedy into everything I've done,' he declares. 'To be serious through an entire evening would bore me. I'm sure if I'd played Ibsen that I'd have tried to find some humour somewhere.' And: 'I've played Julius Caesar and Pope Julius and I wouldn't call them comedy roles exactly. I try to extract what humour there is because it's so goddamn boring if you don't. Actors who don't find the humour in their parts are sometimes tragically dull.' It is simpler to choose parts that are essentially humorous. 'If I have to make the final commitment I'll probably choose to do comedy rather than heavy drama. To me comedy is more truthful than drama. Great emotional feeling is required to make comedy work. Drama can be acted and blurred without great emotional feeling and you can get away with it. You can employ the gimmick in drama. It's impossible with comedy.'

A further constant has been Harrison's refusal to play Shakespeare (a probable cause, in some observers' opinions, of his lack of a knighthood). He recalls that the classical actor was very much on the wane when he began acting: 'Shakespeare wasn't very fashionable then. He was done mostly in the provinces and there were no heroes in the Shakespeare field for me to look up to.'

'It's a purely British conception, designed to glorify Shakespeare, that actors must measure themselves against the great parts,' he told Barry Norman in 1972. 'If I'd been born a Frenchman I could have measured myself against Molière very well. But, except for Ben Jonson, we have no comedy writers of quite his stature.' And, in other interviews: 'I've never been drawn to the Tudor poets. I find the comedy terribly contrived and heavy. I think Shakespeare's comedies are absolutely abominable. Some of the clowns are unbearable. I much

4

prefer Jonson as a playwright – he has an element of the satiric that I like very much. I think the great Shakespeare roles are marvellous but you have to come to them very young. And I suppose I was born much more equipped to play Molière than Shakespeare.'

Only once, in late 1962–early 1963, under the influence of his actress wife, Rachel Roberts, did he succumb to Shakespeare to the extent of doing a sound recording of *Much Ado About Nothing* as Benedick to her Beatrice, and then he tried to make the verse sound as much like prose as possible. (The record was issued in the summer of 1963.) As will be mentioned later, another actress wife, Kay Kendall, might also have overcome his objection to the Bard had she lived.

There is one eminent playwright whose work Harrison *has* constantly embraced – George Bernard Shaw. He knew Shaw slightly, enjoyed his respect as an actor, and has frequently revived his work – it was not just self-protection that, in agreeing to turn *Pygmalion* into *My Fair Lady*, he made contractual provision for key scenes to be retained. Harrison may well be assessed by future theatre historians as the best Shavian performer of our time (and not only in Shaw's plays).

However, coming generations are likely to be as interested in Rex Harrison himself as in his performances on stage or screen. He has led a spectacular private life. In the first place, there is his reputation for temperament. He is not alone, of course, in being thought of as notoriously difficult to work or live with. His good friend Alan Jay Lerner refers to 'a unique approach to human relations'. Joseph L. Mankiewicz, director of four of his films, is quoted as saying, 'He gives everybody problems and he knows it. Everybody knows it.' And Reginald Beck, co-director of one of his lesser films, declares with what sounds like gentlemanly understatement, 'His whole manner is inclined to be offensive.'

But there is the other side of it. Frederick Loewe, composer of *My Fair Lady*, says, 'No one who is a perfectionist is easy to work with. He did everything over and over again – relentlessly.' Vincente Minnelli, who directed Rex and his wife Kay Kendall in *The Reluctant Debutante*, declared: 'I cannot say too much in praise of the Harrisons. They are real troupers. Hard work is their food, their drink, their relaxation. They were an inspiration to cast and crew alike.' And Gene Tierney sounds almost disappointed to record in her autobiography, *Self-Portrait*: 'I saw no sign of Rex Harrison's famous temper. He was always studying his lines, concentrating.'

In his book *The Street Where I Live*, Alan Jay Lerner describes Harrison as 'a human thermostat who changes the temperature of every room he enters, turning summer to winter or ice to steam in a matter of seconds.' And: 'Rex is a man of charm and the unexpected. The most idle remark can suddenly produce a tempest of vituperation that flashes and thunders and passes like a summer storm.'

Harrison admitted to journalist David Lewin in 1961: 'Off-stage I can be far from charming. I am acid. Acid. I have a direct tongue and I say what I think is the truth and I don't give a damn for the consequences.' And he told another journalist, Roderick Mann, ten years later: 'I've still got a temper. I still blow my top. It's part of my character, I suppose. But a lot of that reputation came from the fact that I wasn't very happy. Anyway, I like to think that phlegmatic people can't act as well as temperamental ones.'

But it is, of course, his relationships with women that have attracted the most interest. In this case, his image as a debonair screen lover seems to have become hopelessly blurred and entangled in the public imagination with his personal history. No less than three of his six wives have given us written reminiscences of life with Rex. The suicide of Carole Landis involved him in one of the biggest episodes of Hollywood scandal-mongering. He is – and always will be – 'Sexy Rexy'. Not only has he been typecast in the Casanova mould, but he has contributed to the general impression himself – in the parts he has chosen to play, in beginning his 1974 autobiography *Rex* with an account of his first romantic urge at the age of six, by editing an anthology of love poems, *If Love Be Love* (1979), and by living the kind of life he has.

The appeal he holds for women is well documented. As his second wife, Lilli Palmer, puts it, 'If you're a woman, you know that he knows what it's all about.' And his fifth wife, Elizabeth Harris, has written: 'I found Rex enormously attractive. He enjoy's women's company and his charm, at times, can be overwhelming. I noticed that very few women were unaware of his presence.'

The number of his marriages is hardly unusual in show business – consider Mickey Rooney, Henry Fonda or Elizabeth Taylor for starters, or his good friend Alan Jay Lerner whose eighth wife, Liz Robertson, makes an apposite comment regarding her husband: 'Who would have paid the slightest attention to the fact that he had a string of mistresses? No one. But Alan marries the girls he wants to live with . . . so he makes the news.' Likewise Rex Harrison, who has said, 'I'm a marrying man . . . by that I mean I've never been interested in casual relationships with women.' He also adds, 'I don't like women who are importunate. I like to do my own "chasing", if that is the word.' Admitting to a hatred of being on his own, he has always needed female companionship but, queried as to what he would ask for if he could be born again, his fifth wife, Elizabeth Harris, quotes him as replying: 'Not to be so damned dependent on women.'

Being married to actresses and other figures in the limelight inevitably increases the interest of the gossip columnists, and rows and separations can be much more conspicuous when both parties have access to the media. In Harrison's case, he has been drawn towards women of volatile character, more than likely to sound off in public. He says, 'I don't look for placid relationships with women. That bores me very quickly.' After a first marriage to a young socialite, Collette Thomas, Rex wed three actresses: Lilli Palmer (1943–57), Kay Kendall (1957–59), and Rachel Roberts (1962–71). In 1968 Harrison was commenting, 'I can't imagine being married to anyone except an actress. You must discuss things with someone who knows what you are talking about and understands the problems. It helps so much to have a wife in the same profession.'

Harrison has been wonderfully complimentary about his wives during each marriage and has rarely if ever offered any public criticism of them afterwards. But there were inevitable conflicts in marriages to actress wives with their own careers to pursue or with the strain of subordinating their talents to staying alongside Rex. When he married a non-actress, Mercia Tinker, his present wife, he remarked, 'After five marriages, I have learned a lot. I used to think actors should marry actresses but now I see that is garbage. Actors should be married to wives. From now on, I hope to lead a quiet home life with occasional travel for plays and films.' The travel has proved to be more than occasional but the home life has been frustratingly quiet for the Fleet Street hacks.

In writing this book, I have often incorporated Rex Harrison's quoted comments at the time events happened or shortly afterwards. His views may have changed since then (as indeed they have about the ideal marriage partner), and they may even have been misquoted at the time – but they may provide alternative or additional insights to Harrison's more considered reflections in his 1974 autobiography, *Rex*, which I hope the reader will seek out if it hasn't been enjoyed already. This book concentrates on his career – the theatre performances as others saw them at the time, the film work as it appears to me now.

2
A Lancashire Lad

TO LIVERPOOL WE OWE NOT ONLY THE BEATLES, BUT ALSO Rex Harrison. There was no silver spoon in his mouth but it was a comfortable middle-class environment into which he was born on Thursday, 5 March 1908 in the small town of Huyton, now an eastern suburb of Liverpool (and best known as the Parliamentary seat of former prime minister Harold Wilson). The young Harrison's parents had no connection with show business, except that his mother was said to possess some of the blood of the famous nineteenth-century actor, Edmund Kean (while, if you care to place any importance on it, his date of birth places him under the most artistic of astrological signs, Pisces). He followed two sisters, Marjorie and Sylvia, and was named Reginald Carey Harrison but insisted at an early age on being called Rex ('I heard someone calling for the dog and thought it sounded nice.').

Rex's father, William Reginald Harrison, was some sort of wholesaler connected to the Liverpool Stock Exchange. During the First World War, he moved the family to Sheffield while he worked for a steel firm which was making armour. Young Rex was a sickly boy – it seems that he suffered from tuberculosis of the intestines which cured itself in time, while a severe case of the measles permanently deprived him of most of the sight in his left eye.

He went to prep schools and had some private tuition but later described himself as 'a seedy child, unbright, dull, good at nothing except a bit of cricket'. His parents returned to Liverpool – this time to the Sefton Park district on the northern side – and Rex concluded his formal education by attending Liverpool College for five years, playing more cricket (he was a good left-handed bowler) and developing a passion for the theatre. His parents had often taken him to the theatres of Liverpool and now he participated in the annual school productions. In *A Midsummer Night's Dream*, he was Flute and Thisbe; in *The Blue Bird*, the Maurice Maeterlinck fantasy, he was the Cat, dressed up in a velvety suit.

Ambition was born. He would not become an office clerk or trainee solicitor. He would go on the stage. His father knew someone on the board of the Liverpool Playhouse and Rex was given an interview with the director, William Armstrong.

At this time, the Playhouse had a considerable reputation, both for new plays and revivals. Perhaps because it had to be financially self-supporting, it favoured comedy. The sixteen-year-old Rex was accepted as a student in 1924.

'You were paid thirty shillings a week to understudy and watch,' Harrison later recalled. 'And you took what you were given, which would be all manner of parts; often, in those days, boys of sixteen played the parts of men of sixty. Actors had to learn to play all parts. It's not quite like it is today; then young men in rep had to learn their jobs.' The budding actor was first summoned to participate in a one-act curtain raiser, *Thirty Minutes in a*

Street, playing the small part of a distraught father. 'I had one speech in the play,' he remembers. 'I was to dash on stage and yell "Fetch a doctor. It's the baby!" I rehearsed it for days and then on opening night I was so excited I shouted, "Fetch a baby. It's the doctor!"'

Shaw, Galsworthy, Barrie and Harold Brighouse (of *Hobson's Choice* fame) were prominent among the authors whose work was performed, while Diana Wynyard, Cecil Parker, Sebastian Shaw and Hugh Williams were some of the leading players in the resident company during the two and a half years that Harrison spent at the Playhouse (which, in 1985, is still with us in Williamson Square). His own acting appearances were confined to such minor parts as a footman in Galsworthy's *Old English*, a messenger in John Drinkwater's *Abraham Lincoln*, and blacked-up as the native boy Jimmy Kanaka in the British premiere presentation of Eugene O'Neill's now obscure play, *Gold*.

Eventually, Harrison felt confident enough to offer his services to the actor-managers of London's West End – and sufficiently self-assured to ignore William Armstrong's parting advice that he seek another profession, even though (as he puts it in his autobiography) he only amounted to 'a spotty provincial boy from Liverpool with no classical training'. He had some luck with Jevan Brandon-Thomas, who was playing the juvenile lead of Jack Chesney in a revival of his father's 1892 farce *Charley's Aunt* on the West End stage. It had been decided to send out a touring company in 1927 and Brandon Thomas's son recommended Harrison for the Jack Chesney role. He was engaged at £12 per week, and followed this with tours in other plays such as *Potiphar's Wife*, *Alibi*, *The Chinese Bungalow* and *A Cup of Kindness*, never getting closer to the West End than some of the theatres in the London suburbs.

There was other work to be had on the outskirts of

town – at the film studios where a British quota obligation on distributors and cinema owners stimulated much of the production activity. He turned out for a small part in a football romp called *The Great Game* and sweated under intense lighting for an early colour film of Sheridan's *The School for Scandal* in a walk-on that didn't rate a mention in the credits.

He finally made his debut on Shaftesbury Avenue in the autumn of 1930 when the Old Vic actor Baliol Holloway mounted a rare West End production of Shakespeare, *Richard III*, for which Harrison was assigned several bits. By this time, the actor had become so used to playing sophisticated contemporary parts it was joked that during the performance he answered a question about the time by lifting the chain mail to look at his watch. He much preferred playing a very minor part in the modern comedy *Getting George Married* a few weeks later out at the Everyman Theatre, Hampstead, a former drill hall that was shortly to become a distinguished repertory cinema.

His first real West End part was in February 1931 as an American detective in an imported thriller, *The Ninth Man*, by Frederick Jackson, in which he helped smash an opium-smuggling racket and was allowed by the director, Campbell Gullan, to embroider his part with touches of eccentric behaviour. It paid off, because the eminent theatre critic of *The Sunday Times*, James Agate, after acknowledging that 'a competent cast . . . did all that was possible with the material', added: 'The second detective, whose name escapes me, did rather more by introducing us to a new face, a new personality, and at the moment a new method of entertaining us.' This wretchedly vague compliment didn't help Harrison's 'new face' to catch on in the West End (nor did *The Stage*'s remark that he was 'commendably brisk and energetic') and he was glad of a few months' steady work with a

14

Cardiff repertory company. He concluded 1931 in the touring company of John Van Druten's play *After All*.

In 1932, he toured in *Other Men's Wives* and *For the Love of Mike* (in the latter, a Bobby Howes musical in which he took over co-star Arthur Riscoe's part, he sang for the first time on stage with 'The Prisoner's Song'), then he came back to the West End but only as the understudy to Herbert Marshall in *Another Language*, a play by Rose Franken. In 1933 he travelled in *Road House* and *Mother of Pearl*. He filled in with other work and at least one hotel maître d' was later to recall that Harrison had made an excellent temporary waiter.

He also did more film work in a couple of quota quickies. He appeared in *Leave It to Blanche*, a marital comedy starring Henry Kendall and featuring Harrison very peripherally as a character called Ronnie. He was more effective in a romantic comedy, *Get Your Man*, playing the secretary to a toothpaste magnate. His function in the plot was to run away with the daughter (Kay Walsh) of a dentifrice rival on the day she is supposed to marry his boss's son (Sebastian Shaw, whom he'd known as a star at the Liverpool Playhouse). Dorothy Boyd, the real star of the film, then had a clear field to rush in and get her man with the collapse of his arranged wedding.

Harrison himself was now wed, to Collette Thomas, and living in a small flat in a Mayfair Mews. He was not anxious to go on tour and he found West End roles in a quick flop, *No Way Back* (a turgid melodrama, about a young woman driven to suicide, in which his part was too minor to attract attention), and in a Repertory Players production, *Our Mutual Father*, given a single Sunday night performance in the hope of interesting managements in taking it for a proper run. It was a comedy: he, Ronald Simpson and Basil Radford played three sons summoned to the country house of their 76-year-old father who is thought to be dying – in fact, it was the play that died.

It reflects his standing at the time that he could get a starring role but only out at the Fulham Shilling Theatre in West London (where *No Way Back* had started life earlier in the year). The play was *Anthony and Anna*, yet another comedy and one that had originally been staged at the Liverpool Playhouse while he was there in 1926. Harrison was in his element playing Anthony, a glib, impudent, overbearing type who is allergic to work but occasionally hires himself out as a guest to make up numbers at luncheons, dinners or weekend parties. Anna (played by Carol Goodner), the daughter of an American millionaire, falls in love with him and coaxes him into marriage and management of an inn she buys after he has demanded an outright sum with no strings attached from her father if he takes her on. The play and Harrison received good reviews and a West End transfer was on the cards but, in a further sad indication of Harrison's status at this time, the author, St John G. Ervine, adamantly refused to permit its move to another theatre until a leading man of greater stature was found (it took a year before the play opened at the Whitehall Theatre with Harold Warrender as Anthony).

On 29 January 1935 the Harrisons had a son whom they named Noel. Rex was working on another minor film comedy, *All at Sea*, which starred Tyrrell Davis as a young clerk who uses a legacy of £500 to go on a pleasure cruise and runs into Harrison as one Aubrey Bellingham, who becomes his chief rival for the affections of the heroine, played by Googie Withers. It is the first of Harrison's films known to survive, a single print having been taken into the National Film Archive in 1971 because of his presence and that of Googie Withers, although no viewing copy has yet been made, so it languishes unseen. One contemporary review that bothers to mention Harrison merely comments that he 'overacts', so perhaps *All at Sea* is best left in the vaults undisturbed.

The stage director Campbell Gullan gave Harrison another chance to show his worth in a new West End production, *Man of Yesterday*, starring Leslie Banks. After that it was back to the provinces, touring in the farces *Not Quite a Lady* and *The Wicked Flee*. It was with some relief and rather more astonishment that he was cast in the august company of Marie Tempest, Sybil Thorndyke and A. E. Matthews in the first play by Robert Morley, a slick comedy called *Short Story*, directed by the young Tyrone Guthrie. He played a middle-aged American producer, Mark Kurt.

During the run he also participated in another Sunday performance by the Repertory Players, *Charity Begins*, a comedy which was staged by Henry Kendall. Here he was an architect, separated from his wife, who urged a nice young lady (Cathleen Cordell) to run off with him (her family persuade her to stay and make do with the decent chap played by Nigel Patrick). In his 1960 auto-biography, *I Remember Romano's*, Kendall maintains that Harrison hated the part and wanted to give it up but was persuaded to stay. 'It was just as well he did because on the strength of that performance he got his first big break in pictures.' In fact, Harrison's next two plays had far more to do with his film breakthrough.

Tyrone Guthrie wanted Rex to appear in his Broadway production of *Sweet Aloes*, which had already been a hit in London with Diana Wynyard and was to star Evelyn Laye in America. Harrison was released from *Short Story* to make the trip, his first abroad. 'I was flat broke,' Harrison recalled. 'Our fares were paid, but I had to borrow money to land with, the ten pounds the immi-gration people insist on.' The play was a tear-jerker with Miss Laye as the English Lord's mistress who bears his

17

child but allows it to be brought up by his barren wife (Joyce Carey, who also wrote the play under a pseudonym). Harrison appeared as the Englishman, Tubbs Barrow, who knows the secret and years later arranges for the disturbed mother to meet her son. The little light relief in the play was largely in Harrison's hands. *Sweet Aloes* had an encouraging reception out of town but it was shot down by the New York critics, many of whom singled out Harrison as the sole object of praise. The part of Tubbs Barrow has remained one of his favourites.

The play lingered on Broadway for three weeks, solely to enable the movie studios to get a look at it. Warner Bros. liked what it saw and snapped it up for a Kay Francis vehicle (*Give Me Your Heart*, which reverted back to *Sweet Aloes* for British release). 'I got nibbles from MGM and Warners,' Harrison told journalist Freda Bruce Lockhart in 1937. 'Warners wanted me to play the same part in the film. I made a test and they took a thirty days' option on me. Before the thirty days were up the play was off. I couldn't afford to stay on, even if I'd felt like risking it. So I came straight home.' Roland Young took Harrison's role in the film version.

Back in London, Harrison was greatly relieved to be offered a strong part in an audacious new comedy, *Heroes Don't Care* (which he recalls as the work of two old ladies in Australia). Harrison played Tom Gregory, a member of an Arctic expedition who gets cold feet even before he reaches the Polar regions and delays the party by seducing the glamorous wife (Carol Goodner) of the pompous leader (Felix Aylmer). Audiences laughed at the stuffed shirt and sided with Harrison, who was using the same brand of ingratiating charm he would bring to films like *The Rake's Progress*. They also supported him in his reluctance to yield his place on the expedition to the bossy aviatrix (Coral Browne) who is seeking new fields of adventure. Harrison pinpoints it as one of the first anti-hero parts and it so clearly demonstrated his magnetic personality that on 11 June 1936, the morning after the opening night, a representative of Alexander Korda contacted Harrison to see if he might be interested in signing a contract with Korda's London Films. Even though Korda was the pre-eminent producer of quality films in Britain, Rex was more taken with the size of the remuneration offered – £2,500 a year – and the security of a long-term contract. Unlike a Hollywood offer, it did not prevent him from continuing with his stage career. It was common practice for stars to work on films during the day and appear on the West End stage at nights. However, the deal meant that any earnings from stage work would go to Korda, who could also loan him out to other film producers in slack periods. It was still the best offer Harrison had had to date and he wisely accepted it.

3
A Contract with Korda

ALEXANDER KORDA DID NOT KEEP HIS LATEST ACQUISITION
waiting long. By August 1936, Harrison was out at the
producer's newly built Denham Studios working on a
romantic drama then called *Triangle* but later retitled *Men
Are Not Gods*. Miriam Hopkins was the star, having come
over from Hollywood for her role as the newspaper
drama critic's secretary who becomes the mistress of a
celebrated actor currently starring in *Othello*. Sebastian
Shaw played the thespian and Gertrude Lawrence completed the triangle as his jealous wife and stage Desdemona. The climax of the film has Othello trying to kill
Desdemona for real during a performance until the
screams of Miriam Hopkins from the gallery bring him to
his senses. (Ronald Colman later played another mur-
derous Othello in *A Double Life* and won an Oscar. The
screams that save the day were probably suggested by
Hitchcock's *The Man Who Knew Too Much*.)

Harrison had the fringe part of the newspaper obitu-
arist who adores Miriam Hopkins. As in the case of *The
Ninth Man*, he seems to have persuaded the director
(here, the German émigré Walter Reisch) to let him add

21

colour to a potentially dreary role. He turns his character into a brash, immature, wildly enthusiastic figure, who first bursts in without knocking on A. E. Matthews, playing the theatre critic – he is eager for more space to write his obits, will Matthews oblige and write less? He uses his long, lanky frame to balance ludicrously in the office doorway; he loses his money in slot machines (his other passion besides Miss Hopkins) and practically leaps over the bars on a counter to squeeze an advance out of the newspaper's cashier. He waits in Miriam's doorway late one night for her to return home from a date with the great actor, then after she's gone inside he recites Shakespeare to her loudly from the middle of the street until he is showered by rotten fruit and arrested. She regards him as mad as a hatter and never takes him seriously. He hardly participates in the later stages of the film although Hopkins uses him to deliver her handwritten note of farewell to the actor and he hovers there with a grin on his face, aware of its contents, extracting all the satisfaction he can from the turn of events, telling Sebastian Shaw: 'I'm waiting to see your famous face after you've read the letter.' He is last observed learning from A. E. Matthews that Hopkins has gone to see *Othello* for one last time and he isn't brought back at the end to comfort her after Shaw has been forgiven and taken back by his wife.

'I thought I was foul in *Men Are Not Gods*,' maintained Harrison a year or so later in an interview with Freda Bruce Lockhart. 'Of course, I knew nothing about film acting. I'd done nothing but some quota quickies. The director wanted pace from my part. So I gabbled my head off and really hardly knew what I was doing.' Seen today, though, Harrison's performance brims with assurance. He only needed a less asinine character to make a better impression.

At this time, Harrison was invited to appear in a new

play, *French Without Tears*, written by the then little-known Terence Rattigan. It was a modest production, put on by Bronson Albery to fill a gap at the Criterion Theatre; it had one set and its youthful cast lacked box-office names. Harrison was offered the top salary of £25 a week (except, of course, that it went to Korda). He hesitated. 'I am always indecisive at the beginning of anything and I spend a lot of time making up my mind,' he has said. In the case of *French Without Tears*, he kept Albery dangling while he thought it over, before deciding in favour. The first reading took place on 15 October 1936. The director was Harold French. Gloom set in before the play opened on Friday, 6 November 1936, and some of the backers were desperate to unload their interest. Not all the papers bothered to review it, others thought little of its prospects, and initial advertising was minimal, but somehow *French Without Tears* took off to become the biggest comedy hit of the Thirties, running for 1,039 performances and occupying Harrison's evenings for the next two years, during which time he shot five more films during the day.

The play dealt with a bunch of privileged, sex-starved young men installed in a South of France boarding house to cram up on their French, with Kay Hammond in the spicy role of the heartless man-eater who totally disrupts their studies (Paramount bought the film rights as ideal material for Marlene Dietrich). Trevor Howard played the predatory female's brother, and Harrison, Guy Middleton, Roland Culver and Robert Flemyng were the aroused students.

Even without the play, Harrison's career was gaining momentum. In the same month as the play opened he went to work on his best screen role yet: a romantic lead opposite Vivien Leigh in *Storm in a Teacup*. It introduced Harrison to a more understanding film director, Victor Saville, who helped him relax in front of the cameras without restraining his penchant for eccentric comic behaviour.

Storm in a Teacup cast Harrison as a newspaper reporter, Frank Burdon, who arrives in the Scottish west coast town of Baikie to take up a job on the local rag. Left in charge of filling a page with the views of the pompous, over-bearing local Provost Gow (Cecil Parker), who dictates every word and corrects the page proof, Harrison impulsively scraps the text and reports the man's callous indifference towards the distress of an Irish tinker (Sara Allgood) whose mongrel dog is to be put down because she didn't pay the licence fee. The Provost is standing in a by-election as the candidate for a new nationalist party and has designs on being the first prime minister of Scotland. The populace is stirred by Harrison's article into disrupting a town hall address by the Provost and Harrison later organises a canine demonstration that hilariously wrecks a dinner attended by Parker's political backers.

It falls on Harrison to deliver the film's message. Accused of having discredited the Provost in exchange for a bribe, he grips the back of a chair and fiercely lectures him: 'Listen, Mr Gow, you're not a bad chap at heart but you've got to remember one thing: the people of this country are the most long-suffering on God's earth. They'll put up with humbug, hypocrisy, shilly-shallying and hardship, they'll pull in their belts if they think it's their duty, they'll go to the four corners of the earth and get blown to bits if needs be. But two things they will not stand – bullying and cruelty. And if you've forgotten that, I'll make it my business to remind you!' Put on trial and charged with corruption, Harrison again denounces the Provost in court. The whole of the British press take up the story and turn it into a 'national entertainment'. Comparable in thrust (if not in resonance) to Frank Capra's populist classics of the period (especially

Mr Smith Goes to Washington), it has in Harrison a prickly, self-assured hero rather than a naïve, immature one.

Harrison is involved in some splendid bits of comic business, such as his first appearance in the film when he peremptorily orders Vivien Leigh to rise from a bench, only afterwards revealing that his purpose is to remove the sticky lollipop she has accidentally sat upon and restore it to the bawling child next to her. There are ingenious touches like Harrison's forgetful attempt to light a cigarette in the newspaper office just after being informed that smoking is banned, then later his deliberate defiance of the edict that costs him the remainder of a packet when a compositor responds over-enthusiastically to his offer to have a smoke. Impudent, and also irritable when he becomes newspaper headline material himself, he is far from being a one-dimensional crusader, just as Cecil Parker makes an unexpectedly brave (in the face of a lynch mob) and ultimately repentant villain.

The film received some rave reviews. Basil Wright in *The Spectator* went so far as to describe it as 'the first British comedy from an English studio . . . a film which is, perhaps for the first time, genuinely British' – an odd comment given its origins in a German play and its Scottish more than British flavour, with some cantankerous Irishness from Sara Allgood thrown in!

A modest Harrison gave himself few marks for progress since his disparaging comments on his work in *Men Are Not Gods*. 'I hated myself in *Storm in a Teacup*, too,' he advised Freda Bruce Lockhart. 'I'd only seen some rushes, so I crawled into the Leicester Square [Theatre], because I thought I ought to see the worst. I paid eight and six, I was too scared to ask them to let me in free, and I sat there in agony all through . . . There were only two scenes I didn't mind myself in – the one in the Kursaal, and the one in the car, both fairly serious, I thought they weren't badly played.' The scene in the

Kursaal follows Harrison's denunciation of the Provost and shows him letting off steam on various amusements, his anger turning to delight when Vivien Leigh (as the Provost's daughter) calls him by his Christian name for the first time. Though Harrison was far from conventionally good-looking at the time, with his long, bony face, he shows how charming he can be when he wants and his performance now seems assured and effective throughout.

Certainly Victor Saville had no doubts over his potential as an international star. The director merely rued the fact that there was no quick way of getting him before American audiences in a British picture. 'If I could borrow Luise Rainer [the big Hollywood star of the moment] to co-star in a film with Rex Harrison, I would make this clever British actor as big a personality in America as Tyrone Power or Robert Montgomery,' he told *Film Weekly*. (He suggested that a couple of films with Clark Gable would do wonders for Vivien Leigh, too, little anticipating *Gone with the Wind*.)

Harrison considered that his abilities as a serious screen lover were then in doubt. 'I wish I knew whether the trouble is something I can't help, like my physical appearance, or something I can alter, like my mental attitude,' he mused. 'God forbid I should play serious romantic parts, but I do realise that if you're going to mean anything at the box-office, you must be able to carry an occasional love scene.' He had been tested for the part of Sir Percy Blakeney in a sequel to Korda's 1934 hit, *The Scarlet Pimpernel* (which had starred Leslie Howard), but lost it at the last minute to Barry K. Barnes. Whether Harrison failed to measure up in the romantic clinches or in the three disguises the part required is not known, but *The Return of the Scarlet Pimpernel* did not make Barry K. Barnes a household word when it was released in 1937. (In 1964 Harrison was invited to play the Scarlet Pimpernel on stage but was rightly sceptical as to whether audiences would accept the premise that the aristocrats were laudable and the French revolutionaries all villains.)

Harrison was then assigned by Korda to co-star with Jack Hulbert in a musical comedy tentatively titled *The Playboy*, under the direction of Thornton Freeland. It became *Kiss Me Goodnight*, Arthur Riscoe took over from Harrison, and it was eventually shown as *Paradise for Two* in 1937. Instead, Harrison was loaned out to an independent producer for the key role in *School for Husbands*, a marital comedy that was a British main feature rather than a supporting quota quickie but still only a modest attraction, otherwise the rich opportunity it gave Harrison would have done wonders for his career.

He plays Leonard Drummond, a highly successful author of sexy novels who has lived in Paris and who preys on neglected wives, making his intentions blatantly clear. Even his name as a dinner guest is enough to alarm two dull husbands (Henry Kendall and Romney Brent). They denounce him as a cad and then ask for his advice on handling women. He outlines a 'wife insurance' policy to the pair – they should keep on courting their wives (Diana Churchill and June Clyde) as though they weren't married – but he also suggests they should test their partners by faking a business trip to Paris and coming home unexpectedly.

'I hear you've made love to women on the slightest provocation,' says one of the wives *sotto voce* during the dinner party. 'That's quite untrue,' responds Harrison. 'As a matter of fact, I seldom need any provocation at all.' He adds: 'Some men are independent of women – I need them, their encouragement, their admiration.' Earlier he claims not to understand women: 'I only know they're mysterious and divine,' he says with irresistible flattery. There is no shortage of females ready to surrender to his wiles. As he phones Diana Churchill from his studio, another woman not immediately visible sits facing him in a high-backed chair. 'Was that your latest?' she asks as he replaces the receiver. 'What?' he asks. 'Misunderstood wife?' 'No, no, I understand her perfectly,' he replies. At the end, after cleverly extricating himself from the accusations of the two returning husbands whose wives he has been seeing during their phoney trip, he goes off downstairs to his car – to be hauled inside by some unseen, impatient female.

Harrison went through the film dominating every situation. Henry Kendall and Romney Brent are two gullible, silly ass types whose measure he has all along. In a delicious example of Harrison's control of intonation, he transforms the meaning of an incriminating note, left by June Clyde's Diana Cheswick for her husband to find when she planned to run off with Harrison, by reading it aloud and inserting the pause after 'never' rather than before: 'Fed up with you never. Want to see you again. Diana.' It's crude material, but the actor's brazen treatment almost makes the reading plausible.

The feeble plot, which ensures that the wives never have the chance to succumb to Harrison's advances, makes *School for Husbands* a very minor work as a whole. Essentially, it served to show that Harrison could carry a picture and that fears about his lack of sex appeal were preposterous, but it did not immediately help his career.

Perhaps his role in the expensive Technicolored *Over the Moon* in support of Merle Oberon reflected increasing confidence on Korda's part in his audience appeal, but the film was such a disaster it did nobody's standing any good. Harrison played Freddie Jarvis, the country doctor in the South Riding area of Yorkshire whose great ambition is to go into medical research. Merle Oberon is his girl friend but he doesn't feel he has enough to offer her as a wife until he sells his practice to pay for a honeymoon in Monte Carlo. However, she suddenly inherits £18 million and plans a life of luxury in which she will buy Harrison a fashionable clinic for wealthy hypochondriacs. He decides her wealth has ruined any chance of happiness and so she goes off on her own, to be preyed on by parasites and gigolos. She misses Harrison terribly, calling him an idiot and berating his portrait on her dressing table: 'Dull . . . smug . . . pompous!' Meanwhile, Harrison is easily and unconvincingly tricked into working for a luxury Swiss clinic and becomes the 'star turn' among the female patients – just the kind of life he refused to accept on a platter from Merle Oberon.

With its fashion and travel sequences, exploiting the still rare use of Technicolor, and its emphasis on the Oberon character's experiences, it offered Harrison a very secondary role. There is never any doubt that the two will be reunited at the end – when belatedly the film produces a reasonable competitor for her affections in Robert Douglas's charming heir to a soap fortune who loves her for herself rather than her money, he is not allowed to make any real headway. So there is never any romantic tension and Harrison recognised what was required of him: 'Although there's a great deal of comedy being put in it, it's really the straight hero part, the solid fellow she turns to in the end.' Only at the end does he get a chance to shine: his gentle, sensual handling of the closing romantic scene on a gondola shows his skill as a screen lover.

The comedy that Harrison mentioned is atrocious, the plot feeble, the dialogue leaden. An attempt was made to improve matters by changing directors. William K. Howard, a drama specialist from Hollywood (he had made *Fire Over England* and *The Squeaker* in Britain), gave way to another American, Thornton Freeland. Nothing helped and *Over the Moon* was shelved for a year.

Next Charles Laughton and producer Erich Pommer arranged to borrow Harrison for the second independent production made by their Mayflower Pictures (following *Vessel of Wrath*). It was *St Martin's Lane*, which had an original screenplay by Clemence Dane about life among the buskers who performed for West End theatre and cinema queues.

The original plan was for Harrison to play a newspaperman. No doubt Laughton and Pommer had been impressed by his ease as a reporter in *Men Are Not Gods* and *Storm in a Teacup*. But they decided after preliminary discussions to give him a more substantial role as a successful songwriter and playboy around town, Harley Prentiss. Miss Dane was dispatched to observe him on stage in *French Without Tears* and write the part around his talents. The role of the newspaperman was reduced to a minor one and undertaken by a former reporter, Bartlett Cormack, the American who had worked on the screenplay of *Vessel of Wrath*.

Vivien Leigh was also borrowed from London Films to play the young pickpocket, Libby, who becomes a musical star. She could have started out as a scruffy, Cockney-speaking Eliza Doolittle type of waif but instead she is always a well-spoken, glamorous opportunist. Rex Harrison is first seen standing at a refreshment counter explaining the local slang to Bartlett Cormack; but he is no Henry Higgins eavesdropping on the low life, instead a man about town showing off the area to a visitor. Though impressed by his credentials, Vivien Leigh still can't resist making off with Harrison's silver cigarette case. After Charles Laughton's ugly busker takes her in hand and helps her develop her musical talent with his troupe, she makes use of Harrison to get out of the streets and inside the theatres where she eventually gains stardom.

Both Laughton and Harrison are entranced by her.

Harrison takes her to an upper-crust party, blind to the disapproval of his friends: she dances to his piano playing, then he takes her home and receives a goodnight kiss, after which she laughs cheerfully yet mockingly (knowing that she has him hooked) and goes inside. In this film, though, Harrison is wiser than he was as a doorstep Romeo in *Men Are Not Gods*: he knows that she'll drop him just as she dropped Laughton once he's outlived his usefulness, only his rebuke over her callous treatment of the busker somewhat improbably stings her into seeking him out and trying to make amends. This has nothing to do with logic and everything to do with bringing back Laughton for a lachrymose conclusion to the film (after all, he was the star and producer). As in *Men Are Not Gods*, Harrison drops out of sight.

It's a thin part, but Rex manages to add a certain amount of colour. It helps that he is given a profession instead of being just a wealthy young dandy and there is a glimpse of him in the agonies of composing a song, ruffling his hair in frustration, seated at a piano with tie loose and cigarette dangling from his lip, finally shouting 'I've got it! I've got it!' as he hits on the right tune. (Interesting, but hardly comparable to the build-up to 'The Rain in Spain' in *My Fair Lady*.) Harrison had to learn to conduct a pit orchestra for the sequence in which the number he has just finished, 'Straw Hat in the Rain', is performed in a stage musical. Arthur Johnston, the American composer best known for 'Pennies from Heaven', coached Harrison in using the baton and also wrote the music (Eddie Pola contributing the lyrics).

The Vivien Leigh character has her eyes on Hollywood at the end of *St Martin's Lane*, and Miss Leigh herself went off to play Scarlett O'Hara within a year. Harrison's next film would bring him the offer of a seven-year contract from Metro-Goldwyn-Mayer, even though his role in the company's second big British production, *The Citadel* (it followed *A Yank at Oxford*), was only a modest supporting one.

Robert Donat played the dedicated doctor in this sensitive adaptation of A. J. Cronin's best seller, produced by Victor Saville, and Harrison provided a sharp contrast as the unscrupulous Harley Street doctor, Freddie Lawford, an old student chum of Donat who introduces him to the big money to be made in medicine by adopting the proper bedside manner and stops him from telling a wealthy matron there's nothing wrong with her chest because it's a 'treasure chest' as far as the clinic is concerned. Harrison's charm is clearly being exercised on the nurses and Cecil Parker's equally unsavoury Dr Every observes with amusement, 'You'll notice Freddie's parsing of the word "patient" is always feminine.' This was the same kind of role he had played at the sanatorium in *Over the Moon*, but here it amounted to a vivid cameo thanks to better scripting and Harrison's incisive portrait of a smooth rogue.

French Without Tears was still running but Harrison left the cast, went on holiday for a month, and had soon accepted an offer to star in the West End production of Noel Coward's *Design for Living* opposite Diana Wynyard and Anton Walbrook. Harold French (who had staged *French Without Tears*) was the director. The play was six years old, having premiered on Broadway with Coward (in the role that Rex now inherited), Alfred Lunt and Lynn Fontanne. It had not been a major hit, and Ernst Lubitsch's 1933 film version with Fredric March, Gary Cooper and Miriam Hopkins had also been poorly received. In London, *Design for Living* opened on 25 January 1939 (it was Harrison's first appearance at the Theatre Royal, Haymarket, soon to become his favourite West End theatre), and the production was soundly thrashed by the critics but the public weren't put off and it settled down for a good run.

The play concerns four artistic Bohemians who flit between New York, Paris and London. Diana Wynyard is the successful actress who, with her friends – Harrison's playwright, Walbrook's artist and Alan Webb's house designer, all just as successful in their fields – makes an art out of living as frivolously as possible, unworried by anything, avoiding any deep involvements. Harrison encapsulates the play's nonchalant attitude to life when he makes light of having been to bed with Diana Wynyard's Gilda: 'It was not a deep sexual attraction. It was just a roll in the hay, and we enjoyed it very much.' With the threat of war becoming ever more ominous, it is hardly surprising that the play's flippancy irritated the critics while audiences probably welcomed its pure escapism.

British film production had slumped badly because of the international situation and Harrison was lucky to find starring roles in a couple of the topical spying dramas that were then in vogue. These he shot during the day, supplementing his stage work in *Design for Living*. However, it must have been galling to report to Denham in February 1939 for work on the optimistically titled *Peace In Our Time* for Paramount when the company was about to embark on its lavish film version of *French Without Tears* and decided to give Harrison's old role to their rising Hollywood star, the Welsh-born Ray Milland, although Roland Culver and Guy Middleton were invited to repeat their stage parts. Paramount had dropped the idea of using Marlene Dietrich and sent over contract actress Ellen Drew instead. She was totally out of her depth and even with direction by Anthony Asquith the result was a plodding comedy that lost the sparkle of the stage piece.

It was claimed that Neville Chamberlain's visit to Munich to see Hitler in September 1938 had inspired Harrison's new film and provided the title *Peace In Our*

Time. The film depicts the Prime Minister of Brosnia visiting Slavonia to improve relations and an assassination plot by a group of arms dealers to provoke war as he boards the train for home. Harrison played the famous wise-cracking French special investigator, Jacques Sauvin, who is one jump ahead of the villains at every turn. Most of the action is located on the Simplon-Orient Express between Paris and the Balkans, and a full-size replica of the train was built on a Denham sound stage with 8,000 feet of film shot on a real journey being available for back-projection views through the windows. Valerie Hobson played the woman blackmailed into throwing a parcel bomb at the Prime Minister; John Loder was the third star and supplied the love interest for Hobson. One of the villains, who falls to his death fighting with Harrison on the train, was George Devine, later to cross paths with Rex at the Royal Court Theatre.

The film was in fact a re-make of a French picture, *La Bataille Silencieuse*, and since peace in our time was less and less likely by the time it was rushed into the cinemas in April, the French title was retained and translated, making it *The Silent Battle*. Plump, pug-ugly Michel Simon had played Sauvin originally, with Kate de Nagy and Pierre Fresnay in the other two main roles.

Harrison brought athletic vigour to the part but had more opportunity for introducing a wry edge in *Ten Days in Paris*, which he made at Denham in the summer of 1939 from a Bruce Graeme novel. Here he was a British espionage officer who begins the picture waking up in a Paris nursing home with a bullet wound to his head and a complete loss of memory about his movements over the past ten days. He discovers that he is masquerading as chauffeur cum butler to a French countess to uncover a plot to blow up French fortifications (a topical reference to the Maginot Line). Harrison indulges in light-hearted romantic exchanges with Karen Verne as the countess;

34

ingeniously extracts details of the sabotage plan from a minor spy by imitating William Tell; and ensures that all the villains (led by Leo Genn) perish in the final explosions. A train inevitably featured in the proceedings: this time loaded with munitions and raced by Harrison in a car in his successful effort to prevent it being used to blast a hole in the fortified area.

4
The War Years

ON BRITAIN'S ENTRY INTO THE SECOND WORLD WAR AT 11 a.m. on Sunday, 3 September 1939, all places of entertainment were closed until further notice. Cinemas were allowed to re-open after a couple of weeks but the problems of travel in the blackout and the fear of air raids kept audiences out of the West End in the evenings and crippled the live theatre for much longer.

At the instigation of his agent, Vere Barker, Harrison tried to enlist in the Inns of Court Cavalry Regiment but there were no vacancies. *Design for Living* had stopped but the idea arose of continuing its run in the provinces where playgoers lived nearer the theatres than was the case in London, and so in early October, Harrison, Diana Wynyard, Anton Walbrook and the rest of the cast set off for Liverpool, Newcastle, and other places north of Watford, to find that audiences were tickled pink by the chance to see a star-laden West End success and turned out in huge numbers, enjoying the respite of the 'phoney war'.

While *Design for Living* was packing them in at the Prince of Wales Theatre in Birmingham (bombed in

1941), a new play called *You of All People* was trying out at a rival playhouse, the Theatre Royal. It starred Leslie Banks with the 25-year-old German Jewish actress Lilli Palmer, who had been working in Britain since the mid-Thirties. The two companies shared the same hotel and Lilli Palmer found herself being scrutinised each night in the dining room by Harrison, who was wearing a monocle to improve the poor sight of one eye. The actress's first impulse was to glare at him but, after Leslie Banks had introduced them, they quickly became friends, viewing each other's performances at matinees, sharing their spare time, and driving up together to Liverpool where their plays were running the next week.

During this tour, Harrison was invited to board yet another spy train melodrama. But *Night Train to Munich* was a film with a difference. Then called *Gestapo*, its script was the work of Frank Launder and Sidney Gilliat whose *The Lady Vanishes* (directed by Alfred Hitchcock) had started the craze for such pictures. Because of censorship restrictions, the new film had originally featured another of Europe's mythical states, Ironia, but with the outbreak of war it could be properly identified as Germany. From *The Lady Vanishes*, Launder and Gilliat revived the slow-witted but unflappable, cricket-worshipping Englishmen, Charters and Caldicott, to be played again by Basil Radford and Naunton Wayne. A young Austrian actor who had made a strong impression in *Goodbye Mr Chips*, then Paul von Hernreid, soon to be more simply Paul Henreid, was cast as the principal Nazi menace (a role originally assigned to John Clements). Alfred Hitchcock had gone to Hollywood, but the young Carol Reed made an excellent substitute as director.

Location work was out of the question and the stages at Lime Grove were used for most settings, including a German rural railway station and the Alps, combined with model work. The outside of the studio was briefly transformed into German headquarters and the swastika flag was flown for one shot, resulting in local uproar and useful publicity. Because of the grim mood in England, Launder and Gilliat deliberately emphasised the humorous aspects. As a thriller, *Night Train to Munich* is preposterous, but its wit and energy under Carol Reed's adroit handling ensure that it remains richly entertaining to this day.

Harrison plays a British Intelligence agent who has a front as a sheet music salesman at a resort called Brightbourne, working under the name of Gus Bennett. His real job is looking after a refugee Czech scientist who is working with the Navy. The man's daughter (Margaret Lockwood) escapes from a Nazi concentration camp and comes to Brightbourne, looking for Harrison. 'If you can hear a warbling note like an air raid siren, that's him singing,' says a deck chair attendant. And there on the pier is Harrison in a cardigan, 'the human barrel organ' crooning new songs all day long in a somewhat watery voice to anyone who will listen. Harrison's vocalising becomes the subject of a lively exchange later, after Lockwood has been irritated by his caution in trusting her. He has explained his choice of song plugging as a cover: 'Nature endowed me with a gift,' he declares, 'and I just accepted it, that's all.' Margaret Lockwood responds: 'Pity it didn't endow you with a voice. Nothing that happened to me in that concentration camp was quite as dreadful as listening to you day after day singing those appalling songs!' Harrison feigns dismay: 'With those few words you've knocked the bottom out of my entire existence.' 'Pity I've only knocked it,' she replies. (For a Czech, Lockwood shows a remarkable fluency in English and has no trace of an accent either.)

When the scientist is retrieved by the Germans, along with his daughter, Harrison is raring to go after them. In an exquisitely droll scene during afternoon tea at the Ministry, top officials review the development with glum resignation, exchange reminders about cooking recipes from their wives, and unofficially sanction Harrison's idea for rescuing the Czech boffin.

Harrison spends the rest of the film in a German army major's uniform masquerading as one Ulrich Herzoff with a monocle for his right eye and a comically mechanical, slightly high-pitched way of speaking to suggest a Teutonic accent. He hoodwinks the Germans with Scarlet Pimpernel ease (he did get to play the part after all) and even persuades them to leave him alone in a hotel room for the night with the daughter to exercise his charm on her and induce her co-operation. When he kids her about which of them takes the bed and which the sofa, Lockwood declares, 'You're treating all this as if it were some sort of joke' – which of course is exactly what the film is doing. As Harrison replies, 'No use being intense about it.' The Germans are shown as such a humourless, brainwashed lot that Harrison can even get away with choice observations like, 'Freedom in Germany is a great advance on freedom elsewhere – properly organised and controlled by the State', without arousing their suspicion.

To add tension, of course, the Germans (particularly Henreid) finally become suspicious and cotton on to his masquerade – but only through a slip-up by Naunton Wayne who recognises his old Balliol College chum Harrison on the night train to Munich and helps him, Lockwood and her father escape from the train and make a dash for the Swiss border, hotly pursued by the enemy. Harrison now turns into a resourceful and convincing man of action, sending the others on a cable car across a chasm while he keeps the Germans at bay, then leaping from one cable car to another in mid-air to effect his own escape, leaving Paul Henreid sulking and wounded on

40

the German side like a small boy who's had his ice-cream taken away from him.

Harrison makes a superb symbol of British indomitability: this kind of pluck and resourcefulness will win the war. Whereas Leslie Howard in the following year's *Pimpernel Smith* emphasised intelligence in his daring missions into enemy country, Harrison relies on impudence: our secret weapon is humour. A film so skilfully rude to the Germans and so light in touch could hardly fail to go down well with British picturegoers. It tickled American audiences as well and alerted its US distributor, 20th Century-Fox, to Harrison's appeal, contributing to the company's interest in signing him up later to work in Hollywood.

After finishing *Night Train to Munich*, Harrison joined the Chelsea branch of the Home Guard. British forces were evacuated from Dunkirk at the end of May and a German invasion of England was feared. In July 1940, the month that the German bombing of Britain began, Harrison was asked to take over the role of Adolphus Cusins in Gabriel Pascal's production of George Bernard Shaw's 1908 play *Major Barbara*, then being filmed at Denham. Pascal was apparently dissatisfied with the work of his original choice for the part, Andrew Osborn, and told Robert Morley that he saw 'the face of a tortured Christ' in Harrison and deemed it ideal for the part. The extravagant Rumanian halted filming for a month, then resumed work in Devon at Dartington Hall. Returning to Denham, shooting was continually interrupted by air-raid warnings, whereupon storage space under the concrete floors of the sound stages was occupied as shelters.

Pascal had produced a highly popular and accomplished film of *Pygmalion* (1938) with Leslie Howard and Wendy Hiller under the co-direction of Howard and Anthony Asquith. For *Major Barbara*, Pascal undertook the direction himself with Harold French advising him on the acting and David Lean on camera angles. The result is that *Major Barbara* has a ponderous feel and is often pretty tedious to watch. Shaw's dialogue is frequently scintillating but there's far too much of it – and it pays little attention to consistency of characterisation so that none of the principals emerge as credible figures but are merely vehicles for Shaw's wit and debating skill. Conflict of attitude is pushed to the extreme with Robert Morley as Undershaft, the munitions millionaire who also controls the press and runs the country, and Wendy Hiller as his daughter Barbara, the Salvation Army Major trying to save the souls of down-and-outs.

Cusins is as incoherent and confusing a character as the others but Harrison is lucky that he is specifically conceived as being a flexible figure, a disarmingly honest and penniless scholar of ancient Greece who becomes infatuated on sight with Major Barbara and joins the Salvation Army to worship her. Interested though he is in religions generally, he finds the Salvation Army primarily useful for helping him shed his inhibitions by banging a big drum strapped to his chest. Normally soft-spoken, his voice rings with confidence as he praises the Army to Barbara's father: 'It takes a poor professor of Greek – the most artificial and self-suppressed of human creatures and lets loose the rhapsodist in him – it sends him down the public street drumming dithyrambs' (and he beats the drum enthusiastically). Harrison is quite happy to leave the Salvation Army when Barbara quits in disgust after her father 'buys' it with a huge donation.

On first sight in the film, Harrison is distinctly uncharismatic. His open-air lecture on ancient Greek lacks an audience, he has the look of an untidy academic with overlong hair, pipe and glasses. The actor conveys the naïvely romantic aspect of his character as he takes off his glasses and listens to Major Barbara delivering a sermon, smiling approvingly not at what she says but at Barbara herself spellbinding an audience. Glancing around and seeing the intent gaze of the rest of the crowd, he recovers himself and manages to look suitably serious, putting his spectacles back on. But in close-up his eyes light up again behind the glasses.

Later the Harrison character, somewhat the worse for drink, reflects: 'I am in many ways a weak, timid, ineffectual person . . . but whenever I feel I must have anything, I get it – sooner or later.' He is speaking of Barbara but this sign of willpower gets him the offer of a job in the armaments industry.

Undershaft is desperate for a successor (his partner Lazarus remains curiously unseen and unconsulted), but Harrison never seems a convincing candidate with his academic background and hatred of warmongering. The film somewhat disconcertingly shows us that Undershaft has created a workers' paradise with good wages, a decent home in the countryside, even a place to worship. Furthermore, his factories not only turn out weapons of destruction but also useful things like railway lines, and Harrison is impressed: 'It's all horribly, frightfully, immorally, unanswerably perfect.' Undershaft considers poverty the worst crime of all and he is proud to have conquered that, whereas the Salvation Army has failed. Harrison keeps calling him 'Machiavelli' and 'rascal' but only when Undershaft, having previously suggested that the power of guns can force useful social change, insists that an armourer must on principle sell to anyone who can afford his products, does he really stand exposed as an unscrupulous menace. (In 1941, when the film came out, it was of course difficult to suggest that making weapons was dishonourable, but selling them indiscriminately abroad, even if there is no hint of an actual war in the film, must have seemed deplorable.)

43

Though Harrison speaks of facing 'an abyss of moral horror', he makes a strong challenge to succeed Undershaft and gets the job despite revealing his ignorance of figures (along with a useful skill at bluffing), while Barbara is keen to marry him, live among the workers, and see if men who are not hungry can have their souls saved. Harrison talks of the chance 'to make war on war' but, thanks to Robert Morley's great impact as Undershaft, the film leaves the strong impression that the arms king has won, even though Harrison has the last word, rejecting Undershaft's cheery command that he should report for work at six o'clock in the morning. (Shaw's original screenplay had Undershaft reply by predicting, 'Before a week you will come at six and stay until I turn you out for the sake of your health.') The film also leaves the impression that a more interesting story lies ahead than the one we've seen.

Shaw himself kept a close watch on the sets and performances to ensure fidelity to his intentions. On one visit, Pascal asked him to explain a scene to Harrison and Wendy Hiller. 'The last scene in *Major Barbara* is very high flown – the very last love scene between Cusins and Major Barbara,' recalls Harrison. 'So Wendy Hiller sat down on one side of Bernard Shaw and I sat down on the other while he started to read this scene over – and he didn't say a word – he went on and on – and then all he said was, "Och, what a terrible scene!" He didn't give us any advice, he just closed the book. He probably hadn't read it since 1908.'

Following *Major Barbara*, Harrison returned to the stage to work again with Diana Wynyard and director Harold French in S. N. Behrman's comedy *No Time for Comedy* which had played on Broadway in 1939 with Laurence Olivier and Katharine Cornell. It was a part that helped consolidate his reputation for playing debonair philanderers as he portrayed an author of frothy stage comedies, Gaylord Easterbrook, whose actress wife (Wynyard) scathingly pinpoints him as 'Elusive as a lover, as a husband non-existent,' in conversation with his mistress (Lilli Palmer), the wife of a wealthy banker. The mistress wants the writer to turn his hand to a more elevated, spiritual play while his practical-minded wife waits for him to come to his senses. (Warner Bros had already turned it into a film, converting the playwright into a homespun country boy role for James Stewart.)

The British production tried out in Blackpool during the Christmas week of 1940, then went on a lengthy tour of the provinces. Performances were often interrupted by air-raid warnings – the actors carried on but members of the audience could leave if they preferred. It was, as Harrison vividly recalls in his autobiography, a strange experience playing to people who really had their ears pricked for the noise of planes overhead.

In London, the play opened with a schedule of matinees daily at 2.15 p.m. and 'evening' shows at 5 p.m. on Wednesdays and Saturdays, thus reversing the normal practice. Fortunately, the heavy bombing of London eased off from August 1941 onwards. *No Time for Comedy* carried on and by November performances were beginning at 5.45 p.m. nightly with matinees on Wednesdays and Saturdays at 2.15 p.m.

Although well-known actors were often exempted from war service on the grounds they did more for morale by entertaining the public, and despite the fact that Harrison's impaired eyesight limited his usefulness, he pressed the Air Force for a chance to enlist and was accepted for an officers' training course, reporting to Uxbridge on 4 February 1942. He went on to train as a Flying Control Officer at the Photographic Reconnaissance Unit near Oxford. On 25 January 1943, he used a leave to marry Lilli Palmer at Caxton Hall in Westminster, having been divorced from his first wife since 2 July 1942.

He was then stationed at Uxbridge as a Flying Control Liaison Officer, looking after returning planes that were in difficulties – guiding them to the nearest airfield or arranging a rescue if they ditched in the sea. Harrison's second son, named Carey, was born in February 1944. Shortly afterwards, Harrison was released to make the film version of Noel Coward's play *Blithe Spirit* at Denham. He found it hard to settle down to acting again, especially with a director, David Lean, who had no real flair for comedy or (as yet) much aptitude for handling actors. Despite the film's status as a minor classic, Harrison found making *Blithe Spirit* 'a difficult experience for all concerned . . . there was little fun or relaxation to be had from it'.

He played Charles Condomine, a smugly successful novelist who is working on a mystery story about a homicidal medium and invites a local spiritualist, Margaret Rutherford's Madame Arcati, to a small dinner party, hoping to learn the tricks of the trade. He and his wife (Constance Cummings) and their friends the Bradmans (Olive Carey, Hugh Wakefield) are sceptics, richly amused by the medium – a hearty, bubbling figure not at all put out by their lack of faith. The Harrison character deserves to have his complacency shattered – and shattered it is by the appearance of his first wife who died seven years before – Elvira (Kay Hammond), a catty, fun-loving figure who turns up as a green apparition with red lips, visible and audible only to Harrison and the camera so that his second wife takes some convincing that she is actually there.

Kay Hammond (who had stirred up the males in *French Without Tears*) is deliciously outrageous here, causing Harrison to remark: 'I am pained to observe that seven years in the echoing vaults of eternity have in no way impaired your native vulgarity.' He earns an immediate rebuke from Hammond – 'That was the remark of a pompous ass' – and she is soon criticising him further – 'Nobody but a monumental bore would have thought of having a honeymoon in Budleigh Salterton' – as well as horrifying him with her admission of misbehaviour with a certain Captain Bracegirdle on the moors there. Constance Cummings as the second wife is just as scathing towards him, cueing some delightful business in which Harrison toys with pouring himself a stiff drink at the meal table, opts for water instead, then, as her verbal bombardment reaches full spate, pours the water back and once again goes for something stronger.

His ultimate fate was specially devised for the film, which also opened out the single drawing-room set of the stage original to spread the action over the entire house and make occasional trips outside. But it is essentially a record of the theatrical piece (Kay Hammond and Margaret Rutherford were repeating their roles; Cecil Parker had originally played Charles and Fay Compton his second wife). Brightly Technicolored, airy and fast-moving, the film must have been a tonic in war-time. Yet it suffers from a monotony of tone and smart-alec cleverness. Rex Harrison and Kay Hammond play characters who are themselves putting on acts, conscious of their every word. When, early on, Harrison makes an observation – 'Discouraging to think how many people are shocked by honesty and how few by deceit' – he tells his wife (the second one) that she underrates him by suggesting that he might forget what he has said and won't write it down. The essence of the film is delivery. Performing skill is everything – our pleasure resides in the way Harrison delivers that last epigram mock-casually or Kay Hammond savours the sound of names like Budleigh Salterton and Bracegirdle so that they become humorous. Noel Coward wasn't too pleased with the result but he did extend to Rex the highest praise he could manage: 'After me, you're the best light comedian in the world.'

I Live in Grosvenor Square was an awful attempt to crash the American market by producer-director Herbert Wilcox that ponderously itemised the obvious differences between the British and the Yanks and retailed a mythic image of uppercrust England in its story of a Duke's granddaughter (Anna Neagle) whose affection for her Army Major beau (Rex Harrison) fades when she meets an American Air Force Sergeant (Dean Jagger) – Harrison obtains special leave to contest a Parliamentary by-election for the Conservative Party and is busy campaigning while Neagle and Jagger are cuddling in a haystack. There is one scene in which Harrison becomes justifiably cross at the sudden manner in which the American has usurped her affections but later he goes out of his way as a 'true gentleman' to bring them together.

The film takes nearly two hours to unfold its trite, drearily dialogued story. Its few telling moments are in fact silent ones: Rex Harrison watching his girl and the American at dinner or sitting grimly in the back of a taxi after he has reunited them, and Anna Neagle breaking down after learning (in a typically contrived scene) of Jagger's death in the course of her work at an air base and carrying on with her task of writing out all the details before giving in to her emotions.

The credits are at pains to show that the script was written by an American and a British writer, to suggest a fair balance, but of course it panders to the all-important American market. Yet Dean Jagger is far too ordinary and dull to convincingly sweep Neagle off her feet and it is irksome to watch Harrison denied a chance to make his charm work on her. (An earthier American actor, like John Garfield, might have made it more of a contest with an invitation to a well-bred lady to lower her standards for a change.)

The film seems to regard Robert Morley's hearty,

solicitous Duke of Exmoor as slightly comic but wholly admirable, just as its picture of aristocratic England follows the Hollywood example of *Random Harvest* or *Mrs Miniver* in suggesting a stable, patronising class structure. But could it be that the film – much criticised for its depiction of a phoney England – was in fact ridiculing the privileged class? This would explain the one odd development in the story in which Rex Harrison – very clearly an uppercrust type – unexpectedly loses the election contest to the Independent candidate (a much older, uncharismatic man-of-the-people type, a Labour candidate in all but name) – and this in true-blue Devon, in a seat which has been Tory for three hundred years. In a small way Harrison invites defeat by constantly saying, 'If you don't vote for me, for God's sake vote for someone,' but it is said with the confidence of a person who believes there is nobody else worth bothering about.

The film started production nine months before the Labour Party's startling post-war election victory over Churchill and the Conservatives, so perhaps it cunningly predicted the victory of the common man over his traditional 'betters'. (In fact, the film came out in the same month as the election took place.) It could be argued that Harrison's defeat serves to make him a less worthy suitor but Anna Neagle's switch of affections is already a *fait accompli*. True, it would have been more awkward for her to jilt a victorious MP but on the other hand an election success would have provided him with some consolation. If there was genuine anticipation of social change, it was expressed too subtly for contemporary critics to perceive, but perhaps audiences were wiser and understood . . .

If *I Live in Grosvenor Square* was insulting stuff for the second best light comedian in the world, *The Rake's Progress* which he shot immediately afterwards, early in 1945, made such effective use of Harrison that it estab-

49

lished a firm screen image which would last until the arrival of Henry Higgins. Frank Launder and Sidney Gilliat had already given Harrison's career a leg-up with *Night Train to Munich*. They had turned writer-directors with *Millions Like Us* and Sidney Gilliat had subsequently directed *Waterloo Road* before he took on *The Rake's Progress*. The two earlier films had shown a sympathetic understanding of the working class that was quite fresh in British cinema; now *The Rake's Progress* suggested that, as a result of the war, the idle rich had had their day. Harrison was cast as the archetype of the Thirties playboy, Vivian Kenway, an utterly selfish, debonair scoundrel, the black sheep of his family, whose best talents – enterprise and daring – find a suitable outlet in the Second World War.

The Harrison character lacks any excuse of social deprivation – he is the only son of a wealthy Tory MP (Godfrey Tearle) and automatically goes to Eton and Oxford. He betrays everyone around him – and he gets away with it because he has charm, the particular quality that Harrison could bring to the role. That, plus the cunning way the character is introduced, makes Harrison a fascinating figure and sympathetic for all his faults.

We see him first as a dedicated soldier in the front line – efficient, calm, cheerful. There is tentative criticism from the wireless man accompanying him in the tank who reminds him that their orders didn't extend to crossing a bridge ahead (the subordinate is clearly not keen to risk *his* life unnecessarily); but Harrison sets a better example when he insists on driving over it to find out if it is mined. We then see a newspaper headline about the number one playboy of the Thirties being missing in action and we hear the thoughts of Margaret Johnston's Jennifer Calthrop, a sensible-looking woman, who gently suggests that Harrison was not really a bad person but couldn't help what he was. At the end, after we learn that his tank held the approaches to the bridge for four hours before it was blown up and he was mortally wounded, her voice-over sums him up: 'In peace a misfit, a man who wanted to live dangerously in a world that wanted to play safe. In war, a fine soldier. Perhaps that was his destiny.'

It was this apparent excuse-making that outraged some critics, like James Agee who wrote: 'The film tells the story of one of those irresistibly forgivable and seductive top-drawer skunks, worthless in all of an interminable series of relationships and dangerous in some, who turns out to be just what our side needs once he gets into a war. It is even strongly suggested that the war couldn't have been won without his kind; and it is more slyly suggested that it is the glory and the all-sufficient vindication of the upper classes to have bred such queen-bees.' Launder and Gilliat simply defended the film by saying that the type they had portrayed *did* exist and was instantly recognisable to professional soldiers.

In fact, the film is often harshly critical of its central figure, as when his reckless climbing of the Martyrs' Memorial at Oxford is scathingly contrasted with an ex-serviceman begging for money in the street. (The upper class is savagely attacked in the figure of the inept plantation boss, Sir John.) And Harrison's character ultimately condemns himself: '. . . my type's becoming obsolete. Can't compete with the international situation. Not even news anymore. The Thirties produced us and the champagne's gone flat and we're going out with the Thirties. Nothing to show for it except cirrhosis of the liver and a lot of wasted time.' 'Anyone involved with you faces pain,' he is told and he is brought to the clearest awareness of this when his drunken driving causes his father's death. His 'heroic' demise in the war is a way of redeeming himself and a form of suicide.

It is doubtful if this character ever does anything completely noble or selfless. When the fire-raising Nazi mob outside the Vienna hotel influence him to agree to a marriage of convenience with Lilli Palmer's half-Jewish Nikki, he also has the incentive that she will settle his debts (which he has exaggerated). When he decides not to marry Margaret Johnston after she has cared for him, and deserts her with the note, 'Sorry, darling, I can't', she interprets it as his desire to spare her further pain but it is just as much his old fear of being tied down, especially to the dull suburban existence she offers.

Harrison plays Kenway superbly, with as much humour as possible. For this figure, nothing is to be taken too seriously: even a decision to cut back on his spending with Lilli Palmer has to be celebrated by an expensive dinner. Then there is his earlier response to hearing about the opportunity for an easy life offered by working on a coffee plantation: he has almost dozed off while the family have their discussion over his future, but first one eye opens, then the other, before he gets up and takes matters in his own hands. There is also his comic effort to steal unnoticed into Sir John's conference at the plantation after it has started, and the astonished expression as he stops his descent from his hotel balcony in Austria at the sight of room service being restored. There is the masterful way in which, caught in a lie to Lilli Palmer while on the phone to room service in a London hotel, his voice goes up in pitch for a moment and he clears his throat before he carries on with his order as though nothing has happened.

This was Lilli Palmer's first screen appearance opposite her husband. She starts off with the upper hand as his saviour in the Austrian hotel, inevitably falls in love with him once they are married, and just as inevitably is betrayed. It is a nice ironic touch that she should be driven to attempt suicide in England, her chosen place of safety. Harrison physically injures her as well as his father by his drunken driving; but he leaves the hospital without seeing her – her situation is insignificant compared to what has happened to his father and there's nothing more he could say to her after harming her yet again. She just disappears from the film. (There is a later reference to her having obtained a divorce.)

It is the father's secretary, Jennifer Calthrop (a luminous performance by Margaret Johnston), whose assessments of the Harrison character open and close the film. She understands him, she gently bosses him, but she also succumbs to him despite herself. She later takes the initiative, tracking him down and rescuing him from work as a professional dancing partner in a sleazy ballroom after his father's death. As a practical, intelligent, well-balanced sort of person, her concern and love for Harrison set an example to the audience to regard him sympathetically as well. In his performance, Harrison lets us know that Kenway realises he is hurting people by his actions. In the end he certainly pays for his transgressions. If his death in war has a fault, it is perhaps the touch of making his last action that of drinking champagne (not shown, but reported) – it suggests a reversion to type when really he died a reformed person. But at least it provides an opportunity for a witty and irreverent compliment: 'Typical of him – drinking champagne he hasn't paid for!'

The Rake's Progress is a superb piece of film-making. Even the minor characters are vividly delineated. It gives nothing away to Hollywood in the technical skill it displays. It is far and away the best of Harrison's British starring vehicles. Immediately after it, at what might seem the least appropriate time, Harrison elected to sign a Hollywood contract. And yet of course the very argument of *The Rake's Progress* is that the kind of figure Harrison most vividly represented was finished. And even if such roles *were* going to be available in post-war British films, did Harrison really want to continue playing rakes and roués after having summed up the type to perfection in *The Rake's Progress*?

The actor gave his reason for having gone to Hollywood to readers of the British magazine *Picturegoer* in 1950: 'It was a logical step in my film career. It was a good thing that I should, if possible, become known to the American public, not merely for my own professional sake but also for the sake of future British films I might play in. It is essential that our films have known names. One of the difficulties facing British films in the American market . . . is that our stars, in competition with the Hollywood names, are often not sufficiently well known to attract people into the cinemas. A British star who has been seen in American films has a great advantage.'

Before his trip to the States, though, Harrison was recruited by ENSA to revive *French Without Tears*, for the benefit of British troops who were still stationed in Europe now that peace had been declared, and in the company of Anna Neagle and Roland Culver, he went on tour to bases in Germany, France, Belgium and Holland.

Above:
The first Harrison performance definitely
saved for posterity, supporting Tyrrell Davis in
a quota comedy *All at Sea* (1936) and looking
positively thoughtful about it. Also seen,
another future favourite: Googie Withers.
Whatever happened to Tyrrell Davis?

Below:
In his first Korda assignment, Rex Harrison is
seen extracting every possible ounce of relish
from observing his rival in love (Sebastian
Shaw) read the letter from Miriam Hopkins
terminating their relationship. The film is *Men
Are Not Gods* (1936).

Above:
Rex Harrison as a romantic lead for Vivien Leigh in *Storm in a Teacup* (1937). He considered his right profile the less flattering one.

Right:
On stage in the smash hit comedy of the Thirties, *French Without Tears* (1936), with Kay Hammond, Roland Culver and Robert Flemyng.

Left:
As the ladies' man in *School for Husbands* (1937) with June Clyde (centre) and Diana Churchill as two entranced housewives.

Below:
Night out at a film premiere *(Marie Antoinette)* in October 1938 — Rex Harrison's first wife, Collette, can't take her eyes off him. Also seen are Mr and Mrs Victor Saville (he co-directed Harrison in *Storm in a Teacup* and produced *The Citadel*).

Above:
Harrison discusses a scene in *Night Train to Munich* (1940) with director Carol Reed, watched by Margaret Lockwood. Looking as though he wishes they'd hurry up and get it over with is cinematographer Otto Kanturek.

Below:
Dashing man of action — Rex Harrison fights off the Nazi hordes in *Night Train to Munich* (1940).

Right:
Harrison as Adolphus Cusins in
Major Barbara (1941) with Wendy
Hiller (in the title role) and Walter
Hudd playing her brother,
Stephen Undershaft.

Left:
Seeing is believing: Rex Harrison
tries to point out the green ghost
of his first wife (Kay Hammond)
to his second (Constance
Cummings) in *Blithe Spirit* (1945).

Right:
Rex Harrison's second wife, Lilli
Palmer, appeared opposite him
in *The Rake's Progress* (1945) as
the Jewish refugee who climbs
into his lap in an Austrian hotel
room.

Left:
Rex Harrison with Lilli Palmer (his screen and real-life wife) were on their own apart from the support of *The Four Poster* (1952) in this study of a marriage over nearly half a century.

Right:
Rex Harrison's third wife for a tragically brief period was the talented red-headed comedienne Kay Kendall with whom he appeared in two films, *The Constant Husband* (1955) and *The Reluctant Debutante* (1958).

Left:
Rex Harrison's film with the love goddess Rita Hayworth, *The Happy Thieves* (1961), was made when both their careers were at a low ebb. Unhappily, only Rex's career recovered after this dismal Spanish comedy set among art thieves.

5
Five for Fox

REX HARRISON WASN'T THE ONLY STAR BEING PURSUED BY Hollywood. At 20th Century-Fox alone, Francis Harley, the managing director, and Ben Lyon, the talent chief of the company's British branch, signed up Richard Greene and Peggy Cummins, went after Herbert Lom, and tried to interest James Mason in starring in the forthcoming *Anna and the King of Siam*, based on Margaret Landon's popular 1944 biography. Mason refused the part and it was dangled in front of Harrison as the first film he could make if he signed with Fox for a seven-year contract. Finding the script a challenge and the monetary side appealing ($4,000 weekly for 40 weeks a year), he was further encouraged when Lilli Palmer was offered her own Hollywood contract with Warner Bros. and when Fox agreed that he could spend half the year in Britain, making films there either on loan-out or for Fox itself.

In the autumn of 1945, Lilli Palmer and Rex Harrison took the Queen Elizabeth across the Atlantic and arrived in New York to experience for the first time the high-pressure antics of the American show-biz press who jostled for interviews. (Rex's *Rake's Progress* was running in New York, retitled *The Notorious Gentleman*.) The couple then took the three-day train ride to Hollywood.

Irene Dunne was going to be the main box-office draw of *Anna and the King of Siam* on the American market. The studio waited three months until she was available to play the part of Anna Owens, the British widow who goes to Siam to teach the King's harem of wives and all his children in 1862.

Harrison had yet to work out how he was to play the wily Siamese potentate. He was really far too tall to play an Oriental and he also had to find a suitable accent. He had never even played in a period or costume picture before (except for his bit in *School for Scandal*). He hadn't previously died on screen, but he had a big death scene at the end of this picture. The director was the veteran John Cromwell, who had wanted James Mason to play the part. When Harrison asked for preliminary advice on how to approach the role, Cromwell simply told him to relax and it would all come to him naturally. Cromwell had the classic American director's approach of letting experienced performers find their own way of playing a part to begin with and then responding to what they did on the set. Harrison, though, found it difficult to stay calm until the film started production and hated being cut off from his old acting cronies who might have offered some ideas for this taxing part. According to Lilli Palmer, it was her old drama coach, Elsa Schreiber, who came to Rex's rescue, suggesting a certain kind of wheezy accent and a particular restrained way of laughing. 'For the next three weeks until shooting began, Rex was invisible,' Lilli Palmer records in her autobiography. 'He worked with Elsa from early morning till late at night, until even she groaned, "I'm exhausted. That madman is killing me."'

With eyes turned almond-shaped, his skin darkened, and legs enclosed in a baggy-skirted outfit, he presented

56

his interpretation of King Mongkut to an alarmed John Cromwell who demanded that he stop sounding like a bird imitator and talk in his normal voice (the English voice was often considered foreign enough for American audiences, which is why British actors have played the Germans in many Hollywood war films). Harrison refused to obey Cromwell and the matter went to the studio head, Darryl F. Zanuck, for a decision. Zanuck approved Harrison's interpretation but warned him that it would mean doing without Cromwell's guidance for the rest of the picture. The result was that Cromwell didn't speak to Harrison again and concentrated on Irene Dunne, with whom he had worked many times before.

Harrison's King gives him plenty of scope for displays of petulance, mischievousness and irascibility within a lightly humorous approach. His Mongkut is, in fact, another anxious pupil for Irene Dunne to teach, a dictator who wants to move his people towards more modern ways, a man who will rout her from bed in the middle of the night to know the meaning of a difficult English word, but also a man who forces her to respect traditional Siamese customs, even when they are barbaric. In time, she becomes one of his chief counsellors and they grow fond of each other – the film tickles the audience with the idea of a love affair without actually crossing the racial barriers. The King dies, having earned her lasting admiration: 'He tried so hard, no one will ever know. He was like a little boy sometimes . . . nobody understood, not really.'

What initially verges on caricature is so skilfully sustained by Harrison that his interpretation of Mongkut comes to seem natural to an audience and makes one warm to the character. More than thirty years later, John Cromwell was to see the film again and comment on Harrison's work: 'I was very pleased with his performance – I hadn't remembered it as that good.' It is hard to imagine James Mason being as effective in the part – a more intense, brooding actor, he had no real gift for comedy, and it was the humour of the part that Harrison emphasised to such entertaining effect. But Mason did get his chance to play the part in a 1949 adaptation for American radio.

Two others who remembered Harrison's performance as being most pleasing were Richard Rodgers and Oscar Hammerstein II, who in 1950 invited Harrison to star in their forthcoming musical adaptation of the story, *The King and I*. Harrison had other commitments and the part went to the little-known Yul Brynner, who also starred in Fox's brash, colourful movie version of 1956 with Deborah Kerr as Anna, and has spent years reviving the role on stage with great success. As a result of this (and copyright complications), the earlier film version, with its greater delicacy and charm, has tended to be forgotten.

At the time, *Anna and the King of Siam* was a great success but it didn't provide Fox with any pointers as to what Harrison should do next, except to encourage the executives to view him as a character actor rather than a romantic lead. For most of 1946 Harrison was idle, though still drawing his weekly stipend. Remembering *Night Train to Munich*, Fox did offer him the lead in a war-time spy drama, *13 Rue Madeleine*, but he declined to make another expedition behind enemy lines and the part was later taken by James Cagney (for whom it must have been extensively re-written). Eventually, Harrison agreed to appear in *The Ghost and Mrs Muir*, Philip Dunne's adaptation of a book by Mrs R. A. Dick which was directed by Joseph L. Mankiewicz, the first of four films that the star and director would make together.

In *The Ghost and Mrs Muir*, Harrison played the ghost of the swaggering sea captain Daniel Gregg who haunts

58

the cliff-top Gull Cottage on the English coast at the turn of the century. He died there, having accidentally gassed himself, and now frightens away all visitors until a determined young widow (Gene Tierney) with a small daughter (Natalie Wood) comes to stay. She refuses to be scared off by his hearty laughter and spooky tricks, and quickly wins his admiration, then later his love. She melts his arrogance and arouses his concern for her welfare and happiness.

It is a splendid romantic story that memorably introduces a bearded Harrison by his portrait (picked out in an otherwise totally dark room) and his booming, diabolical laugh. 'I've lived a man's life and I'm not ashamed of it,' he later informs Tierney after he has materialised to her and the film demonstrates his lusty appetite by having him openly appreciate her beauty, finding her 'confoundedly attractive' and shocking her with the comment, after watching her innocently undress and settle down in bed, 'My dear, never let anyone tell you to be ashamed of your figure!' In this chaste Production Code era, it is only because a physical relationship is impossible that Harrison can be so explicit about her charms. The film also ingeniously teases us with an unpermissible four-letter word that Tierney won't utter and reluctantly types as part of the 'unvarnished' autobiography he is dictating to her.

With his gruff, resonant tone of voice, Harrison is vividly convincing as a salty seafarer, outspoken but honest and proud of his profession, even though he is now only a landlubbing ghost. His feelings for the sea mingle with his feelings for the widow when he withdraws to let her lead her own life. He comes to her while she's asleep to impress on her to remember him only as a dream, and leans over her bed, almost kissing her, then goes off to pause at the French windows and lament the life they can't have together – his voice ringing with excitement at the thought of voyages they could have shared. 'What we've missed, Lucia! What we've both missed . . . Goodbye, my darling,' he says, quietly but fervently.

Their reunion after her death, when she steps out of her aged body into his waiting arms as the young woman he first knew, and they go off together out of the house, silhouetted against the sky, is a gorgeous image of romantic fulfilment. Sentimental though *The Ghost and Mrs Muir* is, it has none of the cloying heaviness of that classic spiritual fantasy *Smilin' Through* or the over-wrought intensity of *Portrait of Jennie*, Selznick's ghostly romantic blockbuster that came after this film. It also has far more substance than *Topper* or *Blithe Spirit*, in which smart people exchange wisecracks without really caring about anything. Even the most obvious source of humour – Tierney talking to a Harrison unseen by others in the room who think she's talking to them – is effectively handled. In its modest way, *The Ghost and Mrs Muir* is a complete triumph and it has been fondly remembered over the years, as late as 1968 stimulating a television series in which Edward Mulhare played the ghostly Captain opposite Hope Lange as the widow.

After the racial and physical restraints imposed on his love-making to desirable widows by his first two Hollywood films, Harrison was permitted to play a red-blooded rake of the Old South (1820s New Orleans) in *The Foxes of Harrow*, a sprawling adaptation of a popular Frank Yerby novel for which he had to learn dancing, fencing, judo and card playing. The film tried to emulate *Gone with the Wind* but it lacked Technicolor and its epic pretensions made it seem long-winded and heavy-going; Harrison donned a moustache like Clark Gable (he had great admiration for Gable's style) and tried to bring as much zest to his part as Gable had given to Rhett Butler.

Harrison was playing an Irish gambler of illegitimate

birth, Stephen Fox, who wins a plantation in a card game and forces his way into the landed gentry, marrying a haughty society girl (Maureen O'Hara) and seeking to establish a dynasty like those he knew in Ireland. She gives him a son, conceived before their wedding night on which they quarrel and he storms out, vowing never to enter her bedroom again. There is much further feuding within their marriage-in-name-only until the accidental death of their child and the near loss of their plantation brings them back together. Harrison demonstrates his cool, calmly smiling when the South collapses financially and the Creole gentlemen at the stock exchange panic. Maureen O'Hara is at her fiery, spirited best flinging insults at Harrison and trying to rally the voodoo-fearing plantation workers before his return. But with its claustrophobic studio sets and excess of talk, the film was much less than its stars deserved. Later, there were plans to put them together again in another period drama, *Forbidden Street* (released in Britain as *Britannia Mews*), which was shot in England; but Dana Andrews took over the male leads (it was a dual role) in what turned out to be a sorry mess.

Harrison did make *Escape* in England for Fox. It was an updated version of John Galsworthy's 1926 play which had originally been filmed in 1930 with Gerald du Maurier in the part Harrison was now playing. Harrison's fond memories of the old film version had made him suggest it to Darryl Zanuck as a suitable British project to star him. Zanuck needed to put films into production in England to fulfil promises made under the settlement of Hollywood's dispute with the British government over import taxes. However, an American writer and director were assigned to the film: Philip Dunne and Joseph L. Mankiewicz, both of whom had worked together before with Harrison on *The Ghost and Mrs Muir*. *Escape* was filmed on an amazingly generous budget of $1.6 million on Dartmoor and at Denham in late 1947.

Harrison plays Matt Denant, a gentleman of private means who engages in conversation with a prostitute while strolling at night in Hyde Park, then intervenes when a surly plain-clothes policeman tries to arrest her for accosting. A fight ensues and Harrison accidentally kills the policeman while defending himself. He is sentenced to three years for manslaughter, but finds prison intolerable and during a fog escapes from a working party onto Dartmoor.

He is befriended by a well-bred young woman who first spots him while she is taking part in a fox hunt but doesn't give him away. She later provides him with her fiancé's clothes and a fishing rod as a disguise after she finds him stealing her breakfast in her house. She then encounters him three further times during the manhunt and tries to help him. She is drawn to Harrison on first sight, even as a haggard refugee in a convict's outfit. She has read of his case in the newspapers and accepts his assertion that he was wrongly convicted. She soon falls in love with him and urges him to give himself up for their sake.

It's a screen cliché that a wronged hero on the run will be helped and trusted by a woman on impulse. Here it means something because of the casting of Peggy Cummins in the woman's part. She brings to it an erotic charge that takes her role quite out of the documentary-like realism of the rest. Why she helps him is far more interesting than Galsworthy's dubious comments on the nature of justice.

Peggy Cummins is a prisoner in her own way – prepared to marry a man she doesn't love because she wants to enjoy his wealth, suspecting he is unfaithful to her, and straining under the 'very high standards' set for her by her elder, straitlaced sister and by the unseen fiancé. She tells Harrison she hasn't the faintest idea why she first aids him, then later refers to her sister: 'There's only one way I can make living with her tolerable and that's by doing outrageous things every now and then.'

Her attachment to Harrison goes beyond all reason, all the more so because Harrison does not fully respond to it. It prefigures the heated sexuality that Peggy Cummins was to bring to the *film noir* masterpiece, *Gun Crazy*, made a year later, in which she took the aggressive lead. Contemporary critics of *Escape* found her 'immature' and attributed her help to Harrison as some obscure sporting instinct to give the human fox a chance; but her performance *alone* makes her support for Harrison's convict entirely convincing. There is one scene in an old hut where she catches up with the wounded bedraggled Harrison and urges him to surrender for her sake. 'I want to wait and marry you if you'll have me,' she says. 'There's nothing as poor as an ex-convict's wife – you'll hate it and hate me,' replies Harrison. 'It's the hard way, isn't it? I'll take it, thank you,' she says. 'Because you pity me now?' Harrison asks. 'Because I love you now!' she insists. Here for a moment is a lyrical fervour that a less intellectual director than Mankiewicz might have developed elsewhere. When Harrison collapses, she decides what's best for them and goes off to find a policeman.

But not even her love can overcome Harrison's determination to fight injustice, his refusal to submit to the verdict passed on him in court. The film rubs in the shortcomings of the law, suggesting that irreligious, 'respectable' society is no better than the criminal underworld. A so-called friend betrays Harrison to the police. A used-car salesman tells lies (and Harrison tells him, 'You're an honest citizen, my friend – the kind that sits on juries to judge the criminal class'). The villagers turn into a vigilante mob, pressing unwanted help onto the police. Society is hostile; but as Harrison is really from that society and in fact innocent, the comparison is less apt than if he were a crook. Ironically, it is the police inspector who has most sympathy for Harrison, but his duty prevents him from providing any assistance. (William Hartnell, who normally played crooks, is the inspector, so the casting reinforces the view of society as crooked even if the character's actions disprove the initial impression he makes.)

Only a tragic outcome or an escape to freedom abroad (such as Humphrey Bogart enjoyed in the similarly-themed *Dark Passage*, released the year before) could have satisfactorily resolved the drama, yet oddly the film (following Galsworthy) insists that justice even when unjust is all for the best and Harrison goes back to prison voluntarily with Cummins waiting for him. His change of heart comes when he surrenders to the police to remove from a country parson (Norman Wooland) the choice of saving him (if he lies) or bringing about his capture. It is a gesture as honourable as his intervention on behalf of the prostitute in the park. Yet the parson has no flock to speak of (and the villagers seem defiantly un-Christian), so Harrison's action, splendidly noble as it is, on a practical level hardly seems important enough for him to abandon his cause and to forget his former insistence that he would rather be dead than locked up again.

With its lame finale, *Escape* was not surprisingly a poor performer at the box-office. Darryl Zanuck removed a scene in which Harrison, masquerading as a fisherman on a river bank, debates justice and the law with another angler (played by Felix Aylmer) who turns out to be a kindly judge and who lets him go. It was Zanuck's desire to emphasise the chase and cut back on the talk, and, even for its release in Britain, *Escape* ran a mere 79 minutes.

Returning to America, Harrison found the screenplay

of *Unfaithfully Yours* waiting for him in New York. For a change, it was an original script (all his previous Fox pictures had been adaptations). He had never met the author, the comedy genius Preston Sturges, who had just moved to Fox to become a writer-director-producer, but he read the script and wired his immediate acceptance to Sturges and Zanuck. His part was that of Sir Alfred de Carter, a symphony conductor who suspects his wife of infidelity and dreams up three ways of dealing with the situation. It was an extremely long and complicated role, both in dialogue and in action. Sturges' original choice had been James Mason whom he knew well, but Mason was unavailable and so, as in the case of *Anna and the King of Siam*, Harrison gained a memorable role at Mason's expense. But again it was a part more suited to Harrison with its flashes of temperament and need for a light touch.

Harrison's Sir Alfred is modelled in career terms on another musical knight, Sir Thomas Beecham, as Sturges subtly indicates by giving his character family wealth derived from making laxatives (de Carter's Little Liver Pills?) to match Sir Thomas's fortune from Beecham's Pills. Just as the short-tempered Beecham once barked at an unruly concert audience, 'Quiet, peasants, this stuff is too good for you!' so Harrison concludes a rehearsal by telling the musicians, 'You're much too good for them!'

Harrison's attitude to music in the film is refreshingly irreverent. 'There is nothing serious about music,' he thunders. 'It should be enjoyed flat on the back, with a sandwich in one hand and a bucket of beer in the other, and as many pretty girls around as possible.' He encourages a member of the orchestra to produce a huge pair of cymbals and bring them together in a brazen crash. However, Harrison does regard music as more serious than Hollywood movies, while, learning that a seedy private detective is a great concertgoer, he declares, 'I'd always hoped music had a certain moral and antiseptic power, quite apart from its obvious engorgement of the senses, which elevated and purified its disciples, lifting them out of vulgar professions . . .'

It required some intensive preparation on Harrison's part to be convincing with the baton before an orchestra (though he had had some instruction for a scene in *St Martin's Lane*). Robin Sanders-Clark, a young English conductor, spent seven weeks of evening sessions training Harrison and practising with him, and it was another instance of the actor's dedication to perfectionism. He couldn't read a note of music, nor was he a devotee of the classics (his own taste ran to swing and he had built up a collection of over 5,000 recordings), but he learned by constant repetition, by ear, all the notes of the three pieces he had to conduct, every beat and measure and every gesture he had to make to bring in various sections of the orchestra. 'Sometimes we'd work until two or three in the morning,' Sanders-Clark recalled. 'I first of all had to teach him how to conduct four-in-a-bar, three-in-a-bar, two-in-a-bar, and so on, which I did. And then he had to learn the pieces like he learned lines. So I'd take, for instance, the *Semiramide* Overture and say, "It starts at four bars with a timpani. The fifth bar, the violas and cellos enter, and, on the ninth bar, the horns enter." So he absolutely learned it like that. I showed him where all the sections of the orchestra would be and he had to count mentally. Also, I had an off-camera mike and I would prompt him, always a bar or two bars ahead.'

According to a studio press release, the 110-strong orchestra was very blasé about Harrison at first, the musicians having played under such conductors as Toscanini and Stokowski, but they found that he'd learned his conducting job so thoroughly that they actually followed his beat, gave him an ovation, and huddled together to compose a 'Harrison Fanfare' with which they greeted his appearances on the podium. They also presented him with a commemorative scroll: 'This Fanfare is written for and dedicated to actor Rex Harrison, who, although he cannot read a note of music, by his conscientious application and superb artistry, so perfectly learned every note and beat of Rossini's *Semiramide*, Wagner's *Tannhäuser*-Venusberg music and Tchaikovsky's *Francesca da Rimini* overture for *Unfaithfully Yours*, that we, the 110 musicians of this orchestra, thus commemorate our amazement and delight in his histrionic feat.' Harrison bowed and thanked them, pointed to his coach, and remarked, 'I'm only a Charlie McCarthy to Robin's wonderful Edgar Bergen.'

Away from the concert platform, the Harrison character turns out to be another of Preston Sturges' romantically infatuated saps like Fred MacMurray in *Remember the Night*, Brian Donlevy in *The Great McGinty*, Henry Fonda in *The Lady Eve* or Eddie Bracken in *The Miracle of Morgan's Creek*. But, whereas they were helpless pawns in the hands of an alluring woman and easily led into making fools of themselves, Harrison is solely responsible for the humiliations that descend on him, for his beautiful young wife (Linda Darnell) worships him and has done nothing to provoke him. His fears are founded on the difference in their age and this aspect of the film reflects Preston Sturges' own concern over his close relationship with his young discovery Frances Ramsden, who played opposite Harold Lloyd in *The Sin of Harold Diddlebock* (*Mad Wednesday*) and who was originally set to take the female lead in *Unfaithfully Yours*. (Gene Tierney was the next choice but she was transferred to *That Wonderful Urge*.) Harrison also sees a cultural gap, imagining that his wife prefers movies to concerts and would like to fritter away her time dancing.

In fact, the character Sturges created for Harrison is

very much like the director himself, beginning with a similarity of appearance in their moustaches. Here, uniquely, the male lead in a Sturges film is not naïve and somewhat dimwitted but a thoroughly articulate, cultured, extravagant figure like Sturges himself. Sturges was just as brash and egotistical in his film directing as he makes Harrison in his conducting. Harrison recalls that Sturges 'used to be so amused by his own dialogue that he had to sit behind the camera with a handkerchief in his mouth to stop himself laughing'.

The whole story hinges, delightfully, on a most trivial misunderstanding. Harrison's stuffy brother-in-law (Rudy Vallee) takes Harrison's request to 'keep an eye' on his wife while he is away on a concert tour to mean that he should engage a private eye to spy on her movements. Harrison loves his wife passionately (as their reunion at the airport shows) but can't shake off the suspicion generated by the detective's report that she has been having an affair with his handsome secretary of her own age (Kurt Kreuger).

As he leads the orchestra, he mulls over her apparent infidelity and the music he is conducting stimulates different solutions to the problem. The turbulence of Rossini's *Semiramide* overture gives him the idea of cutting his wife's throat and pinning the blame on the secretary. 'The Pilgrim's Chorus' from Wagner's *Tannhäuser* overture puts him in a generous and forgiving frame of mind in which he accepts losing his wife's affections and writes her a large cheque. Then Tchaikovsky's *Francesca da Rimini* overture suggests a melodramatic solution in which the two men leave to fate which of them shall have her, with Harrison forcing the cringing secretary to play Russian Roulette.

Each of these scenes is prefaced by a technically stupendous tracking shot in on Harrison beginning to conduct, with the camera getting closer and closer, finally going into the pupil of one eye – so that we almost literally enter the realm of the mind. The three sequences have a surreal vividness and exaggeration (not for nothing is there a Dali reproduction – or imitation of his 1938 *Beach Scene with Telephone* – on the wall of the apartment). These tortured flights of fantasy all reflect the character's powerful ego as he dominates their resolutions until his third scheme turns into a nightmare when his confident demonstration of Russian Roulette goes wrong. Sturges had the idea for the dream sequences from noticing years before how a symphony broadcast on a radio in another room had subconsciously affected the outcome of a story he was writing. It would of course be impossible for a conductor to let his mind wander while conducting, let alone improve his performance as is maintained here (it would be more logical – but much duller – to have had a member of the audience stimulated by the music into thinking up the three solutions).

When Harrison tries to put his schemes into practice, he finds that what worked so effortlessly in the mind's eye results only in chaos and confusion. His first resolve is still to murder his wife and he wrecks a hotel room trying to locate the recording machine that his overly-ingenious plan requires. It is a scene of pure slapstick comedy, all the funnier for befuddling a man normally so much in command of his actions – but it is, however, far too protracted and Harrison's foot tugs off the telephone receiver once too often.

Eventually, Harrison discovers that his wife is blameless and he tries to make amends. He begs her not to ask what 'utterly contemptible' notion has been on his mind and he reaffirms his love for her with lyrical extravagance, telling her in a rush of words to dress up in her most vulgar outfit to punish him and saying, 'I want to be seen in your exquisite company. I want the whole world to know that I am the most fortunate of men in the possession of the most magnificent of wives.' He then adds more slowly and with caressing gentleness: 'A thousand poets dreamed a thousand years and you were born, my love.' The film ends.

Few actors have sufficient poetic feeling to say such lines convincingly or the vocal technique to master the rhythm and emphasis. But Harrison thrives on Sturges' intricate dialogue. He can reel off lines like his somewhat contemptuous greeting to his brother-in-law as the latter enters the penthouse suite, 'Now, my dear August, what happy updraft wafts you hither?', relishing the sound of it and making it seem not in the least bit forced but spontaneously in character. Many of these intricate dialogue scenes are done in long takes, like most of the scene in which the wafted Rudy Vallee hesitantly informs Harrison that he's had his wife followed (it runs two-and-a-half minutes before a cut, and is kept visually busy by Harrison finishing dressing and moving around before the camera tracks in on the two men as he becomes increasingly annoyed and talks to Vallee face to face). Harrison also has a somewhat forced line of humour which makes him trip up over American slang, confusing footpads with flatfoots and sluicing with sleuthing ('You dare to inform me that you have had vulgar footpads in snapbrim fedoras sluicing after my beautiful wife?') although it does perhaps indicate an arrogant refusal to master American lingo.

Unfaithfully Yours remains one of the actor's very favourite films and one of the most agreeable he worked on. 'Sturges was a marvellously exciting man to work with,' Harrison has recalled. 'He was very eccentric. He used to direct in a fez so that everybody knew where he was and he couldn't be mistaken for anybody else but Preston Sturges, and he used to have a Doberman Pinscher on the set with him always – it used to bark at

the most important moments. Also it was like a circus –
anybody who was passing the sound stage, he would
beckon them in and he would love to have it a sort of
entertainment, apart from the film itself. Very amusing
man.'

In one sequence, Harrison accidentally sets fire to his
dressing room at the concert hall while trying to burn the
detective's report on his wife, and he and other characters use fire extinguishers and hoses to douse the fire.
The scene turns into a comic free-for-all with the cast
turning jets of water on each other, ignoring the fire, and
this spread to Preston Sturges and the crew joining in
and being soaked as well. Harrison caught cold and had
to work with a high temperature and take penicillin jabs
to avoid holding up the production.

The film was a very expensive undertaking because of
a huge cast (that included the 110-piece orchestra hired
for three weeks) and the very considerable salary that
Sturges drew as writer-director-producer. The budget
was around two million dollars. There was considerable
optimism that *Unfaithfully Yours* would repeat the box-
office success of Sturges' *Hail the Conquering Hero* and *The
Miracle of Morgan's Creek*. Sadly, it drew thin audiences: it
was 'much too good for them'. With hindsight (and
perhaps even without it), a film that took classical music
seriously and depended so much on highly sophisticated dialogue was hardly likely to appeal to the mass
market, who might also not have warmed to the Harrison character – irascible, overbearing and ready to murder his wife.

Over the years, *Unfaithfully Yours* has become
accepted as a comedy masterpiece and it has even
received the rare accolade for a box-office flop of being
re-made. Before his death, Peter Sellers had signed to
undertake Harrison's old role; renamed Claude
Eastman, it was eventually played by Dudley Moore and

the new *Unfaithfully Yours* on its appearance in 1984 proved to be a moderately effective piece, considerably simplified in plot. Its main drawback was its inability to make the cuddly, diminutive Moore ever seem really intent on killing his wife (now played by Nastassja Kinski). Harrison, by contrast, thoroughly convinced as a man who would like to do away with his wife, gleefully slashing at her body with a razor in his fantasy (and lit to look even more maniacal), making his version of *Unfaithfully Yours* truly a black comedy.

Part of the original film's poor reception is sometimes attributed to the Carole Landis suicide, which occurred between the completion of the film and its release, as the gossip mongers made much of Harrison's involvement with her.

Harrison had been less than popular with the Hollywood press all the time he had been there. On *Anna and the King of Siam*, he missed an interview with a leading columnist because he was too preoccupied working out how King Mongkut would eat a bowl of rice (the studio publicists turned it to advantage by issuing a story about his absentmindedness). There was much made of an occasion when he appeared on a radio show and refused to deliver a crack likening King George VI to an American millionaire socialite of the time.

The actor strongly objected to the two ogresses, Hedda Hopper and Louella Parsons, whose syndicated columns and radio broadcasts were so widely disseminated that they were feared and courted. Harrison was particularly incensed to observe Gene Tierney being reduced to tears when Hedda Hopper tore into her for withholding the information that she was pregnant. He said that the real power in Hollywood lay with 'a coterie of highly paid journalists'. He described the result: 'One of them went on the air and with heavy sarcasm called herself a "moron" and then proceeded to make me look so unsavoury a character that it would have surprised my worst enemy. Do you wonder that at such a time I said in an interview: "Hollywood and I have no future in common – and I doubt if Hollywood has a future at all"?'

Harrison was less than enchanted with the studio system that put films into production to keep the sound stages occupied and the theatres supplied with a steady stream of new product regardless of whether the script was ready or the casting satisfactory. He also found that, compared to Alexander Korda's London Films, the scale of the 20th Century-Fox operation was formidable: he could get to see Darryl Zanuck for a quarter of an hour but he rarely got anything settled in that time. So he was more than interested when playwright Maxwell Anderson approached him to appear as Henry VIII in his forthcoming Broadway production *Anne of the Thousand Days*.

During the shooting of *The Foxes of Harrow*, Harrison had met Carole Landis, who was then estranged from her fourth husband. While he was filming *Escape* in Britain, she had come over to make two films of her own, *Noose* and *The Brass Monkey*, and their friendship had flourished. (Lilli Palmer had remained in Hollywood, tied up with filming.)

Harrison continued to see Landis once they were back in Hollywood. Lilli Palmer flew east to join her married sister in New York. On 4 July 1948, Independence Day, Harrison dined with Carole at her Brentwood Heights apartment, then left to visit an old friend from *French Without Tears* days, Roland Culver. The following morning he talked to Maxwell Anderson about *Anne of the Thousand Days*. He later telephoned Landis, who hadn't been seen all day by her maid, and drove over to investigate, only to find her dead body on the floor in a bathroom. An empty bottle of pills and a note to her mother clearly indicated suicide. Harrison went off to try to find his own doctor, then called the nearest hospital and the police before returning to her place.

The actress's death and the exposure of her relationship with Harrison made newspaper headlines. The gossip columnists and gutter press tried to turn it into a scandal, hinting that Harrison might have removed a note addressed to himself or that some action of his might have caused her to take her own life. It was not then known that Miss Landis had tried to commit suicide several times before. Lilli Palmer flew back from New York and joined her husband.

Even if Harrison had endeared himself to the gossip mongers, it is doubtful whether they could have resisted exploiting the Landis tragedy. They began calling Harrison 'Sexy Rexy', much to his annoyance (in reply, he would sometimes comment, 'The formation of my eyes may be sexy but what I think really fools people are the bags I have under them'). Harrison wasn't alone in having ruffled Hedda, Louella and their ilk. Other British stars in Hollywood like James Mason and (later) Stewart Granger didn't play ball with them either. And it is worth remembering that Hollywood was not that well disposed towards Britain generally. Beginning with films like *Blithe Spirit*, J. Arthur Rank had been having some alarming success in eroding Hollywood's dominance of the world market, and the British government had only recently withdrawn the punitive 'Dalton duty' on American film income from Britain (the richest source of foreign revenue) which had caused Hollywood to slash budgets and cancel or postpone projects with resultant loss of work. In addition, the Zionist movement in America had stirred up considerable Anglophobia in its protests at British policy in Palestine.

Harrison felt a distinct lack of support from 20th Century-Fox in the aftermath of Carole Landis's death. The studio must have concluded that the actor could never be turned into a major box-office asset. The simplest solution under the circumstances was to dissolve the contract and allow Harrison to go back to the stage in *Anne of the Thousand Days*.

6
Escape from Hollywood

REHEARSALS FOR *ANNE OF THE THOUSAND DAYS* DID NOT
start until 15 September 1948, so Harrison first accompanied his wife to Paris where she was to make the film
Hans le Marin.

Deborah Kerr had been the first choice to play the part
of Anne Boleyn in the stage play but MGM refused to
release her and the part went to Joyce Redman. The
production was an expensive one, eventually costing
$300,000, and there were considerable difficulties
staging the play in the intricate manner that Maxwell
Anderson wanted, using revolving stages, a series of
flashbacks and short episodes in a somewhat filmic manner. The original director, Bretaigne Windust, was soon
reported too exhausted to continue and former stage
director H. C. Potter raced in from Hollywood and
quickly set about simplifying the structure, ordering
new sets from designer Jo Mielziner, and condensing
three acts into two with Anderson's willing co-operation. All this was done in two and a half weeks
prior to the postponed Broadway first night on 8
December 1948 with the last changes being made a

77

couple of hours before the curtain went up. Despite its traumatic gestation, the play was rapturously received by critics and audiences and occupied Harrison for most of 1949 on Broadway and then on a tour of the Midwest and Canada.

The play was still far from orthodox in form, with a series of brief scenes, but the powerful performances of Harrison and Joyce Redman gave it shape and strength. Playing Henry VIII, Rex was barely recognisable with false cheeks, a bearded face, and a portly body padded with foam rubber. His characterisation of the lusty monarch made him less of a glutton than was the case in Charles Laughton's classic screen portrayal. The Harrison humour did something to soften the strutting arrogance of the King and the result was a complex portrait of a man not only bawdy and cruel but also concerned to be a wise ruler. Back on stage for the first time in seven years (except for reviving *French Without Tears* to entertain the troops), Harrison had the great satisfaction of winning the Antoinette Perry award for the best dramatic actor of the season. He may have had greater satisfaction still in being presented with the award by none other than Hedda Hopper, the gossip queen who had pronounced his career 'dead as a mackerel' only a few months before. It all served to show that in New York private matters did not interfere with the appreciation of talent. It was twenty years before *Anne of the Thousand Days* was made into a film with Richard Burton playing Henry and Genevieve Bujold as Anne.

Lilli Palmer meanwhile was starring in a Broadway revival of Shaw's *Caesar and Cleopatra* opposite Sir Cedric Hardwicke. The pair of them roped in Harrison to appear in a one-night charity performance of Shaw's *The Dark Lady of the Sonnets* which Hardwicke directed with Lilli as the Dark Lady and Rex in Elizabethan costume as the Bard. If Harrison had to play Shakespeare, this was the way he preferred it – written by Shaw.

Harrison made his debut on American television with a personal appearance on NBC's *Saturday Night Revue* and followed this with an acting appearance on the same network's Chevrolet Tele-Theatre in a dramatic fantasy called *The Walking Stick*. He played a diffident assistant bank manager whose personality is transformed when he inherits a fancy cane. He becomes a well-dressed dandy, so full of himself that the cane trips him up to teach him a lesson. The narration to this whimsical piece was provided by the cane itself, which helped Harrison thwart a bank robbery, earn promotion to manager, and win the hand of a girl.

Kurt Weill came up with an intriguing project at this period: he was thinking of a new English version of *The Threepenny Opera* for Rex Harrison, was convinced that the actor could sing well enough, and discussed a collaboration with Alan Jay Lerner, but nothing came of it.

Alec Guinness had brought T. S. Eliot's verse play *The Cocktail Party* to Broadway early in 1950. Harrison saw it and eagerly accepted an offer to star in the London production by the same director, E. Martin Browne. It opened in May 1950 and Harrison was seen as 'An Unidentified Guest', the key figure who involves himself in the romantic triangle consisting of a barrister (Ian Hunter), his wife (Alison Leggatt) and the other woman (Margaret Leighton). In particular, he tries to help the mistress find salvation. The Guinness interpretation had accented the supernatural, God-like aspect of the character. To the reviewer from *The Stage*, Harrison suggested 'a confident and competent professional psychiatrist rather than a manifestation from another world' and this raised a doubt: 'Whether Mr Harrison, normally so light and volatile a comedian, is quite the man for the psychiatrist's part may be open to question. But he plays it with great dignity, seriousness and intelligence, with a cool sense of humour peeping through now and then.'

The stylised, sometimes rhyming dialogue and the emphasis on the souls rather than the hearts of its troubled characters made it 'theatre of cerebration' to be regarded with respect rather than enthusiasm. It prompted one wit to change Harrison's soubriquet from 'Sexy Rexy' to 'Holy Harrison'. The actor himself noticed a difference: 'Not many people ever came round to see me after *The Cocktail Party*. I used to sit and stare at myself in the mirror and you felt as if you'd been sitting in a cold bath for three hours. Your head had been occupied enormously but you weren't allowed to give emotions to that piece. Eliot came to rehearsals and his metre in his head was very strong . . . I found it awfully difficult to find a metre in it.'

Harrison resumed his film career in Britain with *The Long Dark Hall*. It was a small independent production based on an American screenplay by Nunnally Johnson, originally written for Universal and somewhat similar to his 1944 *The Woman in the Window*, as both films concern a meek, respectable figure involved with a glamorous young woman and death, and both had unsatisfactory gimmick endings. Certainly this new picture would have better suited Edward G. Robinson, the star of *The Woman in the Window*, than it did Harrison.

Here Rex was required to play a suburban businessman called Arthur Groome who has a wife (Lilli Palmer) and two children. He also has an affair with a chorus girl (Patricia Wayne) and when he finds her murdered at her Earls Court lodgings he runs away in panic. Subsequently questioned by the police, he at first denies all knowledge of the dead woman to spare his wife's feelings, then admits the truth. Charged with murder and put on trial at the Old Bailey, he is found guilty and sentenced to death by hanging. The real murderer (Anthony Dawson) watches the proceedings with relish and pens a letter to the police to arrive after the execution, boasting of how he has hoodwinked them. Only an arbitrary plot twist saves Harrison from the rope to be eventually reunited with his forgiving family. He has suffered enough.

Denied his usual chance to assert himself, even more a prisoner of circumstances than in *Escape*, Harrison could only give a technically sound but monotonously subdued performance. Not surprisingly, he regards it as one of his worst pictures.

Later in 1950 he and his wife returned to Broadway in a new comedy by John Van Druten, *Bell, Book and Candle*, which the author himself directed. It was a slight fantasy in which Lilli Palmer played modern-day witch Gillian Holroyd who uses her magical powers to bewitch a publisher, Shepherd Henderson (Rex Harrison), and keep him from marrying a woman she detests. But when the witch falls in love with her victim, she loses her supernatural skills. *Variety's* reviewer, 'Hobe', said: 'The couple, as a sort of junior Alfred Lunt and Lynn Fontanne, play with deft, disarming assurance, providing the principal vitality to a whimsy that starts engagingly, but presently fades into innocuous banalities.' The same scribe added that the play 'provides the Harrisons with several captivating love scenes, which are played with diverting realism (and which staid suburban matrons can comfortably relish, since the stars are married in private life)'. The eminent arbiter George Jean Nathan reluctantly attached the word 'charm' to their performances: 'It is generally an overworked word and analytical readers are inclined to sicken of it. But I don't know any other to describe the performances of Lilli Palmer and Rex Harrison, who contribute a large share of it to the evening. In addition to expertness, both have that uncommon quality which, like whipped cream on borscht, adds to the relish of what technically they boil so well, and about which Barrie noted, "If you have charm, you don't really need to have anything else; and if you don't have it, it doesn't matter what else you have."'

Six out of eight principal New York reviewers praised the play and put it firmly in the winners' circle so that it kept the Harrisons busy until the end of May 1951 when they could slip away for a holiday at Portofino on the Italian Riviera where, on a hillside site they had spotted during a summer break two years before, they had paid for a house to be built.

Gabriel Pascal had signed Harrison to play Julius Caesar in his latest Shaw venture, a production of *Androcles and the Lion* for Howard Hughes at RKO in Hollywood; but, true to Pascal's past form (compounded by interference from Hughes), the film ran into problems and had to be temporarily shut down. When it did get underway six months later in September 1951, Harrison was committed to another film in Hollywood and Maurice Evans inherited the role of Caesar.

It was not the Hollywood establishment that beckoned Harrison to return. It was a maverick producer, Stanley Kramer, who came under intense pressure for wanting to use him and Lilli Palmer in a film version of Jan de Hartog's play *The Four Poster* which had been a great success on Broadway for the husband and wife team of Hume Cronyn and Jessica Tandy. What Kramer offered was a laudable attempt to make a different kind of film. Instead of the usual 'opening out', the film essentially restricted itself to just two characters like the play and to the same single setting, a bedroom (with the eponymous bed), venturing only momentarily onto the landing outside. According to Lilli Palmer, Kramer tried to get out of using Harrison and he was then asked to sign a conciliatory letter to Louella Parsons and refused, before the producer went ahead with them. *The Four Poster* was made in a theatrical fashion – completely rehearsed before any scene was filmed, then shot in two weeks entirely in sequence – a method which turned out to be, in Harrison's words, 'a terrible experience'. Often, complete scenes were shot in takes lasting from seven to ten minutes (although in editing other shots from different angles were inter-cut). And so the film was faithful to its source material, but did this make sense given that it *was* now in a different medium?

The Four Poster tells the story of a couple from their wedding night in 1897 to the death of the surviving partner forty-five years later. The couple are not recluses and big events do happen outside the bedroom, such as the First World War, a long cruise together, and the building up of the neighbourhood. These are conveyed in cartoon form by the UPA studio (creators of Gerald McBoing Boing) and Harrison and Palmer are depicted in caricatures silently participating in them. There is considerable wit in the drawing and, given the expense of animation, it was probably no cheaper than staging the key scenes with actual performers, using back projection and similar cost-cutting methods. But it seems unnecessarily artificial and constricting to present a scene like Harrison's dismissal as a schoolteacher in cartoon form, or to keep the couple's son and daughter as well as the 'other woman' off screen. It means that we only know the pair in a limited way and that Harrison has to resort to an unlikely slip of the tongue to impart to us in the last supper scene the information that Lilli Palmer is dying.

It throws an enormous strain on Palmer and Harrison, and the material they are given is too ordinary to work. The nervousness of Palmer on the wedding night, the row over Harrison's infidelity, the loss of the son in the Great War – these are all clichéd episodes, as are the conceptions of Harrison and Palmer, he always selfish and weak, she consistently long-suffering and cleverer. Changes in their appearance provide some variety –

Harrison is clean-shaven for the marriage, then has a rakish beard and moustache as a successful author, a moustache only in later years, and then is white-haired and clean-shaven again in old age. But the camera is hard to fool and the two players are too old for the early scenes and not frail enough (a fault that could have been remedied by slower movements) in old age.

Perhaps the most effective episode has Harrison tell Palmer that he intends going off with another woman, whereupon Palmer persuades him to stay by pretending that she too has a lover and arousing his jealousy, only to give the game away when she relaxes prematurely after they kiss and her relief is apparent. Here, as in most other scenes, it is Lilli Palmer who has the greater range of emotions to convey. Harrison expectedly relishes his caddish and cantankerous moments but remains too brisk in the scene in which his plan for them to die together goes astray. After her demise, when she appears to him as a vision, seduces him to his own death, and they become their younger selves again in the hereafter, the theme of love eternal is bland and unaffecting: the similar conclusion to *The Ghost and Mrs Muir* was much more powerful.

Next, Laurence Olivier invited the Harrisons to star in his Broadway re-staging of Christopher Fry's *Venus Observed* (Olivier had played the lead in London), and this opened in February 1952. Rex played the greying, distinguished-looking Duke of Altair whose great passions in life have been women and astronomy. He invites his former lovers to the observatory in a wing of his mansion so that they can observe a total eclipse of the sun. He has decided to marry whichever of the women his son (John Merivale) selects, but a new arrival on the scene (Lilli Palmer) distracts him.

Of course, the play's quality resided in the complex language of Fry's text with its sections of ornate verse.

On stage virtually throughout, Harrison rose to the challenge, causing *Variety's* reviewer, 'Hobe', to comment: 'Whether or not he fully understands everything Fry is getting at, he gives the impression of doing so. And, what's more important, he gives the playgoer the illusion, however temporary, that he too grasps what it's all about.' And of the play generally: 'Nearly always it is saved by Harrison's magnetic, elucidating performance in the principal role. So *Venus* comes across as an interesting and enjoyable, if not always completely comprehensible, evening.'

Looking back on his appearances in the Eliot and Fry plays, Harrison told interviewer Michael Coveney: 'These plays were very difficult, and very different to anything I'd done. The Eliot was very precise; he made the maximum effect with almost the minimum amount of words. It was very sparse, in a sense, unlike Fry, who would use word-images. He was very flowery, Fry, in his use of words. So they were totally different in style, and I found that the Fry was the most difficult to learn. He used extraordinary images, Fry, and gave marvellous shapes and patterns to his words. But it was very hard on the actor!'

For the premiere show in the *Omnibus* series on American television in 1952, Rex starred again as Henry VIII in *Trial of Anne Boleyn*, a short play that Maxwell Anderson derived from *Anne of the Thousand Days*. This time it was Lilli Palmer who played the hapless Anne. *Omnibus* also included a dance number, excerpts from *The Mikado*, and a dramatised William Saroyan story as a cultural feast for late Sunday afternoon consumption. It was tasty enough to launch *Omnibus* successfully on its long run.

To help promote the theatre, the Harrisons joined other stage celebrities appearing as themselves in the film *Main Street to Broadway* which told the story of a young playwright's attempts to succeed on the Great

White Way. Rex and Lilli were filmed strolling along 44th Street discussing the phenomenon of the three-decker sandwich and the difficulty of consuming such a thick wedge of food. The film was of such limited appeal to movie fans and theatregoers that it did negligible good to the coffers of the Council of the Living Theatre which was promised twenty-five per cent of the profits. It leaked onto the British market three years later.

The Theatre Guild, which had staged *Venus Observed*, now made Harrison an intriguing proposition: would he like to star in and direct a New York production of the London stage success *The Love of Four Colonels* by Peter Ustinov? Harrison accepted the challenge and the play opened in New York in January 1953. His debut as a director was a success.

Ustinov's play featured four Colonels in Occupied Europe – British, American, French and Russian – who are offered an opportunity by Harrison's agent of the Devil to make love to Lilli Palmer as the legendary Sleeping Beauty. There were four plays-within-the-play in which each Colonel was seen with his concept of the beauty and these were parodies of Shakespeare, modern American drama, French Restoration comedy and Chekhov. Harrison and Palmer appeared in wildly different costumes for each episode; Harrison even wore different noses as well as a huge plaster cast on one leg and a flowing wig for the French period sequence, a ragged white beard, white coat and monocle for the Russian, and a jester's costume for the British.

During try-outs Harrison decided to eliminate appearances by the Colonels' wives that had been a feature of the play's finale, and 'Hobe' in *Variety* felt this contributed to the weakness of the second half, but again he had praise for Harrison: 'If there was any doubt of it before, *Colonels* should establish Harrison as the most expert and ingratiating light comedian on the stage

86

today . . . he picks up the show from his initial entrance and gives it an electric quality whenever he's on thereafter.'

The Theatre Guild had also engaged Harrison and Lilli Palmer to star in radio and television adaptations of a 1930 play by H. M. Harwood, *Man in Possession*, which had originally been a big hit with Leslie Banks. The couple first performed it around 1951 for Theatre Guild on the Air and then again when the Theatre Guild went into American television for the US Steel Hour in 1953.

Rex took the meaty role of the ex-Cambridge wastrel, Raymond Dabney, recently out of prison, who obtains a job as a bailiff's emissary and is assigned custody of the effects of a young widow (Lilli Palmer) who is in debt. He covets the lady, who is engaged to his brother (Robert Coote), and allows her to retain her property while he masquerades as a servant in the mansion and tries to win her for himself. It made for unusually elegant television fare.

At the end of the year, Jack Warner at Warner Bros. decided to risk the ire of the gossip queens and invited Harrison to play in *King Richard and the Crusaders*, a film of Sir Walter Scott's *The Talisman* that was part of a revival of interest in Scott's work following the success of MGM's *Ivanhoe*. Harrison was offered a character role, that of a Saracen ruler, but he was given top billing ahead of Virginia Mayo, George Sanders (as King Richard) and Laurence Harvey (the romantic hero) and doubtless knew that he could steal the picture as the chivalrous but crafty Sultan Saladin. Filmed in the new CinemaScope process with WarnerColor and Perspecta Stereophonic Sound, it was an action spectacular for kids of all ages and it didn't have to be good. In fact, as Harrison has since said, it was 'absolutely rotten' – but it was a real hoot.

Blacked up and bearded, wearing long robes and

dashing about on horseback, hissing and bowing in a somewhat Japanese style, Harrison actually proves to be more of a gentleman than King Richard, who is seeking to drive him from the Holy Land and has brought along his blonde cousin Lady Edith (Virginia Mayo) to watch the fun. Richard behaves with the cruelty and bloodlust of an Eastern barbarian ('War, war, that's all you ever think of, Dick Plantagenet!' says Virginia Mayo in a classic rebuke at the end) while Harrison displays a European sophistication and prudence. He tricks his way to the ailing King Richard's bedside, offering to restore him to health if he will stop fighting, and mixing a medicinal brew in the manner of a fashionable Harley Street specialist. Unfortunately, Harrison is captivated by the beauty of Miss Mayo (convincing enough, for she did have some special appeal to the Eastern eye: a Sultan of Morocco once described her as 'tangible proof of the existence of God'), and he pads around her tent playing a lyre and singing to her. The real villains are among the Crusaders and it takes the combined efforts of Harrison and Laurence Harvey's Scottish knight to save Richard's life. At the end, Miss Mayo falls into the arms of Laurence Harvey since Harrison's dark skin effectively rules him out and he rides off without complaining, a gallant gentleman to the end.

After that, he must have been relieved to receive an offer from Sidney Gilliat to star in his new comedy, *The Constant Husband*, playing a man who wakes up in a Welsh hotel bedroom, having completely lost his memory. It was meant to be a saucy, Gallic-style comedy of mounting embarrassment as Harrison slowly discovers to his horror that he has at least seven wives in different places, all of whom want him back – especially Kay Kendall's redheaded fashion photographer and Nicole Maurey's temperamental circus artiste. Charged with polygamy at the Old Bailey, Harrison is defended by yet another woman, Margaret Leighton's Miss Chesterman, who predictably decides at the end to become his next wife.

It could have been an amusing reversal of Harrison's screen image – the great lover who only wants to be left alone in his prison cell. But the Launder and Gilliat team were no longer the inventive groundbreakers they had been in the Forties, the film is so innocuous it gained a U certificate, and one is left feeling Harrison would have been much more interesting playing the polygamist *before* he lost his memory. It was a long way from the subtlety and quality of *The Rake's Progress*. Part of the problem may have been diagnosed by Sidney Gilliat in his recent comment: 'I'm fascinated by the film whenever I see it, because it's in an absolutely consistent style. It is over-directed to exactly the same degree with everyone: everyone does more than I should have let him or her do. If it had just been toned down it would have been a better picture. As it was, it looks as though we all enjoyed ourselves, but it hasn't got quite the high comedy tone that I really intended. I just pushed it a bit too hard. One is apt to do that with Rex because Rex is not an over-player . . .'

Harrison then turned stage director again to put on the London production of *Bell, Book and Candle*, once more starring himself and Lilli Palmer. He worked with playwright John Van Druten to Anglicise the work, changing the first name of his character from Shepherd to Anthony Henderson and the setting from New York to Knightsbridge. Once again the play was deemed slight but there was nothing but praise for the work of the two stars. As Ronald Barker put it in *Plays and Players*: '. . . it is a very amusing evening in the theatre, thanks to the Harrisons. They play with a delicate, feather-weight touch which is a joy to watch. They transform this ordinary dialogue into something which passes for wit.' (They succeeded, then, where James Stewart and Kim Novak failed in the 1958 film version.)

While the run continued, Harrison accepted an offer to direct Dame Edith Evans in Arthur Macrae's adaptation of a French boudoir farce, *Nina*, by André Roussin (whose *The Little Hut* had recently been a big hit). As Harrison candidly reveals in his autobiography, there were problems with the casting of the principal male roles of husband and lover. Dame Edith couldn't adjust to the work of two less precise performers and suffered a breakdown in Liverpool just before the try-out. (It could be relevant that Gloria Swanson had come to hate the play before she opened in it on Broadway in 1951 and had to be forced to stay on for its short, forty-five performance run.) Coral Browne replaced Dame Edith, Michael Hordern took over the lover's part, and the play ran into more difficulties, opening in London not only in July, which was a bad time of year anyway, but during a heatwave. Dame Edith's name on the front of house display would have ensured an audience but it was a lost cause without her, so flimsy and old-fashioned were the complications of the play's storyline. Harrison refers to it as 'a failure on my part which still makes me shudder' although *Variety's* London reviewer ('Clem') described the play as being 'superbly directed by Rex Harrison' and 'staged . . . with a light touch'. And, fortunately for Harrison, the greatest success of his life was just around the corner.

7
Enter Henry Higgins

In October 1954, Rex Harrison received a phone call from New York asking if he would be interested in starring in a new Broadway musical, then to be called *Lady Liza*, based on the George Bernard Shaw screenplay for *Pygmalion*, the 1938 film produced by Gabriel Pascal. It was Pascal who had originally put forward the idea of turning *Pygmalion* into a stage musical and he had first interested Rodgers and Hammerstein in writing it, before he engaged Alan Jay Lerner in the spring of 1952. He was later compelled by financial problems to sell his rights and he died in 1954, never knowing that his idea would achieve even greater success than his own grandiose predictions. Alan Jay Lerner was now working on the musical adaptation with composer Frederick Loewe and producer Herman Levin. They had already decided that the part of Eliza Doolittle, the Cockney flower girl of Covent Garden, should for a change be played by an actress of the right age (Shaw's stage directions stated Eliza to be eighteen, but much more mature actresses, like Wendy Hiller in the film version, were traditionally cast). They had approached Julie Andrews, who had only just passed eighteen and who was the rage of Broadway in *The Boy Friend*, to take the part. For Professor Henry Higgins, the master of phonetics, they had contemplated asking Noel Coward and from there it was but a short step to considering Rex Harrison, although Michael Redgrave and Ray Milland were also kept in mind as possibilities.

When Harrison expressed a firm interest, Lerner and Loewe arranged to visit London in January 1955 to show him the songs they had written and to discuss it further. As usual, the actor took his time reaching a decision. He knew for one thing that a previous attempt to musicalise Shaw had been a disaster and he had so much respect for the playwright that he wanted to avoid anything that would damage his reputation. He was concerned about the risk to his own career in tackling a musical, and whether his voice would be good enough. Loewe found a piano and Rex sang a verse of 'Molly Malone' after which he was deemed vocally passable. 'His voice had a tenor timbre,' Lerner subsequently recollected, 'which meant it would carry over an orchestra and, we later discovered, his sense of rhythm was faultless. He is instinctively musical.' Lerner ran the film of *Pygmalion* and persuaded Harrison that Leslie Howard's portrayal of Higgins was not the definitive one – that Howard had been too charming and romantic, aware too soon of his feelings for his protégée. Lerner wanted to make Higgins more callous and genuinely taken aback when, having taught Eliza to speak like a Duchess, she fears for what will become of her. Harrison could make Higgins more irascible and disagreeable. Harrison liked the idea.

'Several factors were involved in my decision to do the show,' he later reminisced. 'First, there was Shaw, and the fact that I had guarantees in my contract that certain passages of Shaw would remain. The second factor was my genuine faith in the talents of Alan Jay Lerner. I must say, however, that in the beginning it was a most visionary project. The one number in the show at that time which was in the final version was "The Rain in Spain". Instead of "Ordinary Man", which was written later, I had a number called "Please Don't Marry Me", which was thrown out.'

Harrison finally agreed to take on the part early in February 1955, while he was appearing in *Bell, Book and Candle*, and plans were made to start rehearsals in New York towards the end of the year on the assumption that his current play would by then have exhausted its appeal with London audiences. But it continued to show such strength that the run had to be terminated by special arrangement. In the meantime, Harrison took singing lessons – at first trying unsuccessfully to improve his voice to grand opera pitch, then evolving with a musician called Bill Low the strategy of 'talking on pitch'. 'It means that you don't sing but you hit the notes with your speaking voice,' explained Harrison. 'It's really an excuse because I couldn't sing.'

'Often all of us would sit around the piano and sing Gilbert and Sullivan together,' he recalled. 'What Loewe was doing was listening to which notes I could sing and which ones I couldn't. It turned out that my range was about two notes, so they did the numbers around those two notes – three at the most. Six months passed, during which time Julie Andrews was signed, then Lerner and Loewe presented me with fresh material: "Ordinary Man" and "Why Can't the English?". Later came "I've Grown Accustomed to Her Face", and the start of rehearsals.'

Lerner comments in his book, *The Street Where I Live*: 'I realised that the secret in writing for him was to make certain at all times that the lyrical and musical line coincided exactly with the way one would speak a line. For example, "Let a woman in your life and your sabbatical is through'' was composed in such a manner that it could either be spoken or sung without altering the music. It had nothing to do with range; only that. Fritz [Frederick Loewe] and I also slowly began to realise that his songs, most of which could be classified as comedy songs, had to be built on a strong foundation of emotion.'

Cast rehearsals were scheduled to start on 3 January 1956 in New York so that the English players – who also included Stanley Holloway as Eliza's father and Robert Coote as Higgins' chum, Colonel Pickering – could enjoy Christmas at home. But Harrison arrived a short while before the holidays to have more time to prepare with the director, Moss Hart, and with Lerner and Loewe.

During rehearsals, Harrison kept a copy of Shaw's play with him to ensure that they weren't straying too far from the original text and he became, in his own words, 'a damned nuisance, clinging to Shaw like mad'. Lerner had to pretend that some of his new material was actually taken from other writing by Shaw in order to get it past the star. 'There were tremendous rages and stalkings off during rehearsals,' recalled Moss Hart, adding: 'The key to Rex is he's not a frivolous man . . . What he achieves he gets from digging, digging. Once I discovered this, I could forgive him a good deal.'

'The one thing that gave me an absolutely terrible time was learning the lyrics,' Harrison has since said. 'There's just no finding your way back when you blow a line – you have to keep on because the damned orchestra won't stop.' In fact, the first time that Harrison performed the musical numbers with the full pit orchestra, just prior to the first preview performances out of town, there was a major crisis because the star found it difficult to hear the melody. The solution was for Harrison to go straight into his songs without waiting for a cue or changing tempo, leaving it to the orchestra leader, Franz Allers, to ensure that the music started with him. 'I broke a convention between the singer and the conductor,' explained Harrison. 'The singer, so-called – I don't consider myself a singer – has always followed the conductor for the beat. But I never looked at the conductor. It would have put me off. It would have really confused me, because I tried to do something which started a vogue in musicals, pretending the orchestra wasn't there.'

In all, rehearsals lasted six weeks and exposed a weakness in Harrison's role. 'I had nothing much to do between the first number of the second act and the last number. To remedy this, while we were still in rehearsal, Lerner and Loewe wrote "Why Can't a Woman Be More Like a Man".' The show, with its title set as *My Fair Lady*, finally opened for the first of nine try-out performances at the Shubert Theatre, New Haven, during a blizzard. *Variety*'s 'Bone' covered the event: '*My Fair Lady* is going to be a whale of a show when they get it functioning within normal bounds. On the basis of a premiere that ran 30 minutes overtime, the musical contains enough smash potential to assure it a high place on the list of Broadway prospects. . . As the callous Prof. Higgins, who sees in the flower girl only a challenge to his skill with phonetics, Harrison comes through with a highly polished and engaging performance, demonstrating how to "talk" a song when vocal talents are not all they might be.' Rex had one of his numbers, 'Come to the Ball', which followed the Ascot sequence, dropped to shorten the show.

From this first glimpse, few doubted that *My Fair Lady* would be a Broadway hit and word of mouth was such that, by the time the show reached Philadelphia to continue its pre-Broadway try-outs, seats were changing hands at a premium. Local reviews were raves, audiences gave it a tumultuous reception, and the play did three weeks of (to quote *Variety*) 'smasheroo' business before moving on to the Mark Hellinger Theatre on Broadway, where it opened on 15 March 1956 to unanimously rapturous notices and became the biggest stage success in years. *Variety*'s reviewer 'Hobe' declared that 'Rex Harrison and Julie Andrews are delightful co-stars. Harrison is handicapped by his lack of a singing voice, but he succeeds in putting over his numbers effectively, making expert use of his ingratiating comic acting talent and even whacking over a sort of climax in talking his songs. His straight scenes are, of course, superb, combining the humour and attractiveness of Higgins without losing the arrogance of the character.'

In a 1965 article on Rex Harrison for *Films in Review*, Rudy Behlmer maintains that 'although he "talked" his songs, few in the audience were aware of the fact, and many believe to this day he is possessed of a first-rate singing voice and an impeccable melodic sense, so expert was his delivery of the lyrics'. Certainly by the time Harrison repeated his performance for the film version of 1964, this method of delivering songs had become so accepted that it no longer seemed forced or unusual, but just different – with an emphasis on the lyrics that, in this case, were well worth hearing.

By September 1956 it was impossible to purchase seats for less than six months away except on the black market and long queues formed to wait overnight for the standing room that was sold on the day of the performance. 'I would come out of the theatre,' Harrison recalled years later, 'and see people with blankets and thermos flasks camping for the night, outside, waiting to be first in line to get tickets the following morning. Never happened before. Don't suppose it will again.'

During the run, Harrison found time to do a television special called *Crescendo*. His masquerade as an Englishman on his first-ever visit to the United States was the flimsy excuse for a potted history of American

96

music. Rex teamed with Louis 'Satchmo' Armstrong for the number 'That's Jazz' while Julie Andrews and Stanley Holloway performed a medley from *My Fair Lady*.

Harrison had originally signed on to do *My Fair Lady* for nine months but he remained with the production for ninety weeks, until late November 1957, and was said to be earning £2,000 a week for his work. He also earned his second Antoinette Perry (or Tony) award, for Best Actor in a musical, although it could not be arranged for Hedda Hopper to present it to him again. The first actor brave enough to follow in Rex Harrison's footsteps was another non-singer, Brian Aherne, who went out with the first touring company of *My Fair Lady* in the spring of 1957. Harrison left the production to give himself a breather before he played it again in London. The actor who succeeded him on Broadway was Edward Mulhare (who also picked up another old Harrison role when he played the sea captain in the television series *The Ghost and Mrs Muir* some years later).

During the run of *My Fair Lady*, on 23 June 1957, Harrison married Kay Kendall, the actress he had met while filming *The Constant Husband* and for whom he had split up with Lilli Palmer. He already knew from her doctor that Kay had an incurable form of leukaemia that would kill her within eighteen months or so, but she was never told and Harrison willingly made it his job to look after her because of his great love for her. 'The next two years were without doubt the worst and yet the best years of my life,' he declares in his autobiography.

Kay Kendall had made her name in *Genevieve* (1953) in which she delighted audiences with her effervescent personality, especially in the trumpet-blowing sequence. She had rare gifts as a comedienne and made a terrific partner for her husband on the one occasion they were properly matched, in the film version of William Douglas

Home's *The Reluctant Debutante* which was such a mild piece of fluff it would have been nothing without them. Although the picture was set in London, most of the filming took place in Paris early in 1958 either because there was a lack of studio space in England (delay was impossible since Harrison had to be available to start rehearsals for the London production of *My Fair Lady* on 7 April) or to help Rex's tax position. Harrison and the film's director Vincente Minnelli hated the script that had been prepared by an American writer and William Douglas Home was drafted to write a new screenplay, staying a day or so ahead of shooting.

Harrison and Kendall played Lord and Lady Broadbent – Jimmy and Sheila – who return to London after an absence of several years to present his American-born daughter Jane (Sandra Dee) to society. Most of the film concerned their efforts to prise the daughter away from John Saxon's humble drummer (who plays at coming-out balls) and focus her attention on more suitable husband material in the form of Peter Myers' aristocratic bounder.

The impression the film gives is of Harrison faithfully supporting Kendall. He is constantly to one side of her, trying to get a word in edgeways, waiting with amused tolerance as she prattles on, or declaring 'Well done, darling' or 'Bad luck, darling', always the anchor she can rely on to support her wild manoeuvres or sympathise with their failure.

One remembers images of Harrison holding a drink for his wife as she gabs with her friend Mabel (Angela Lansbury); of him quietly getting drunk in one corner of the ballroom while Kendall tries to arrange Sandra Dee's love life; and of him straining to hear Lansbury's ripe gossip over the sound of the band. There are many moments like these when he has no actual lines to speak and Vincente Minnelli recalled: 'This, as was only natural, bothered him – and what bothered him, bothered Kay. Finally, we reached a compromise. "Try it," I said. "Then, if you don't like what you see, Home is on hand to remedy the situation." Harrison liked what he saw. Some of the most hilarious and brilliant scenes of the film find him speechless.' And Minnelli concluded: 'Harrison is one of the great pantomimists of our generation.'

In *Reluctant Debutante* there is even a moment of physical comedy reminiscent of *Unfaithfully Yours* in which Harrison is spying through a keyhole and falls down when the door suddenly opens. As Minnelli described the film's approach: 'The parents behave like teenagers – and the teenagers behave like adults.' Unfortunately, the director had little success in coaxing mature performances from Sandra Dee and John Saxon.

The Reluctant Debutante was a rare opportunity for Harrison to don top hat and tails in a contemporary setting. Its very title suggested an apology for dwelling on the aristocratic ritual of presenting debutantes to the Queen, a practice that was about to be abolished as undemocratic and therefore could be celebrated one last time. It was unfortunate for Harrison that, as far as contemporary subjects were concerned, the kind of milieu in which he flourished best was not one that mass audiences were greatly concerned about.

The West End had waited two years for *My Fair Lady*. The cast album from the American production, not officially available in Britain, had been imported in such quantity that musical devotees knew what was coming and could hardly contain their excitement. An earlier production would have been possible but it would have meant taking a risk with a different cast. Now Harrison, Julie Andrews, Stanley Holloway and Robert Coote were all ready to recreate their Broadway parts with Mrs Higgins the only major role that was recast (being given to Zena Dare) although the many supporting parts went to British performers.

The play's opening on 30 April 1958 was a major news event. It was given unprecedented space and emphasis in the British press: as a news item on the front page (where some of the reviews also began), as a centre picture spread in the tabloids. A Royal Command Performance three nights later with the Queen and Prince Philip renewed the press coverage. Some of the critics resented the amount of advance ballyhoo and the fact that Americans had purloined a British play but most of them were forced to agree that it was as good – or nearly as good – as it had been made out to be. Audiences flocked to the huge Theatre Royal in Drury Lane (Covent Garden) and the play ran there for over six years (twice as long as *Oklahoma!*).

Variety's London reviewer ('Myro') even considered the new production possibly better than the New York one: 'The slightly larger dimensions of the stage give greater depth to the production numbers and the chorus has been slightly strengthened on this account . . . Rex Harrison . . . the exponent of impeccable English, shows, too, that he has a sharp ear for dialect and his mimicry of Miss Andrews' accent is magnificent.'

Harrison stayed with Henry Higgins for eleven months. He later observed: 'I don't think anybody realises the agony that actors go through if they play a thing for a long time. It becomes meaningless after a while. If you've done it eight times a week for a year, two years, your mind is apt to wander a little bit and if it wanders for a second and you think "What am I going to have for supper?" in the middle of it all, you don't know where you are for a minute, then you catch it again. But it gives you such a mental shock that for a week you're terrified it's going to happen again. It's not fun. At the end of Drury Lane – this was my third year, mark you – I used to have to have the lyrics at the side of the stage

100

before I went on, because I knew them too well – they made no sense any more. Long runs are very hard on actors.'

During the time he was performing *My Fair Lady* in London, Kay Kendall expressed an interest in starring in a play she had found, *The Bright One*, by the actress Judy Campbell (using the pseudonym of J. M. Fulton). This would be Kay's West End starring debut and Harrison went into partnership with impresario Jack Minster (an old friend from Liverpool Playhouse days) to present the play, with himself directing.

Kay appeared as a botany teacher, Agatha Purvis, who drowns while bathing in Greece. Her body is taken over by the spirit of the nymph Echo, and the god Zeus causes complications by pursuing her back to England where, in her new human form, Echo has married an Englishman (Michael Gwynn). It was a whimsical fantasy, shot down by the critics for being too slight and lacking in laughs although the performances of Kay Kendall (sparkling as always) and Gladys Cooper (as an eccentric great-grandmother) were praised. Furthermore, it was staged at the cavernous Winter Garden Theatre, a white elephant soon to be torn down (but handily close to the Theatre Royal where Harrison was appearing daily). *Variety*'s man in London, 'Myro', referred to 'uninspired direction by Rex Harrison' and added: 'He gives the impression of making the play largely a star vehicle and that results in an uneven quality.' It had to come off after a few performances.

On leaving *My Fair Lady*, Rex went to Paris to be at Kay's side while she filmed *Once More With Feeling* opposite Yul Brynner, a comedy directed by Stanley Donen for Columbia. Kendall's illness now became much worse and disrupted filming. Harrison took her to Italy once she had finished her part and then brought her back to the London Clinic where, after a week, she died on

6 September 1959, aged only thirty-two. It was a tragic loss – for Harrison, for the theatre and cinema. Kay had even overcome her husband's dislike of Shakespeare and they had plans for doing *The Taming of the Shrew* at Stratford.

'After Kay died, I just wanted to work, anything that came along,' he has said. 'I can barely remember what I did during that first year. The only therapy was work.' While Kay had been filming in Paris, Harrison had seen a hit play by Jean Anouilh, *L'Hurluberlu*, and he agreed to perform in it on Broadway. It was retitled *The Fighting Cock* and opened, under direction by Peter Brook, for a try-out in Philadelphia in November 1959. Harrison was to look back on it as one of his greatest mistakes. 'It's a very obscure play about de Gaulle – I fell in love with it and wanted to do it. They didn't understand it at all in America. I put on a nose, I put on the eyebrows, I put on the boots. I had to take them off in Philadelphia. It was just hopeless. That was a hideous error on my part.'

The Harrison character is simply known as The General. He is a retired soldier, a vague and ineffectual romantic who is waging a losing battle to preserve the old code of values against the rising decadence of the 'maggots', the ordinary people. Harrison avoided presenting the figure as a buffoon and made him seem touching and sympathetic. As *Variety*'s 'Hobe' said: 'Without losing any of the ironic humour of the part or the situation, Harrison makes the silly but dauntless old idealist-bumbler a genuine and wistful character. If the portrayal hasn't the glitter of his original Prof. 'Enry 'Iggins of *My Fair Lady*, it's because the part lacks the same surface quality. If The General isn't his most successful performance to date, it may conceivably be his finest.'

But it was dubious material commercially and such compliments as this must have been little consolation as the play struggled along for two and a half months, taking Harrison into the 1960s, while Edward Mulhare played to full houses as 'Enry 'Iggins in a nearby theatre. Ironically, Rex was still the Professor to television audiences when he was seen in a tribute to *The Fabulous Fifties* in which he and Julie Andrews pretended to be back at the Shubert Theatre, New Haven, getting their act together at rehearsals – she struggling with a Cockney accent, he learning to talk-sing 'I'm an Ordinary Man' in front of an orchestra.

Television also claimed Harrison for a couple of taped one-hour shows. *Dear Arthur* had a script of distinguished pedigree (Gore Vidal out of Ferenc Molnar via P. G. Wodehouse) that resulted in quality entertainment with Harrison playing a smooth rogue who provides his daughter (Sarah Marshall) with a fictitious husband to make her youthful admirer in the Monte Carlo smart set compete harder for her affections and then finds that the absent Count he has created becomes a bit of a public nuisance. *The Datchet Diamonds* presented Rex as a stuffy gentleman of Victorian England who is down on his luck – his money-making schemes have failed and his fiancée (Tammy Grimes) has run out on him. But then he stumbles across a fortune in stolen gems and displays pluck in warding off Robert Flemyng's master criminal and his two accomplices.

As the closure of *The Fighting Cock* became imminent, Harrison was encouraged to find that Hollywood still had some use for him, even considered him a suitable partner for Doris Day – not, alas, in one of her frothy comedies, but in a mediocre thriller called *Midnight Lace*. Natasha Parry (wife of Peter Brook) was also recruited from the cast of *The Fighting Cock* for a supporting part.

Midnight Lace was based on a British stage play and kept its London setting but the stars never left Hollywood and doubles were shown getting in and out of taxis near landmarks in the capital. The film revived the cycle of thrillers in which women were elaborately driven mad for their money (Claudette Colbert in *Sleep, My Love* and *The Secret Fury*, Merle Oberon in *Dark Waters*, Joan Crawford in *Sudden Fear*). David Miller had done so well with this plot before (he directed *Sudden Fear*) that he was hired to do it all over again.

At the beginning of *Midnight Lace*, Doris's Kit Preston is threatened by a mysterious voice in foggy Grosvenor Square that taunts her and threatens to kill her. We hear the voice so we know she's not imagining it, whatever anyone else says. Nearly killed by falling girders outside a building site, threatened over the telephone when she is alone, she is suspected of making a fuss to gain more of her husband's time and attention. She has been three months married to Rex Harrison who has delayed their honeymoon to Venice because of pressing business problems and who even breaks lunch dates with her on the same pretext. Seemingly considerate (he buys her a diamond brooch), he in fact undermines his wife's confidence in little matters like handling British money. Prime suspects are the housekeeper's sponging son (Roddy McDowall) and the builder (John Gavin) who hasn't fully recovered from disturbing experiences in the war. But, just as you expected, it is really Harrison, in cahoots with his mistress (Natasha Parry), who is behind it all, trying to unhinge his wife so that her murder will pass as suicide.

Harrison makes a debonair villain, of course – and one who, instead of making an attempt to escape, accepts defeat gracefully, quietly telling his wife how he has deceived her (sweat breaking out on his forehead) and calmly accompanying the police away. But, all the same, how vexing that such a skilled farceur should have been required to threaten Doris Day's life rather than her perpetual virginity.

Doris used some frightening experiences in her own

past life to make her terror convincing – and put herself under such strain that at one point she collapsed and production had to be suspended for several days. She found Harrison a great help: 'A darling, witty man, Rex, whose light sense of humour helped me keep my sanity balance throughout the rough part of the picture.'

Doris returned to comedies thereafter while Harrison went back to the stage to test himself where it was 'all happening', at the Royal Court in London. He told journalist Cecil Wilson: 'I was fascinated by the new school of playwrights – the Weskers and the Pinters and so forth – and also these progressive new theatre companies like the Royal Court's. I met George Devine and he asked me if I would like to do a play there. I said I would. Then I went to Italy for a holiday at my villa in Portofino and while I was there George sent me this Chekhov script.' It was Chekhov's first play, *Platonov*, never previously performed in Britain, and Harrison donned a beard to appear as the eponymous schoolmaster whose life is disrupted by the various women who throw themselves at him. *Plays and Players'* reviewer Caryl Brahms referred to 'the game of tennis which Mr Rex Harrison plays with his lines – the restless, split-second volleying of phrases. Beneath the shambles of his hirsute and lined exterior there lies the wary pacing of the panther', and concluded that Rex's Platonov was 'almost too good to be true'.

Playing Anna Petrovna, the general's widow who pursues the schoolteacher with amorous intent, was Rachel Roberts, later to become Rex's fourth wife. For her, the daughter of a Welsh baptist preacher and a woman of fiercely anti-establishment views, the aura of her celebrated co-star was intoxicating. In her posthumously published diaries, she describes the man she found at that time: 'Rex crackled. He seemed charged with electricity. Tall and hooded-looking, dressed in blue dog's tooth tweeds and blue cashmere sweater, thin and suspicious, lithe as an electric eel . . . Rex cut such a dash. There was something Edwardian about him, something silky and ruffled.' And: '. . . Rex fascinated me. Underneath the glitter, I saw the widower making a brave attempt to carry on – Kay Kendall had died only a year before, so appallingly young – and I admired his guts for doing so. I know that, for Rex, I represented the "new blood" of the London theatre. The Royal Court was at its zenith.'

Having been very modestly paid for the fixed six-week run of *Platonov* (which did exceptionally well at the box-office, thanks to Harrison's drawing power), he was receptive to an offer to co-star with Rita Hayworth in an American film to be made in Madrid under the title *Once a Thief* but eventually released as *The Happy Thieves*. It was based on promising source material, Richard Condon's novel *The Oldest Confession*, and it does have a perky performance by Harrison as a nattily-dressed, fast-striding art thief called Jim Bourne, but Rita Hayworth as his more honest confederate (and, later, wife) is listless, the film is ugly to look at (and shot on the cheap in black and white), while a director of broad comedy like George Marshall was misplaced handling such potentially chic material. The vein of black humour lays undisturbed and Harrison is unable to get far enough into his character to make sense of his sudden reformation at the end, when in order to refute Hayworth's accusation that he lacks a heart he goes to jail rather than send an accomplice there. In Britain, the film bypassed the national critics to be quietly dumped on a few luckless cinemas, coupled with a western revival, *Vera Cruz*, in an effort to drum up business.

A far more interesting film project came to grief. Producer John Stafford had made *The Stranger's Hand*, *Loser Takes All* and *Across the Bridge* from the work of Graham Greene and he had now entered into a partnership with

Greene to film the writer's first play, *The Living Room,* which had starred Eric Portman in 1953. The pair had signed up Samantha Eggar, sensing her star potential, and Rex Harrison was set to head a cast that included John Gielgud, Flora Robson and Rachel Roberts under the direction of Michael Powell. United Artists were to release the film and production was due to start in London on Monday, 31 July 1961, but it all fell through. Another equally illustrious cast (headed by Richard Attenborough) was brought together by Michael Powell to make *The Living Room* a few years later but once again the project wouldn't take off.

It's not clear when Harrison pulled out but he was quickly involved with the Royal Court again, declaring 'The theatre is my serious work and I make films for the money' and 'I like to think that the money I make in films enables me to take uncommercial chances in the theatre.' Nigel Dennis's specially commissioned play *August for the People* was certainly uncommercial as far as Shaftesbury Avenue was concerned, with its vitriolic portrait of the ruling classes and gibes at all kinds of values sacred to the right wing. Harrison played Sir Augustus Thwaites, the aristocratic owner of a stately home who is forced to let in visitors at half a crown a time and who thinks of democracy as 'a disgusting thing'. The character has been described as 'advancing through Fascism into madness'. Rachel Roberts played his mistress. The work seems to have had responsive audiences when it first opened at the Edinburgh Festival but at the Royal Court in Sloane Square it was certainly not popular with critics and Harrison felt uncomfortable in it, finding it muddled and in part unplayable. One can't help wondering if he was happy advancing Nigel Dennis's viewpoint but, as far as worthwhile contemporary plays went, he was restricted in what he could do.

8
From Sloane Square to Cinecittà

EVEN BEFORE *AUGUST FOR THE PEOPLE* HAD MOVED FROM Edinburgh to the Royal Court, Harrison was approached to play Julius Caesar in *Cleopatra*, the 20th Century-Fox epic that was about to go into production.

There had already been an abortive start at Pinewood in September 1960 with Elizabeth Taylor in the title role under Rouben Mamoulian's direction and with Peter Finch as Julius Caesar and Stephen Boyd as Mark Antony. This had collapsed owing to bad weather and the near-fatal illness of Taylor in March 1961. The wave of public sympathy and the Oscar she won for *Butterfield 8* made her a hot name and Fox were anxious to get *Cleopatra* rolling again. Joseph L. Mankiewicz was pulled off work on a film of Lawrence Durrell's *Alexandria Quartet* to write and direct the historical epic of old Alexandria and Rome. Producer Walter Wanger first sought Trevor Howard to take over the Caesar part but this proved impossible and Wanger records in his diary entry for 16 August 1961 (subsequently published in *My Life with Cleopatra*): 'I asked JLM in Rome and recommended Rex Harrison who, I think, will be better in the long run. JLM agrees so we are going after him.' Wanger told the authors of *The Real Tinsel* the reaction he had from Spyros Skouras, head of Fox: 'Skouras threw up his hands and said he'd resign from the company before he'd have Rex Harrison. Rex Harrison couldn't act. He was no good. The press hated him. Well, you see, they had him under contract and had handled him very badly. Skouras said, "Look at this crazy Wanger. Look at what he wants to do. Let me show you what we've lost on this man." He showed me all the books!' But, against the date 11 September 1961, Wanger's diary notes: 'Negotiations finally concluded for Rex Harrison to play Caesar at $10,000 a week, plus expenses, a car and driver, and co-star billing.' Elizabeth Taylor was receiving $50,000 a week and expenses.

Richard Burton was signed to play Mark Antony. Like Harrison, he was tied up in a play, the highly successful Lerner and Loewe musical *Camelot* on Broadway, but Hollywood money spoke and the stage producers agreed to release him for $50,000. In Harrison's case, *August for the People* was originally set for a four-week run at the Royal Court and George Devine was opposed to releasing him because of the harm it would inflict on Nigel Dennis's reputation if the play terminated early. However, he finally agreed that *August for the People* should do only eleven performances (the alternative of re-casting Harrison's role apparently did not arise, or perhaps the play wasn't viable without him) and Harrison had to help finance the return of the preceding production, a highly successful revival of Arnold Wesker's *The Kitchen*. According to Harrison, *August for the People* was doing poor business anyway, although *Plays and Players* refers to packed houses (perhaps there was a surge of business after the early closing of the play was announced). Anyway, Harrison reflects in his autobiography that he should have stayed with the play for its full month and kept 20th Century-Fox waiting.

There was a considerable element of trust in Harrison's trip to Rome for *Cleopatra*. Mankiewicz had no finished script to show him but their past association on *The Ghost and Mrs Muir* and *Escape* and the writer-director's reputation (*All About Eve*, *Julius Caesar*) were enough for him. And perhaps it was a measure of his unhappiness with the Dennis play that for once he didn't hesitate and 'dived right in'.

Harrison quickly researched Caesar's life with his usual thoroughness and communicated his views on the character to Wanger and Mankiewicz. (He credits Thornton Wilder's novel *The Ides of March* with giving him a lot of the feeling of the character.) Production proceeded fairly quietly until January 1962 when Burton arrived to shoot his first scenes with Taylor and they embarked on the love affair that became a worldwide sensation from April 1962 onwards. Harrison had completed most of his scenes but remained in Rome as a stopgap available for use on the many occasions when Taylor and/or Burton weren't working. Production costs spiralled because of bad weather, the absence of a completed script (Mankiewicz was shooting by day and re-writing by evening and at weekends), and Elizabeth Taylor's tardy arrivals on the set (Fox eventually sued her for $120 million for her conduct during the making of the film).

Even before Burton joined the production, the Fox front office had been trying to cut costs. In December 1961, Harrison returned from a visit to London to find that his dressing room caravan had been withdrawn and his chauffeur wasn't being paid. He summoned Walter Wanger and production manager Sid Rogell and, according to Wanger, began by telling Rogell, 'I treat my servants better than I am about to treat you' and proceeded to give the hapless executive the 'worst lacing'

111

the hard-boiled Wanger had ever heard. Harrison not only got his way, he received an ovation from the company when he came onto the set.

The film was supposed to open with the Battle of Pharsalia in which Caesar fights the army of a fellow Roman, Pompey, but it was running so far over budget that the studio saw another opportunity to save money. As Wanger records for 4 June 1962: 'Rex Harrison called. He has heard that the studio is thinking of cutting out the Pharsalia sequence and he believes so strongly that the scene is necessary he is willing to underwrite the cost of filming it himself. A magnificent gesture!' Fox eventually allowed two days for hurriedly shooting it in the hills of Almeria in Southern Spain but the results were so unsatisfactory it was re-shot in February 1963.

The scene opens the film and not only provides a suitably spectacular introduction but is important to an understanding of Caesar: it enables him to register his humane feelings at the loss of life, it demonstrates his military prowess, and it sets him up as a formidable figure for his appearance at Alexandria in the next scene where the huge set of the palace and harbour again shows the film to be of truly epic proportions. The opening scene was also intended to establish Mark Antony's staunch loyalty towards Caesar but, even though his presence at the battle is referred to, he is never seen (as by this time Burton was unavailable, shooting his next film *The VIPs* in London). If Harrison *had* paid for Pharsalia, it would have set him back quite a penny, given the huge number of extras spread over the landscape (although the actor did earn at least half a million dollars from the film).

Cleopatra ended up costing $31 million, the most ever spent on a motion picture to that time, and Fox's future rested on the box-office outcome. The film ran at least six hours in edited form and Darryl Zanuck, who returned to Fox and took over the company from Spyros Skouras, resisted the suggestion of releasing it in two halves and instead had it cut down to four hours for its premiere.

It is difficult now to recall the frenzy of excitement that accompanied the unveiling of *Cleopatra* in the summer of 1963. Its American premiere became a world news event and other premieres were razzle-dazzle occasions with Fox labelling its London debut 'C-Day' and television providing live coverage of the opening night. The Burton–Taylor affair had been perhaps the top news story of 1962 in terms of the space it had obtained, and in most places audiences flocked to see the pair in the film that had been the cause of it. Fox was saved, and *Cleopatra* even broke into profit a few years later.

In fact, *Cleopatra* is neither the best nor the worst of historical epics. Its spectacle is certainly glorious, its script is often interesting, and its first part is generally impressive, reflecting the fact that Mankiewicz was fresher when it was made and had yet to run into the more severe problems of the production. Harrison later commented: 'I was very, very lucky to be in the first half of the picture. Joe hadn't reached his climax of despair at that point.' In any case, the second part is inherently weaker, dramatically: Mark Antony comes to the fore after Caesar's murder but proves to be a feeble successor, dominated by Cleopatra and failing as a politician, soldier and lover, eventually committing suicide. In addition, Burton gives a thoroughly monotonous performance, though it is only fair to add that his part was the one most severely cut by Zanuck. Harrison ran away with the acting honours, winning an Academy Award nomination for his work and restoring himself to full Hollywood favour as a 'hot' name.

Harrison's Caesar is a masterful interpretation, fully conveying the charismatic qualities of the man. He commands with shrewdness and wit and a certain arrogance, in a somewhat Shavian conception of the part, but is also thoroughly ruthless and ambitious. He is a civilised man appalled by battlefield losses or the gift of an enemy's head, but egotistically concerned at how history will view him, immediately dictating his lament for the waste of battle to ensure it doesn't pass unnoticed. He is a clever tactician who resists the provocation of his enemies and manipulates their actions to his advantage. He is a man who makes short shrift of unnecessary pomp and ceremony, abridging a speech with a couple of 'etceteras and etceteras' (quite different from Harrison's fond use of the same phrase as King Mongkut in *Anna and the King of Siam*). But his weaknesses are his epilepsy and his longing for a son and heir – and it is these the equally clever Cleopatra uses to advantage, winning his trust by seeing him through an epileptic fit and providing him with a baby boy. There is not a great deal of passion to the relationship, partly because of the way Harrison approached the part: 'I could never quite believe that Caesar, with all the political and military problems that were on his mind at the time, was so absolutely obsessed with Cleopatra. It seems against his character. So I resisted as much as possible the pressure to play it that way.'

Harrison was the right age to play Caesar but Cleopatra should have been a vivacious, flirting figure of nineteen. Instead, as played by Elizabeth Taylor, she appears hard and calculating, quite without the exotic allure that Vivien Leigh sometimes suggested in the 1946 *Caesar and Cleopatra*, and horribly shrill when rejecting Harrison's advances ('I promise you will not enjoy me like this'), so that she seems a fit subject for his wit rather than his passion. (When she speaks of rubbing him up the wrong way, he replies, 'I'm not sure I want to be rubbed by you at all.') Their later love-making registers as plain relief at finding someone to relax with – an extension of their respect for each other as master strategists and mutual trust as equals with compatible ambitions. Regrettably, a vital motivating scene at the tomb of Alexander, in which Cleopatra fires Caesar with the ambition to rule one united world and succeed where Alexander the Great failed, is missing from the much shorter version of the film that quickly replaced the four-hour cut at the premiere.

Mankiewicz succeeds admirably in providing Harrison with dialogue that is not stilted yet not too modern in sound, but his staging of the film is dull so that the characters remain in long shot, at a distance. Take Caesar's insistence on picking up the bundle that contains his child, holding it aloft, acknowledging his paternity against the advice of his lieutenants, crying out, 'I have a son! I have a son!' This might have been reinforced with a track-in or close-up but instead is observed from afar. And Caesar's growing megalomania, his sense of infallibility, is not explored at all. The reasons for his assassination and why Cleopatra sees it as a vision in a fire were lost in the post-premiere cutting. As it stands, the assassination of Caesar is viewed mute as Cleopatra's flame-fringed vision and so Harrison concludes his appearance at a disadvantage, robbed of his last words to his attackers and diminished by the way the scene is shown (happening elsewhere and not wholly dominating the frame). Still, it makes sense structurally to handle his demise from Cleopatra's position as she is the focus of the film and the link to the second half.

During *Cleopatra*'s production, Rex Harrison married Rachel Roberts in Genoa – she was his fourth wife, the date was 22 March 1962. She won an Oscar nomination for her work in the British film *This Sporting Life* to parallel the one Rex received for *Cleopatra*. He lost to Sidney Poitier in *Lilies of the Field*, she to Patricia Neal in *Hud*.

9
The Film of My Fair Lady

THERE WAS NEVER ANY DOUBT THAT HOLLYWOOD WOULD make a film of *My Fair Lady*. But it was forced to wait until the stage show had had its full innings. Finally, a screen version was permitted for release in 1965 or later, and there was fevered bidding for the film rights. Arthur Freed, that most innovative of Hollywood's musical producers, desperately wanted to obtain them but he couldn't persuade an ailing MGM to offer enough, and veteran studio boss Jack L. Warner beat off all the competition to secure the rights for a staggering $5.5 million plus a percentage of the gross after $20 million was reached in rentals. For Jack Warner, money was no object: he wanted to make *My Fair Lady* as his swan song, a final production that he would personally supervise before retiring from Warner Bros.

For Rex Harrison, there was the prospect of consolidating his success in *Cleopatra* if he played Henry Higgins again, and the fear that the part would become permanently identified with some other actor if he didn't. But would Harrison even be asked? His performance in *Cleopatra* had been lauded but it was Burton and

Taylor who had been the real draws and Fox had those figures to prove that American audiences didn't like him. He was now thought of as primarily a stage actor. Anxious as he was to get the part, he decided the best strategy was to sit and wait in Portofino rather than get lost amidst the rush of big stars putting their names forward for Jack Warner's consideration. Jack had shown his respect for Rex's talents by bringing him back to Hollywood for *King Richard and the Crusaders*, and hadn't been disappointed. Perhaps Jack would come out in his favour again.

With so much money already spent on the rights and a natural desire to end his reign at the studio on a high note, Jack Warner had every incentive to play safe. And play safe he did when he signed George Cukor to direct the film – a veteran of proven artistry who could also be relied upon to make a commercial picture and to respect the values of the stage original (he had previously made *A Star Is Born* at Warner Bros.). Warner's first casting ideas were to offer Cary Grant the part of Professor Higgins and to try to lure James Cagney out of retirement to play Alfred Doolittle, the scrounging father of Eliza. Cagney admitted to a 'slight tug' towards acceptance (he was offered a million dollars) but, as he puts it in his memoirs, he couldn't summon up sufficient interest. As for Grant, his celebrated reply was, 'Not only will I not do it, but if you don't use Rex Harrison, I won't go to see it.' Grant later added: 'Once something has been done to perfection, why interfere with it?' and 'I just didn't think anyone could do it better than Rex Harrison.' Even though he could have trusted Cukor to get the best performance out of him (they had made the memorable *Holiday* and *Philadelphia Story* together), Grant was probably right, After all, a million or so people had seen Rex Harrison on the stage; he had done numbers from it on television; and he had been heard on the immensely successful cast album. Comparisons were bound to be made and Grant was no more a singer than Harrison, lacked his acerbic edge, and, as Alan Jay Lerner observed, had an inappropriate Cockney strain in his voice.

Jack Warner then see-sawed to the other extreme and sent George Cukor out to see the hotly-touted newcomer Peter O'Toole on the location of *Lawrence of Arabia*, the film that made him a star. O'Toole was reported as saying, 'I want to do *My Fair Lady* – it's a marvellous part,' and, according to some reports, seemed almost certain to get it in October 1962. But a few years later, O'Toole told *Playboy*: 'The simple fact is that someone from Warner Bros. approached me about *My Fair Lady*, and I said I thought they were potty and that the only man who could and should play Higgins was Rex Harrison.'

Next, Cukor called Harrison in Portofino, asking him to come to Hollywood and make a screen test. Apparently, Jack Warner's main fear – fuelled by the way he had looked in *Cleopatra* with a grey wig – was that he had aged too much to play the part. Somehow, a couple of candid Polaroids taken by Rachel Roberts, showing a thin, toupee-less Harrison, were sufficient to gain him the role without the audition when she sent them to Cukor in Hollywood.

Stanley Holloway had also been signed to repeat his stage part as Alfred Doolittle. Jack Warner baulked at going the whole hog and taking Julie Andrews as well. He felt he needed box-office insurance and so he signed Audrey Hepburn and gave her top billing and a million dollar fee, even though she could not sing well enough for the part and was too old. According to Harrison, George Cukor wanted her for the part. Julie was bitterly disappointed but fortunately the Walt Disney studios were happy to star her in *Mary Poppins* and, had she done *My Fair Lady*, she wouldn't have been available for another little picture called *The Sound of Music*. . . In the outcome, she had a chance to display her versatility. 'Of course I wanted to play Eliza. But in a way it's a good thing to have to play a different role,' she said. 'I'd have been stuck as Eliza Doolittle for the rest of my life. People will at least know I can do something else.' For doing something else in *Mary Poppins*, she won the Academy Award for Best Actress while Audrey Hepburn didn't even receive a nomination for *My Fair Lady* (probably because the film industry as a whole disapproved of her casting).

For Harrison, then reckoned to have played Higgins 1,006 times on the stage, there was one problem in playing it yet again. 'The only danger was that I would give what is called a stagy film performance – in other words, it would be too projected. In films, you shouldn't project – obviously – to the extent that you have to in the theatre. I thought I might have got into an ugly trap of getting used to projecting. But there were about four years in between the last performance I gave at Drury Lane and the time I made the film. I found it quite easy to adapt it to the screen.' Playing opposite a new Eliza, a new Colonel Pickering (Wilfrid Hyde-White) and many other new faces also sharpened his responses but, as it turned out, the film adhered very closely to the play and Harrison had little new to learn. 'I didn't try to tamper with *My Fair Lady*,' said Cukor. 'It was perfect on stage.' It was obviously possible to open up the indoor settings but there were no gusts of realism, such as shooting the highly-stylised Ascot sequence in a natural outdoor setting, apart from the grievous (though fortunately fleeting) error of showing real horses thundering past the camera during the number to clash with the artifice of the rest when they should only have been heard.

The film of *My Fair Lady* is essentially a record of the stage play and of Harrison's stage interpretation suitably

120

scaled down for the closer eye of the camera. (He did make one other adjustment: 'Audrey Hepburn is more delicate than Julie Andrews, so I tempered my interpretation, and was a more agreeable Higgins.') The head-on cinemascope set-ups are akin to looking at performers on a stage. The pleasures afforded by the film are real enough but they tap few of the greater possibilities offered by the cinema. Whatever Arthur Freed might have done, Alan Jay Lerner concludes that he would have made a much different film of it.

Harrison insisted on doing his musical numbers live, using a throat mike and being covered by two or more cameras, instead of the normal practice of singing to a pre-recorded playback. The new musical director, Andre Previn, had to adjust to Harrison just as Franz Allers had on Broadway. Mona Washbourne, who played Professor Higgins' housekeeper, Mrs Pearce, recalled: 'Words are very important to Rex, and for that reason he didn't always keep absolutely dead in time with the music. This used to upset Previn. Rex was elastic in his phrasing, dropping back and then catching up with the music. Previn would say: "You're out of the beat again", and Rex used to reply: "I catch up in the end – what are you worrying about?"'

In Rex Harrison's hands, Professor Higgins is a smugly superior human being who relishes the challenge of taking someone 'so deliciously low, so horribly dirty' (his words savour the depths to which Eliza has fallen, from which he must elevate her) and turning this 'draggle-tailed guttersnipe' into a Duchess – when all she wanted was to become a better kind of flower girl and work in a shop instead of the open. He drives Eliza mercilessly to achieve his ends and ignores her basic needs (he feeds the last strawberry tart to his pet bird rather than to the ravenous Eliza) as well as her feelings (she swallows one of the marbles he has put in her mouth to improve her elocution and he merely remarks that there are plenty more).

His ostensible aims are admirable in the context of the period: to liberate Eliza from the gutter and realise her 'divine gift of articulate speech'. 'What could possibly matter more than to take a human being and change her into a different human being by creating a new speech for her?' he asks. 'It's filling up the deepest gap that separates class from class, and soul from soul.' In the 'Why Can't the English?' number, he rails against class distinctions based on speech and he delivers the lyrics with a thrust and passion that shows the strength of the Professor's convictions. He rightly contrasts his own noble aspirations with those of the rival phonetician Zoltan Karpathy, described in the lyrics as 'That blackguard who uses the science of speech/More to blackmail than to teach'. And his purpose is stated most eloquently (in a speech that is not Shaw: it is by Alan Jay Lerner and it is better than Shaw) at 3 a.m. in the morning when Harrison relaxes his guard and makes an uncharacteristically gentle attempt to encourage Eliza: 'I know your head aches. I know you're tired. I know your nerves are as raw as meat in a butcher's window. But think what you're trying to accomplish. Just think what you're dealing with. The majesty and grandeur of the English language. It's the greatest possession we have. The noblest thoughts that ever flowed through the hearts of men are contained in its extraordinary, imaginative, and musical mixtures of sounds, and that's what you've set yourself out to conquer, Eliza. And conquer it . . . you will.'

With a long sigh, he goes back behind his desk and slumps into the chair, covering his face. The pause in the last sentence he speaks is masterly, emphasising a conviction that his long sigh immediately afterwards contradicts. But this quieter, more rational approach works, of course, inspiring Eliza to say her 'rain in Spain' text correctly. Harrison sits half up. She repeats it. He sits all the way up. The wonderfully jubilant musical number 'The Rain in Spain' follows (marred only by the obvious and ridiculous dubbing of Audrey Hepburn at the very moment when her voice is the cause of celebration).

And yet Harrison's Higgins is also deluding himself with his talk of high ideals, since he is as much concerned to play a joke on society, thrilled by the risk when he infiltrates Eliza, a mere commoner, into the aristocrats' ball. He insults Eliza with relish, his only excuse being the patently untrue one that he treats nobody else better. (Despite looking suitably thin and scraggly, Audrey Hepburn's awkward attempts to act crude early in the film make Eliza too comical for Harrison's heartless treatment of her to arouse much audience concern.)

And Harrison also fools himself into thinking he has no need for a woman. His convincingly alarmed description of the havoc a woman would cause in his life in the number 'I'm an Ordinary Man' (more self-deception in that title) persuades us that he has by sheer willpower excluded all need of the other sex. In the number 'Why Can't a Woman Be More Like a Man?' (official title: 'A Hymn to Him') he further denounces women for their moods and tantrums. In fact, he never openly admits that he does love Eliza, knowing only that he desperately wants her back after she has stormed out of his life because of his display of ingratitude over her triumph at the ball, expressed in the number 'You Did It' (incidentally, the film offers the bonus of the full lyrics compared to the stage version).

Too regal and refined earlier, Audrey Hepburn comes into her own once she is as good as a Duchess – and she registers poignantly the feelings of Eliza on being ignored by the Professor, or treated to his withering contempt ('You presumptuous insect!') when she dares suggest that she won for him the bet he made that she would go undetected at the ball, or realising that she can't ever go back to her life in Covent Garden.

'What I liked most about [*My Fair Lady*] was the fact that it was less of a romantic love story than a battle of wits,' George Cukor said. And so it becomes when Hepburn's Eliza uses her newfound confidence and linguistic abilities to torment Harrison's Professor Higgins in front of his mother, even threatening to join up with the detestable Hungarian linguist, Karpathy – provoking him to reach out and start to throttle her, only to throw up his hands in despair and collapse into a chair. Her revenge on him is highly relishable. It is odd, though, that she says so emphatically, 'You shall not be seeing me again.'

Harrison shows a new tenderness in the memorable 'I've Grown Accustomed to Her Face' although in other parts of the number he relapses into his old characteristics (delight at the thought of a failed marriage to Freddy, a handsome admirer; pleasure at the image of her crawling back to him; flaring anger as he imagines slamming the door in her face).

In the marvellously handled closing scene, as Harrison listens to a recording of her voice and Hepburn silently returns, switches it off, and speaks the lines herself, the way that Harrison's face brightens as he realises she is actually there, then stiffens again as he lies back and demands his slippers, seems to provide a happy ending on the Professor's terms: she will continue to pick up his slippers, put up with his tempers, fetch and carry for him. It is hard to imagine the Professor has reformed but Hepburn has proved to herself that he does need her and perhaps that is enough. Cleverly, Hepburn's face is blank and there is nothing to actually denote surrender in what she does.

Shaw, of course, did not want Eliza to end up with Higgins. He had strongly disapproved of the way Leslie Howard had played the Professor – 'the public will like him and probably want him to marry Eliza, which is just what I don't want'. Here, for once, Shaw had written a convincing emotional relationship between the sexes and just couldn't see where it led. At least, he couldn't have accused Rex Harrison of being too sympathetic, and at least it is Eliza's considered choice to return to him.

George Cukor was full of praise for Harrison's work: 'Rex's performance, I think, is the most dazzling piece of work, even better on the screen than on the stage.' He added: '. . . the real difference between *My Fair Lady* on the stage and screen and *Pygmalion* on the screen and in most stage productions lay in the casting of Rex Harrison. Eliza was usually played by one of those overpowering actresses, and Higgins became an almost subsidiary, rather weak character. In the British film Leslie Howard did him charmingly as a romantic, but Rex hit the fanaticism, the possessed quality, and this made him infinitely touching and original.'

Cukor also uses Harrison's lanky frame to good comic effect, sprawled across chairs, with his feet up on a fireside bench, and has a marvellous head-and-shoulders-only shot of him over the back of the bench seat when he pauses in his pacing up and down to stare at Hepburn as she discusses his failings with his mother who readily sympathises with her.

As demanding a critic as the late Kenneth Tynan, reviewing the film in *The Observer*, found Rex 'incomparable': 'Give him a simple, helpless line like: "Damn Mrs Pearce, and damn the coffee, and damn you!" and he will make it sound as elegantly yet majestically final as a trio of crashing chords at the end of a symphony. His eyes are mere slits and his stance is preposterously angular;

but he exudes that combination of the aggressor and the injured, the schoolmaster and the truant, which adds up in Britain (and elsewhere) to erotic infallibility. From the opening words of a number such as "A Hymn to Him" ("What in all of heaven can have prompted her to go?") you know that you are in absolutely safe hands; a supreme performer is in charge, steering you as a master helmsman steers his yacht.'

Douglas McVay later made an explicit comparison between Harrison's stage interpretation and his approach on film: '. . . Rex Harrison's definitive portrait of Higgins . . . on celluloid proves even more blandly, breezily, incomparably relaxed than on-stage. Any fractional deterioration of *finesse* in his *quasi-parlando* treatment of his numbers is more than balanced by a general increase of expansive confidence and humour.'

Brian Aherne, who played Higgins after Rex Harrison, felt that Harrison in the film was tending more to sing the lines than speak them as he had on stage, and preferred the latter approach (which is, as he mentions, still to be heard on the New York cast album).

Harrison was again nominated for the Best Actor Academy Award. He was competing with Richard Burton and Peter O'Toole (both for *Becket*), Anthony Quinn (for *Zorba the Greek*) and Peter Sellers (for *Dr Strangelove*). This time Harrison won, as did many other members of the *My Fair Lady* team: George Cukor (Best Direction), Harry Stradling (Best Colour Cinematography), Gene Allen, Cecil Beaton and George James Hopkins (Best Colour Art Direction and Set Decoration), the Warner Bros. sound department, Andre Previn (Best Music Adaptation) and Beaton again (on his own) for Best Colour Costume Design. Clearly, with the omission of even a nomination for Audrey Hepburn, the industry *was* making a point on Julie Andrews' behalf.

My Fair Lady had cost $11.5 million to produce, so the

total expenditure including the rights was $17 million even before a penny was spent on promotion and prints. But Warners had no need to worry: a record sum of over $8.4 million was in the tills from advance booking in the United States alone, and the film went on to show a healthy profit. And Rex Harrison was placed at the pinnacle of his fame as an international movie star.

10
The Movie Star

REX HARRISON SPENT THE FIVE YEARS FROM 1964 TO 1968 responding to the demand from film producers for his talents in the wake of *My Fair Lady*.

He first went to London to take part in *The Yellow Rolls-Royce*, written by Terence Rattigan (who had given Harrison his first big success with *French Without Tears*) and directed by Anthony Asquith (the distinguished film-maker who had directed the film version of *French Without Tears* and *The Winslow Boy*, another Rattigan hit). Harrison featured in the first episode in which, as the Marquess of Frinton, a Government Minister, he sets the eponymous vehicle off on its career when he buys it from a showroom as a belated anniversary present for his wife (originally to be played by an English actress, but rewritten when Jeanne Moreau was cast to help attract the European audience). Tipped that his wife is having an affair with one of his staff, the handsome junior diplomat played by Edmund Purdom, he discovers them in the back of the Rolls in the car park during Royal Ascot while his horse is busy winning the Gold Cup. Fearful of scandal, he can only act by arranging for the lover to be

129

posted abroad and by disposing of the car. He sends it back, offering as an explanation only the words, 'It displeases me', said in a weary, saddened tone that exactly captures the distress it has innocently caused, forfeiting its master's affection like a dog that has soiled a priceless carpet.

At this short length, characterisation is minimal but the sequence rests firmly enough on the shoulders of Jeanne Moreau (living up to her screen image of the hot-blooded Frenchwoman) and Rex Harrison (the model of dignity and reserve). A slight but pithy anecdote, it had the benefit of a brevity that later episodes lacked.

Harrison then unknowingly set in motion the screen-writing career of William Goldman (Oscar winner for *Butch Cassidy and the Sundance Kid*) by dropping out of the British caper comedy *Masquerade*. Cliff Robertson replaced him and William Goldman was brought in for the rush job of adapting Harrison's dialogue to suit an American actor. *Masquerade* was undistinguished and inconspicuous. Harrison had done better by fulfilling an earlier agreement to play opposite Charlton Heston in a new 20th Century-Fox epic, *The Agony and the Ecstasy*, under Carol Reed's direction in Italy. That, too, proved to be undistinguished (despite a script by Philip Dunne) but it was highly conspicuous, a roadshow attraction in 70mm and good to look at (photographed by Leon Shamroy, who had shot *Cleopatra*).

Charlton Heston played the artist Michelangelo and Rex Harrison the warrior Pope, Julius II (1443–1513). 'Now there's a part!' Rex is quoted as saying, 'A Renaissance bull of a man, an unpopelike pope, fighting duels, siring illegitimate children.' He it is who orders the sculptor to cease work on ornamental figures for his tomb and instead paint the barrel-shaped vaulted ceiling of the Sistine Chapel, his private shrine in the Vatican. 'It was built by my uncle, Pope Sixtus. That's why it is called the Sistine,' he informs the artist (who, unlike the audience, knows it already). The rest of the film shows the long struggle to finish the ceiling, a drama punctuated by almost music-hall repartee with the Pope bellowing on his way to Mass each morning 'When will you make an end?' and the artist shouting back, 'When I'm finished!'

Since we know it will be completed, and since the details of its execution (although conscientiously presented) are of little dramatic interest, the film plays up the 'odd couple' relationship of the two men, taunting, quarrelling, bargaining, scheming to outwit each other – for Heston's headstrong Michelangelo considers himself a sculptor rather than a painter, is unhappy with his early design for the ceiling, and later has to badger the churchman for materials to complete the work, while Harrison's Pope is engaged in a desperate battle to preserve his power over the Papal States and fears that he will die without seeing the painting finished. There is an amusing and unforgettable scene in which the Pope is on the battlefield, enemy cannonballs exploding all around, and Michelangelo interrupts him to show him preliminary sketches for his new design; the Pope studies them and comments, 'I planned a ceiling – he plans a miracle!', then turns to his subordinates and barks, 'What are you waiting for? Attack!' Only the Pope's needling (such as threatening to bring in a rival to finish the job if Michelangelo won't continue) keeps the artist at work, and (in the kind of old-fashioned dramatic counterbalance that shows how skilfully calculated an entertainment this is) the favour is returned when Michelangelo arouses the Pope from his deathbed to complete *his* task of driving the French and German invaders out of Italy. According to Hollywood, the Pope's assessment of the Sistine ceiling was 'This work is greater than the both of us', whereas he really thought it looked a bit dull and could do with some more gold paint on it. Neither Heston nor Harrison looked anything like the people they were portraying but they make a good team, Heston's earnest peasant-like strength opposed to Harrison's authority of bearing and wit.

The film benefited from some real-life competition between the two stars. According to Harrison, 'Heston very politely and very nicely made me feel that it was extremely kind of me to be supporting him . . . I did everything I could to make myself believe that the picture was about Pope Julius rather than Michelangelo.' (*My Fair Lady* had not yet been released, nor had Rex won his Oscar.) He and Heston literally tried to out-stretch each other, with Heston always contriving to tower over him. In this light, some of Heston's diary entries in *The Actor's Life* make interesting reading. Early in the shooting he writes: 'Rex requires careful handling, but he'll be damn good in the part.' Then at the end: 'I think he's fine as the Pope, worth all the megrims.' Editing the diaries for publication in 1976, he added, 'Rex is a very gifted performer. He also has the temperament of a thoroughbred racehorse . . . highly strung, with a tendency to snort and rear and kick at the starting gate.'

Harrison had always admired Ben Jonson for his satiric viewpoint (much preferring his work to that of Shakespeare) and this helped dispose him favourably towards the latest project of Joseph L. Mankiewicz, as did the genial and (more often than not) successful collaborations they had in the past – for Mankiewicz proposed to film an updated version of *Volpone*. Even though Mankiewicz's script was unfinished and filled a suitcase, Harrison teamed up with him for the project which was filmed at Cinecittà in Rome and went through several titles before being released as *The Honey Pot*.

The Harrison part was that of Cecil Fox, a legendary

modern-day millionaire who lives in old-world luxury and isolation at a seventeenth-century palazzo on the Grand Canal in Venice. After a rare excursion to view in solitary splendour a production of his favourite play, *Volpone*, Fox is inspired to think up an ingenious plot to trick three former mistresses into believing he is a dying man and he recruits William McFly (Cliff Robertson) as his confidential secretary to bring off the plan. Although all three women are supposed to be wealthy, they are sure to be attracted by the prospect of gaining his fortune, and so they are invited to visit him on his deathbed and to stay for the subsequent reading of the will.

Susan Hayward was cast as the hypochondriacal Texan widow, Edie Adams played the bosomy, fading film star with tax difficulties, and Capucine appeared as the haughty, hard-up princess. Maggie Smith had a key role as the Texas lady's nurse (a part that Rachel Roberts, Harrison's wife, had been anxious to play). But the only really fascinating role belonged to Harrison as the master manipulator, relishing his highly literate dialogue (especially the monologues on how to outwit time, an obsession of the character). His great regret is not having become a ballet dancer and the supposedly dying man is seen gracefully pirouetting around his room (Harrison was, of course, doubled in long shot). Really penniless, and forced to murder Susan Hayward's Texan (the only one of the women who has actual wealth), he is finally caught out and performs a dance of death into the canal.

Vastly overlong, far from being especially witty or intriguing and dully shot, *The Honey Pot* was distressingly poor to come from the author and director of *All About Eve*. In particular, compared to the understanding of the feminine psyche in that film, the three former mistresses were too coarsely grasping and unpleasant (so that Harrison seemed sympathetic by contrast and only properly matched in his scenes with Maggie Smith).

133

The three women had fantasy scenes with Harrison that were cut out to reduce the running time. Susan Hayward, dressed in a buckskin outfit, imagined herself cradling Harrison as a dying prospector out in the desert, first comforting him, then shouting into his ear, 'Be you dead, Ceece?', next ripping open his saddle-bags so that the gold pours out. A fully restored version of *The Honey Pot* does not amount to an archival goal of any priority. The film's lack of box-office appeal did not become apparent until after Harrison had completed what had all the signs of a sure-fire hit, the big musical *Doctor Dolittle* for 20th Century-Fox.

Producer Arthur P. Jacobs thought he couldn't go wrong using two of the key elements that had made *My Fair Lady* so successful. He engaged Alan Lay Lerner to write a script and to come up with song lyrics based on the children's stories by Hugh Lofting. Then, even though Lofting had drawn his Doctor Dolittle as a tubby, balding bear-like figure with a bulbous nose, Jacobs interested Harrison in playing the part, for which in one respect he seemed obvious and ideal casting: having played the master of a thousand dialects so well in *My Fair Lady*, he was clearly suited to playing a man who could speak 498 animal languages. After fifteen apparently unproductive months, Lerner was replaced by Leslie Bricusse and Jacobs persuaded Harrison to stay with the project after showing him part of the screenplay and some of the songs that Bricusse had come up with. Next the producer engaged Richard Fleischer to direct, even though he was not a musical specialist, because he had a reputation for quiet efficiency. Fleischer went to Portofino with Jacobs and came away bearing Harrison's approval.

The next development is related by Jacobs in John Gregory Dunne's book *The Studio*: 'Then Rex says, "Goodbye, sue me, I'm not going to do it." . . . We have a picture called *Doctor Dolittle*, twelve million going in, and no one to play Dr Dolittle. We scratch around and come up with Christopher Plummer. The studio liked him, he'd been in *The Sound of Music*, but it was no secret we were in a jam and we had to lay out $300,000 to get him. So Fox wires Rex something like, "As per your request, you have been relieved of your *Doctor Dolittle* assignment and replaced by another artist." Next day his agents call, Rex didn't mean it, he just wanted a few changes, and so on and so forth. So we pay off Plummer, he's got us over a barrel with a nice legal contract. But Rex is back and we're ready to go.'

In the beginning, Harrison makes a strong impression as Dr John Dolittle, the West Country medic of the mid-nineteenth century who tires of his human patients and decides that 'Animals are so much more fun!' With the encouragement of his thinking parrot, Polynesia, he learns to talk to the animals. We see him trying to extend his expertise to the goldfish by blowing bubbles into a tank (the smallest bubbles he can manage seem like shouting to them). We see him out and about, shaking a leg to communicate with the cows. We see him in a study full of animals including Chee-Chee, the chimpanzee who has learned to cook. If Harrison had an actor's fear of appearing with animals, it proved unjustified here: there are so many of them, but individually they do so little that no scene-stealing occurs. (The introduction of mythical creatures is varyingly successful: the two-headed llama, the pushmi-pullyu, is cleverly done but the Great Pink Sea Snail is weakly realised.)

Having cleared the hurdle of establishing Harrison's extraordinary rapport with animals, the film then seems content to amble through the rest of its two hours and thirty-two minutes of running time without making any further impression at all, except for the exuberance and agility displayed in the circus number 'I've Never Seen

Anything Like It in My Life', led by Richard Atten-borough's circus proprietor Mr Blossom when he sees the pushmi-pullyu. (By contrast, Harrison's musical numbers fall flat, despite the intelligent content of the lyrics, because the rhymes are nowhere near as catchy and memorable as those by Alan Jay Lerner for *My Fair Lady*.) Melodramatic sequences like the Doctor's arrest for apparent murder or his being threatened with the death of ten thousand screams by African natives are ponderously set up and neither thrill nor amuse. Additionally, the image of the black leader is insulting, while Harrison proves physically miscast talk-singing to Sophie the Seal and kissing her before dispatching her into the Bristol Channel to return to her husband at the North Pole: whereas a fat, ugly man like Lofting's origi-nal would merely seem comic fondling a seal which is dressed in bonnet and shawl, for a man as debonair as Harrison to be uttering what is almost a love song ('Isn't it a pity you're a seal?') seems disturbingly perverted. Later it transpires that he is meant to look as though he is with a woman so that he can be accused of having thrown her over the cliffs. When, with the help of the magistrate's dog, Harrison clears himself of the murder charge by demonstrating that he can communicate with animals, he is then declared insane (a judgement that also might have stuck better had a less prepossessing character actor played the role).

Harrison further seems the wrong actor to play shy when confronted by Samantha Eggar's spirited Gen-eral's niece. After she survives a shipwreck and is recov-ered in her underwear, Harrison tells her how terribly glad he is to see her but then retreats by saying that's only because there's so much work to do. When she presses him in song to say whether he likes her or hates her, he has just time to admit 'I think I like you' before they're conveniently taken captive by the African tribe.

However, in what seems to be the farewell scene in which he dispatches Samantha Eggar back to England in the Great Sea Snail, he manages to be diffident and touching as he confesses, 'I'm not very good with people. I'm all right with animals. I don't know why', shyly looking down, his voice full of regret. One glimpses that Harrison might have gone against type and convincingly presented the character as a diffident, easily embarrassed and inadequate figure taking refuge from life in the world of animals.

But principally the Leslie Bricusse script is apt to fall back on the egotistical aspects of the Harrison/Professor Higgins persona. When the Doctor first thinks about learning to speak to animals, he says, 'If I can succeed, I'll be the greatest animal doctor in the world' and this suggests that he is more interested in the renown it will bring than in the work itself. A misogynistic streak appears on a sea voyage when Harrison declares that the ship is no place for a woman: Samantha Eggar replies, 'Then the simple answer is to treat me like a man,' to which he responds, 'I intend to,' and we see her scrubbing the deck and doing the other heavy work. But no aspect of the Doctor's personality is really explored and no amount of smooth playing on Harrison's part can overcome this deficiency.

Doctor Dolittle was a troubled production. Problems with the weather in England (where Castle Combe, inland in Wiltshire, was expensively converted into the film's seaside Puddleby-on-the-Marsh) and with the training of the animals, not overlooking the cost of shooting in Todd-AO and compensating Christopher Plummer, meant that the film went fifty per cent over budget, costing $18 million (more than *My Fair Lady*) by the time it was finished. Harrison insisted on following the slow and expensive procedure he had so successfully adopted for the musical numbers in filming *My Fair Lady*.

He declined to mouth the lyrics to a pre-recorded play-back but was recorded live to a piano accompaniment (the full orchestra was added later). With the cost of 70mm prints and advertising amounting to a further $10 million, the film needed to earn $28 million to break even. Although the appeal of the musical numbers was an unknown factor, the lasting popularity of the Hugh Lofting stories and the widespread interest in merchandising tie-ins created optimism even when sneak previews showed that audiences were only lukewarm about the picture.

Doctor Dolittle had its world premiere in London in December 1967, closely following *Camelot* and just preceding *Half a Sixpence* in the Christmas line-up of big attractions. It had fancy premieres in Copenhagen, Paris, New York and Los Angeles with Harrison making personal appearances accompanied by Chee-Chee and Polynesia. Fox spent lavishly in a campaign for Academy Awards in the hope of winning some and lifting its commercial prospects. Incredibly, the film gained a nomination for Best Picture – there were others for Best Cinematography, Art Direction, Sound, Original Score and Song ('Talk to the Animals'), Editing and Special Visual Effects. But it was found out in the actual voting – the only Oscars it won were for Best Song and Best Special Visual Effects. *Doctor Dolittle* brought in merely $6,215,000 to Fox's coffers from North America and probably a similar amount from the rest of the world. It was a colossal flop, but at least it had plenty of company – there was also *Star!* and *Darling Lili* (Julie Andrews couldn't always draw them in either) as well as *Half a Sixpence* and others.

While *Doctor Dolittle* was in production, Harrison agreed to star in Arthur P. Jacobs' next project, a musical version of *Goodbye Mr Chips*. Then Harrison went to Paris for his next picture and Jacobs and the proposed director

Gower Champion went over to confer with him. According to Jacobs in *The Studio*, 'We drive out to his house in the country and he meets us at the door. "Marvellous day," he says. You know the way he talks. "Marvellous day. Bloody Mary, anyone, Bloody Mary." He gets us the Bloody Marys and then he says, "Now let me tell you why I'm not going to do *Mr Chips*." That's the first we heard about it. It was all set. Well, Gower looks at me, picks up his attaché case and says, "Sorry, I'm going to the airport, I'm going home." It was all set. *All set.*' Jacobs went ahead and filmed it, with Peter O'Toole getting his opportunity to step into Harrison's shoes, but Herbert Ross became the director.

Harrison was in France making *A Flea in Her Ear* for 20th Century-Fox, an improbable venture for a Hollywood company even if Feydeau's sex farce had been a big hit in its London National Theatre production with Albert Finney, and the director, Jacques Charon, and adaptor, John Mortimer, had been engaged to work on the film version. The plot has Harrison as an elegant barrister at the turn of the century who becomes impotent when his wife (Rosemary Harris) suggests that nine years of marriage means that they will be together always. She wrongly suspects him of infidelity and arranges for her married friend (Rachel Roberts) to test him with an invitation to the Coq d'Or, a notorious rendezvous for illicit love. Harrison is not interested and sends a friend in his place, then has to go there to warn him that the woman's husband is in hot pursuit. The porter at the hot-sheets hotel is an exact double of the barrister, providing Harrison with a dual role (but, rather surprisingly, the two characters never meet). As the drunken, half-witted, low-life employee, Harrison is woefully unconvincing, but this is in part because he has to stay near enough to his other character for the wife to think the porter is her husband. On stage, it was possible; in big screen close-up, evidently not.

The action is frantic but obstinately unamusing. Fox presumably entertained hopes of repeating the success of *Irma La Douce* but in Darryl Zanuck's words, the film was 'A catastrophe! An absolute bust everywhere.' It is not hard to see why: the film dissipated the artifice and compactness of the stage set with real Parisian exteriors and many more interiors, and was obviously unable to draw on the great pleasure of watching a really well-oiled farce in the theatre, which is the appreciation of the skill in timing and choreography needed to open doors, faint away and hide in closets on cue.

For once, Harrison had no plans after *A Flea in Her Ear*, saying, 'I do know what's around and, really, I'm not that keen on any of it.' His next film (again for 20th Century-Fox) was the result of a 'dare': he and Richard Burton agreed to play ageing homosexuals in a film version of Charles Dyer's stage play *Staircase* after Burton phoned to say, 'I'll do it if you'll do it.' Paul Scofield and Patrick Magee had starred in the London theatre in this story of a gay marriage under pressure (Eli Wallach and Milo O'Shea had done it briefly on Broadway). An intimate, low-budget film adaptation might have had some chance of success but instead the film became a wildly expensive production with a gimmick. Although the odd couple live in the seedy Brixton area of South London, the entire picture was made on sets in Paris to protect the tax position of Richard Burton and to enable him to be near Elizabeth Taylor (who was making *The Only Game in Town* there to save taxes, forcing Fox to also rebuild Las Vegas in France). Burton was reported as receiving one and a quarter million dollars for *Staircase* while Harrison's fee was a reputed one million.

The gimmick was having two such celebrated heterosexual actors play the gay barbers of Brixton. This made it almost impossible for the actors to be convincing, as was vital if their dramatic predicament was to be moving rather than uncomfortable. Audiences were not at all curious to see how well Burton and Harrison had impersonated characters so far from their own natures and the film was a box-office disaster (as was *The Only Game in Town* for its own reasons).

In *Staircase*, Harrison and Burton have spent thirty years together and their relationship has degenerated into continual bickering and friction, but after several crises they realise they cannot get along without each other. They appear grotesque misfits, inviting ridicule rather than sympathy, as they fret over their wrinkles and expanding waistlines or enviously watch a young boy and girl strip in the park with Harrison squealing to Burton, 'Ooh look, Harry, they're making love,' as though they themselves did nothing comparable.

At one time Harrison saw his part (named after the author, Charles Dyer) as 'a marvellous piece of writing' with 'all sorts of colours in it'. 'The lines are contrived to carry the rhythms of homosexual speech. Burton and I just batted them at each other for sixteen weeks. I had to draw very much on the emotional side of my make-up. Charlie was an enormously emotional creature. He spent a lot of time weeping, in anger or depression.' Harrison elaborated to interviewer Catherine Stott on the approach they took. 'We were not heterosexuals *sending up* homosexuals – we felt very sympathetic towards their dilemma. We were both terrified of over-playing, or looking as though we were being camp or rampant queers. It was damn difficult to keep my part within the realms of total reality. I found it impossible to push through the sort of emotions that Charlie had and to keep in my head that he was anything – homosexual, heterosexual or goat. He was just a man in dire distress.' As the more extrovert and flamboyant of the two men, a former actor lamenting a passed-up career (but still doing the odd television commercial), Harrison gives a performance that does tip over into the extravagant – it reminded one critic of Bette Davis in her heyday – and Burton emerges with more credit as the less aggressive, more sober Harry. With its downbeat treatment of two tragic figures and lack of any sensational scene to compare with that of *The Killing of Sister George*, the film proved to have little appeal to anybody.

'They made it a much harsher picture than both Burton and I thought it would be when we agreed to do it,' said Harrison afterwards. He is subsequently quoted as blaming producer-director Stanley Donen for the film's failings: 'I'd seen Paul Scofield in it and loved it. But I was terribly upset by the script. Donen had dirtied it up. When I tried everything to get out of it, Fox threatened to sue me for a million dollars, and after seeing the final cut I wished I'd paid the million and never done it.' He refers to it in the same disparaging terms in his autobiography, *Rex*.

11
Going with the Times

THE LATE 1960S AND EARLY 1970S WERE A DIFFICULT TIME for Harrison professionally (and personally, with his separation from Rachel Roberts in December 1969). The box-office disappointment of *Doctor Dolittle* and the rejection of *A Flea in Her Ear* and *Staircase* came at a time when the film industry in Hollywood was in disarray because of over-spending and film production in Britain was in difficulties as well. Several interesting film projects for Harrison just wouldn't take off while one good offer that he did receive, which might have restored his box-office standing – the chance to play the title role in *Scrooge*, a musical version of Charles Dickens' *A Christmas Carol* – was lost when he withdrew on doctor's orders.

George Cukor had been interested in making two more films with Rex after *My Fair Lady*. One of them offered the intriguing prospect of Harrison as the middle-aged Casanova in *Casanova's Homecoming*. 'It is rather moving,' declared Harrison. 'The poor fellow never learned to move with the times. His tragedy was his failure to adapt. And if you don't go with the times you're – well, finished. He was a man utterly obsessed with his past. What a tragic waste – middle age is such a marvellous time of one's life. Despite the reputation I have in some quarters I certainly don't view myself as a Casanova at all, but the man certainly fascinates me.'

Cukor and Harrison had also wanted to film Michael Bradley-Dyne's 1964 play *The Right Honourable Gentleman* in a screen adaptation by John Osborne. Rex would have portrayed Sir Charles Dilke, the famous Liberal statesman of the Victorian era, a potential prime minister, whose career was wrecked when his sordid extra-marital affairs were exposed in the divorce court. Anthony Quayle had played Dilke on stage. Then in April 1969, some three years later, Harrison was again proposing to play Dilke, only this time in a film that would be derived from Roy Jenkins' 1965 book *Sir Charles Dilke: A Victorian Tragedy*. The film would apparently not have been sympathetic to Dilke, finding him guilty of serious misconduct. 'He must have been,' said Harrison. 'They all were. It was an incredibly shady period.'

Harrison also made plans to work in films behind the camera as a director and producer. 'I want to direct,' he said in 1969. 'I've had a lifetime of acting, and the feeling has been growing on me – especially after a long spell of working – that I would like to become more than just a hired actor. As time goes by, I've found that I have been playing a larger part – talking to the director, going through the script – so it's a development.' He bought the rights to *Graceless Go I*, the tragi-comic novel by Anthony Storey about a middle-aged psychiatrist, and engaged Storey to adapt it for the screen. He then had hopes of filming it in early 1970.

While that was brewing, Harrison went back to the stage for the first time in eight years. He hadn't been short of offers. He was invited to play Henry VIII again in a musical comedy, *Something About Anne*, for the

Broadway stage. Rachel Roberts would have co-starred and he was asked to direct it as well. He pondered the idea and declined. There had also been talk of him doing Anthony Shaffer's *Sleuth* (the proposed part went to Anthony Quayle) but instead he gave his support to a new playwright, George Hulme, who had created a work called *The Lionel Touch*. It is easy to see the superficial appeal of the play, giving Harrison the opportunity to play a lovable rascal called Lionel Farleigh, a 57-year-old failed painter living in Brighton with his wife (Joyce Redman, his Anne Boleyn in *Anne of the Thousand Days*) and their three children. A totally irresponsible roué and conman, he lives by the motto, 'I Came, I Conned, I Conquered', tells his long-suffering wife, 'I'd do anything for you – except regular work' and frankly answers his son's question, 'Did it ever occur to you that sex might not be the be-all and end-all of life?' with the one word, 'Never'. On the day featured in the play, Harrison has to raise £200 to meet mortgage payments and stay out of jail.

The trouble seems to have been that the play allowed Harrison to charm his way through without ever suggesting that his attitudes were harmful or that his approach to women was deplorable. In *Plays and Players*, Stanley Price commented that 'his smug delight in his own caddishness comes across as rather pathetic and juvenile; a middle-aged naughty boy practising adult vices of thoughtlessness and egoism . . . it is clearly conceived by author and star, hand in glove, as a charming little comedy in which the generation gap is bridged by an elderly swinger, and in which poverty and selfishness don't hurt anybody provided you've got style, baby.' Harrison shared the dissatisfaction with the play and continual attempts were made to improve it by changing lines.

The Lionel Touch's run was limited because Harrison

had signed to star in the film *Scrooge* (another Leslie Bricusse adaptation, this time of Dickens, for which recitative numbers to suit Harrison had been devised). However, Harrison felt too unwell to continue with *The Lionel Touch* after the announcement of his separation from Rachel Roberts and it was at this point that he also withdrew from *Scrooge* to take a complete rest (Albert Finney inherited his part).

Over the next two years, while Rachel Roberts obtained a divorce (in March 1971) and he married the former wife of actor Richard Harris, Elizabeth Harris, five months later, his career seemed largely at a standstill. Part of the time he spent travelling around the world with the fifth Mrs Harrison. There had been a suggestion that he would co-star with Vanessa Redgrave in the historical drama *Nicholas and Alexandra* but the leads ultimately went to fresher faces, Michael Jayston and Janet Suzman, when the film was made in 1971.

Now in his sixties, Harrison realised that he had little chance of starring in films for the modern teenage audience being weaned on graphic sex and violence, though to his dismay he was offered work in a horror film. He toyed further with the idea of becoming a film producer and thought he saw suitable material for modern tastes in a story called *Pride of Lions* that he bought from David Pursall and Jack Seddon, commissioning them to develop it into a full screenplay. 'It is very violently anti-war,' explained Harrison, 'but I will not make it anti-American. It shows what happens to young people trained only to kill. It is totally contemporary.' He saw Henry Fonda and his son Peter as ideal casting.

The would-be producer also purchased film rights to a novel by Angela Huth, *Nowhere Girl*, which he planned to film on the Continent. He interested Shirley MacLaine in starring under his direction. In the tricky financing circumstances of the time, all Harrison's producing plans withered and died, although *Nowhere Girl* was still a possibility for production two years later when he had encouraging talks with Sarah Miles and Donald Sutherland about doing it.

Harrison was still very attractive as a star name to British television and he agreed to give his first major performance there reviving his 1960 stage role in Chekhov's *Platonov* for BBC TV's 'Play of the Month' drama slot on a Sunday evening. As he wryly commented afterwards, 'I did it because I was asked to do it. Many actors would do more if they were asked.' It was the kind of subject that the cinema would never have made, and this was an opportunity to bring the work to a mass audience. Nothing was changed: it was simply the play on television.

'*Platonov* is a genuinely funny play,' he told *Radio Times*. 'I always like doing funny plays or serio-funny. . . It has a marvellous vitality, a great sprightly quality which will encourage people to see more Chekhov.' It introduced the actor to the concentrated techniques of the medium – five weeks of rehearsal, a day of blocking for the camera, a day in which the first hour was shot, a second day of blocking, then a further day shooting the other hour.

He emerged from it to win renewed acclaim for his performance as the bearded, vodka-soaked village schoolmaster, Platonov, with Sian Phillips taking the role of the attractive but poverty-stricken widow, Anna, who is the most important of the three women outside his marriage who become involved with him (this was the part that Rachel Roberts had played). Opinions varied from, 'Director and actors together swept through the play with fine confidence' (Peter Fiddick, *The Guardian*) to the view that Harrison 'makes most of the other actors on the set seem stagy' (T. C. Worsley in *The Financial Times*) but praise for Harrison was constant. 'Here is an actor who – with the face becoming more expressive the older, more rubbery, it gets – becomes even stronger in presence yet retains the elegance of touch for which the matinee idol was somewhat mindlessly lauded. He played the quicksilver range of Platonov's character with apparent ease,' declared Fiddick.

An intriguing challenge arose when Alan Jay Lerner came to him with *Lolita*, the stage musical he had written from Vladimir Nabokov's novel with music by John Barry. The production had already played an unsuccessful try-out and now Lerner was proposing to re-write it entirely to suit Harrison. He, of course, would play Humbert Humbert, the middle-aged lecturer in love with a twelve-year-old girl (James Mason had done it in the discreet film version). Harrison's comment was: 'I'm very fascinated and I'd like to do it. They've got a totally different conception of the theme than the novel and are working to come up with something funny. The great thing with this subject is to keep it in comedy and that's a difficult thing to do. It is a very delicate subject and if it comes off it has got to be amusing. It is a tight-rope walk. If it is not funny then it is absolutely revolting. The girl, too, has to be right. She makes the running.' But *Lolita* proved to be stubbornly stage-resistant. Even when another distinguished writer, Edward Albee, tried a straight play adaptation in which Donald Sutherland starred in 1981, it proved disastrous.

The stage musical *Man of La Mancha* had revived interest in Cervantes' seventeeth-century classic *The Adventures of Don Quixote* from which it was derived. Peter O'Toole was set to make the film of *Man of La Mancha* and the BBC came to an agreement with the Hollywood film company, Universal, to make a two-hour television film from Cervantes' original novel to take advantage of the wave of interest in the subject. Rex Harrison accepted an offer to star in the production, which was filmed on the plains of La Mancha in Spain during the summer of 1972, with Alvin Rakoff directing.

Elizabeth Harrison accompanied her husband to the location. In her book *Love, Honour and Dismay* she remarks: 'I am never less than awed by Rex whenever I watch him work. His dedication is total; he drives himself as well as others mercilessly.' She adds: 'During the whole time we were in La Mancha he was in considerable pain. He had broken three ribs in a fall a few weeks before in Portofino. . . He had to mount his horse by means of a step-ladder; he would remain in the saddle for hours since it was too painful to dismount between takes.'

Harrison described his feelings about the character he was playing. 'Don Quixote is the anti-hero who keeps on losing – but he is a courtly man who always wants to be all things that are pleasant. It is a romantic story, but I do not see him as a dejected forlorn figure at all.' In fact, Don Quixote was a 'marvellous character . . . with a great relevance to the present age. He was a drop-out, a hippy, who hated his own time and his tragedy, of course, was that the Establishment won. The White Knight, the priest, tells him, "You're not a knight, you're a nut" and he dies because he can't face reality.'

Clad in armour, with a white, trimmed beard, Harrison breathed life into the part of the self-proclaimed Spanish knight who dreams of helping the oppressed by reviving the glory of Knight Errantry despite the objections of those who want him to behave sensibly, and who travels the countryside with his squire (played by Frank Finlay), tilting at windmills, until he is finally compelled to confront reality. And yet, as Harrison's Don says, 'The truth lies in a man's dreams . . . perhaps in this unhappy world of ours, a wise madness is better than a foolish sanity.'

Madness and sanity were themes that Harrison pursued when he personally optioned Pirandello's 1922 play *Enrico IV* and supervised a new translation with the director Clifford Williams. The revival, titled *Emperor Henry IV*, opened in Toronto in December 1972 and went on to Los Angeles, Boston and Washington before reaching New York at the end of March 1973.

Harrison played the wealthy Italian aristocrat who, twenty years beforehand, dressed up as the tyrannical German emperor Henry IV for a pageant, was knocked on the head, and has thought of himself as being that ruler ever since. Thanks to his money, the servants have humoured him all these years and a completely eleventh-century atmosphere has been created inside his palace. When an old lover and a former rival for her affections turn up to investigate whether he is as mad as he looks, they are forced to take part in the charade. Rex had no problem handling the displays of charm and temperament required, but the part did present an odd challenge: 'There are no bounds or lengths to which I cannot go because there's no naturalism in the part except where I wish it to be. In other words it's unnatural acting that is required in this case.'

Clifford Williams was full of praise for Harrison's work: 'Rex is not exactly in his first flush of youth and he has worked like a slave on this. He is masterly. It is a character way outside the things he has done on that famous wit and charm. He may be regretting all the time he has spent on films.' Elizabeth Harrison observed that her husband was very nervous about taking on the role: 'It is a massive, complex part and a formidable challenge to any actor, even to one of Rex's considerable talent. I know that it often made him physically sick with fear and apprehension. It amazed me. He could have chosen almost any play he wanted . . . Yet he drove himself to play the Emperor.' Furthermore, it was a commercial risk, certainly not the kind of play to draw his admirers of *My Fair Lady* days. But after the experience of *The Lionel Touch*, he had clearly decided to reaffirm his credentials as a serious actor with material of accepted merit, and to use his drawing power to bring back from obscurity a work he admired.

The next job he undertook was the dictation of his autobiography before he returned to England for the promising part of the irascible, blind, lawyer father of the playwright and barrister John Mortimer in the television film *Voyage Round My Father*, based on Mortimer's auto-biographical play. Production started in November 1973 with Alvin Rakoff directing and Frederick Brogger pro-ducing. Besides Wendy Hiller (the star of *Major Barbara*), the other leading players were Edward Fox and Alastair Sim. Regrettably, after two weeks on location and six days of shooting at Elstree, the production ran into insuperable cash flow problems and was closed down. There were hopes of resurrecting it, even in the follow-ing February, but it was not until 1981 that *Voyage Round My Father* was finally made with only Alvin Rakoff (now producing as well as directing) still on board and with another illustrious cast comprising Laurence Olivier, Alan Bates, Elizabeth Sellars, Jane Asher, Raymond Huntley and Esmond Knight.

It had always been Harrison's intention to bring *Emperor Henry IV* to London and in early 1974 he did so, for a limited three-month season. He and Clifford Williams took the opportunity to reinstate some cuts they had made for the American production before Harrison's first entrance (he is the last character to appear) when it had been feared that audiences there would become impatient for his arrival. It was felt that British audiences were more tolerant of the plodding introduc-tory scenes. Also, in London the play was more simply titled *Henry IV*, and Harrison insisted on good seats being available at a price within reach of students. He was gratified by one of the best sets of reviews he had ever received, and by the drama students who gathered at the stage door to discuss the part with him after performances instead of wanting his autograph.

True to his tastes, he rejected an invitation to tour America in *King Lear* during the summer of 1974, but he did agree to return to Broadway in a play by Terence Rattigan called *In Praise of Love*. The author had based the work on his personal knowledge of Kay Kendall's brief time with Harrison, and it had already been staged in London with Donald Sinden and Joan Greenwood. Harrison appeared as an egocentric critic and novelist who conceals from his beloved wife (played by Julie Harris) the fact that she is in the terminal stage of an incurable illness. 'Of course it won't be easy to do,' Harrison remarked the month before rehearsals began. 'And yet, you know, the memories of Kay are no longer painful ones – I wouldn't have missed a moment of the life we shared.'

If the basic situation was familiar, the detail was much different. Here the wife is an Estonian-born woman who fought the Nazis and escaped when the Harrison character married her so that she could reach England and safety (Rattigan seems to have been remembering Lilli Palmer in *The Rake's Progress*). Also, the couple have been married for twenty-eight years; and there's a son, pre-occupied with his own problems and unaware of his mother's proximity to death. Harrison enacted a selfish figure of dry humour who has always taken everyone for granted and he continues to let his wife wait on him hand and foot to avoid alarming her about her condition, but he comes to love her deeply for the first time. Even those critics who found the play sentimental and insubstantial acclaimed the performances of Julie Harris and Rex Harrison, and *In Praise of Love* ran for nearly six months, closing in May 1975.

There were rumours of a rift in Harrison's latest marriage and these were confirmed in August when Elizabeth Harrison told reporters in London that she was filing for divorce on the grounds of irreconcilable differences, while Rex informed the press in Nice that he was deeply distressed by the steps his wife had taken and that he was going off in his yacht to get away from it all. Mrs Harrison was granted a decree nisi on 16 December 1975 when the petition was not contested.

It would seem as if, in 1976, Harrison decided to accept cameo roles in films if the money was good or interesting travel was involved. This was also the year when he appeared on American television in a series of popular commercials for Aspen, a new car from Dodge Motors, for which it was said he received a million dollars.

In the case of *The Prince and the Pauper*, a Mark Twain yarn filmed in England and Hungary, he appeared again with Charlton Heston, who was doing a cameo as Henry VIII, and worked for Richard Fleischer, who had directed him in *Doctor Dolittle*. He played a member of the court, the Duke of Norfolk, who persuades the King not to punish an urchin boy after he has accidentally entered Westminster Palace. Later he comes across the boy again (or so he thinks) and has him hustled out of the grounds (but in fact the urchin has changed clothes with the young Prince Edward, who looks exactly like him, and it is the heir to the throne who is ejected, leaving the pauper to take his place). For other reasons, Harrison is later bundled off to the Tower to await execution, only to be pardoned when the King dies and the pauper occupies the throne. The picture foundered on the vapid, prissy central performance of Mark Lester, a last minute choice for the dual role, and on the stolid direction by Fleischer. Understandably, Harrison seemed somewhat subdued, although (for those who hadn't rushed out when the end approached) he narrated a witty epilogue describing in anachronistic terms the fate of the various characters (the pauper becomes a successful thief or 'chairman of the board') and mentioning his character's enthusiasm for cutting off heads after having come so close to experiencing it himself.

Another all-star classic costume caper in which Harrison was caught up was a re-make of the 1939 version of *The Man in the Iron Mask*, based on the nineteenth-century Dumas novel. It was shot in Austria and after much delay released as *The 5th Musketeer*. Cornel Wilde, Lloyd Bridges, José Ferrer and Alan Hale (Jr) appeared as the ageing D'Artagnan and the three musketeers and Harrison was their good friend, the elder statesman Colbert, who gets strung up by the wrists in a cell for his part in opposing the barbaric Fouquet (played by Ian McShane). It was hardly a role that required a star 'name' (the minor character actor Walter Kingsford had handled it in 1939) but the film also stuffed in Olivia de Havilland and Helmut Dantine for good measure. The actual leads in the film are Beau Bridges (dual role as Louis XIV and his brother Philippe), Ursula Andress and Sylvia Kristel. Unfortunately, the film forgot to include imagination and languishes in deserved obscurity.

If Harrison's standards in film work had slipped, he still took his stage career seriously and in 1976 helped the Chichester Festival Theatre in Sussex revive an obscure French farce, *Monsieur Perrichon's Travels*, to mixed reviews from the critics. The large Chichester stage can dwarf some actors but, under Patrick Garland's direction, Harrison made his presence felt as the vain coach-builder Perrichon, a self-made man who believes that his holiday trip to the Matterhorn with his wife and daughter is of such earth-shattering importance that he should give speeches at railway stations, record his impressions on paper, and receive headline treatment in the press. He is too much the petty businessman, watching the cost of the trip and assessing its value in enhanced prestige, ever to relax into the part of the cultured man to which he aspires. His dignity is upset when a ruddy, bewhiskered army major (played by Keith Michell) challenges him to a duel. A spectacular surprise effect produced Harrison hanging from the rafters at the back of the auditorium, to represent him having fallen down the Matterhorn.

In Harrison's hands, Perrichon became less of an idiot, more of a supreme egotist. The interpretation was not to all tastes. R. B. Marriott in *The Stage* commented: 'Rex Harrison gives a stylish, witty performance as Perrichon. One feels, however, that the part calls for a different style of acting: something more vulgar and robust, something with a tinge of silliness. Mr Harrison naturally suggests intelligence and taste.'

In 1977, the actor returned to his favourite source of stage material, the work of George Bernard Shaw, and played Julius Caesar in Shaw's 1906 comedy *Caesar and Cleopatra* on Broadway and read a selection from Shaw's theatre criticism at the Edinburgh Festival.

The new production of *Caesar and Cleopatra* had a troubled history with the original director, Noel Willman, being replaced by Ellis Rabb during the Washington try-out period. Co-star Elizabeth Ashley was potentially capable of bringing out the kittenish sexuality of Cleopatra better than Liz Taylor, but the play seems not to have cohered properly on this occasion and the production quickly folded. *Variety*'s critic, 'Hobe', was even drawn to remark: 'Harrison, normally a master of high comedy acting, gives an impression of only partial interest, without his usual concentration and casual precision. It's almost as if he were standing aside and impersonally observing his own performance.'

The Edinburgh appearance reunited him with director Patrick Garland for five afternoon performances of *Our Theatres in the Nineties*, a one-man show derived from three collections of Shaw's criticism of the great actors of the 1890s. 'It's marvellously vigorous stuff, of extraordinarily high quality,' said Harrison. 'Shaw held the theatre very high, he was always hoping for better things. He tried to get the actors to be more honest in their acting but they did nothing about it. He was impatient because he had high ideals. If there was someone like him writing today then leading actors would be extremely concerned.'

There was a glimmer of a good movie early in 1977, something 'rather like an Ealing comedy', but that was another casualty of financing problems. Instead, Harrison agreed to head a small contingent of actors from the western world, travelling to Southern India for what was said to be the first full cinema co-production between America and India, an extravaganza called *Shalimar*. He was in the company of John Saxon and Sylvia Miles while on the Indian side there were two top box-office heart-throbs, Zeenat Aman and Dharmendra, as well as a favourite character actor, Shammi Kapoor.

Harrison's role of Sir John Locksley bears a superficial resemblance to his Cecil Fox of *The Honey Pot*: here again he is a recluse (this time on an island in the Indian Ocean), pretending that he is dying, summoning visitors and teasing them with a chance of obtaining great wealth. But this Harrison is far from penniless and is really a villain in the tradition of Count Zaroff practising his most dangerous game. He has been a thief by profession. His biggest triumph was seizing the Shalimar ruby, worth $135 million, but he has spent twelve sleepless years worrying about losing it, so he invites the world's greatest thieves to try to outwit his security arrangements, confident that they will die in the attempt and he can then rest easy. He has had his palace booby-trapped and covered by closed-circuit television as well as guarded by a small army. He watches with genuine admiration on his bank of television monitors as the

156

mute John Saxon and trapeze artist Sylvia Miles make their attempts and perish. He kills two others who want to back out, but sees the self-invited petty thief and ultimate hero Dharmendra make his worst fears come true.

Regrettably, the whole piece is handled by director Krishna Shah as flatly as one of the *Man from UNCLE* episodes he had directed in Hollywood. Harrison gives as adequate a performance as his prosaic lines permit and remains cool and commanding amidst some wildly exaggerated, loudly dubbed supporting performances and the often meaningless pyrotechnics of the special effects department. What he doesn't do is bring any humour or expression of relish to his crazed character. He makes a very humdrum villain compared with Leslie Banks in *The Most Dangerous Game* and the film, poor as it already is, becomes poorer still for his one-note interpretation.

Apart from the action sequences, every scene in the film was shot twice, in English and Hindi. Contractually, Harrison was spared learning his lines in Hindi although Sylvia Miles read hers with the help of an 'idiot board'. With added songs and dances, the Hindi version ran a good hour longer than the one prepared for the English-speaking market, and it was widely seen in Indian cinemas, even reaching the United States to play at Manhattan's only Indian-language movie house, the Bombay Cinema. However, the English version found no takers for British or American exhibition, and was only picked up for videotape release.

More exotic location work was involved when Rex worked yet again for the ever-active Richard Fleischer (who replaced the original director, Richard C. Sarafian) on the dismal adventure yarn *Ashanti*. Filmed in Kenya and Israel, it starred Michael Caine as the doctor desperately trying to recover his black wife after she has been abducted by slavers in West Africa. Urbane and cheerful, Harrison popped up as a member of the Anti-Slavery Society, putting Caine in touch with William Holden's helicopter pilot (another cameo role) and with a tribesman who is also chasing the same slave-trader.

Then it was back to the more sophisticated environs of Broadway and top billing opposite Claudette Colbert in the first American production of the William Douglas Home comedy, *The Kingfisher*, which had opened in London in May 1977 with Ralph Richardson, Celia Johnson and Alan Webb. The director and designer of the original production, Lindsay Anderson and Alan Tagg, repeated their work in New York and George Rose rounded out the cast of three when the play premiered in December 1978 as butler to Harrison's bachelor novelist, who entertains an old flame (Colbert), just widowed after fifty years of marriage. The couple spend two hours debating whether they should or shouldn't get hitched while the butler watches apprehensively, unwilling for his domain to be invaded by the lively, strong-minded widow. 'Hobe' in *Variety* was once again ready with praise: 'Harrison gives an expertly projected comedy portrayal of the selfish but disarming novelist who's determined not to let the enchanting lady slip away on this long-delayed reunion. As usual, his timing and shading of the lines is brilliant.'

During the play's run, at the turn of the year, Harrison married for the sixth time, to a middle-aged brunette, Mercia Tinker, who was involved in social research in New York. Like his previous wives, she soon noticed Harrison's obsession with his craft. In the last week of *The Kingfisher*'s run on Broadway, she discovered him pacing the stage after a performance, working out in his mind if a scene would play better done another way. He declared himself keen to go on exploring a part until the very last night.

A second literary endeavour was concluded in 1979: an anthology of 'tender, sweet and often humorous thoughts on love' selected by Harrison and issued under the title *If Love Be Love*.

In 1979 Harrison also journeyed to Holland for another unpromising film assignment, playing a German called Klaus von Osten in a glum melodrama then called *Mario Puzo's Seven Graves for Rogan* to emphasise the involvement of the author of *The Godfather* in providing the basic story. The film is a pointless and very belated addition to the cycle of Forties films in which Americans conducted personal vendettas against those responsible for killing loved ones in the Second World War (Dick Powell in *Cornered*, Alan Ladd in *Captain Carey USA*). Harrison is the Nazi colonel who, in the last days of the war, is responsible for killing Edward Albert Jr's wife, forcing him to give away secret codes, and then having him shot in the head. Miraculously surviving, Albert sets out to murder all those concerned, working his way up to Harrison who three years later is a judge being groomed, with Allied approval, to become the next Chancellor of Germany. Harrison is seen ironically sentencing a murderer, expressing the hope that the man will earn his own forgiveness. Confronted by Albert (who has been spotted but finds him alone in the courthouse with miraculous ease), Harrison has only time to mutter the words, 'You are far more terrible than in my dreams', before he is executed. It is the only indication that the Harrison character has been at all conscience-stricken.

Harrison received top billing, although his footage is brief – confined to the opening interrogation scenes and the end of the picture. As a German officer, he is grave and businesslike rather than a ranting brute; as a judge, he is believably eminent and patrician in white bow-tie and robes. But neither the script nor his performance give us any insight and, deprived of scope for a glint of

159

humour, Harrison brings nothing distinctive to the part beyond his name. As in the case of *Shalimar*, his participation was not enough to ensure a proper cinema release – and it was not until 1983 that the film surfaced in some American movie houses as *A Time to Die*, while British Harrison fans had to seek it out on video cassette. The actor has since concentrated on stage work.

12
Full Circle

IT WAS BOUND TO HAPPEN AND IT WAS SUCH 'AN astronomical offer' that Harrison didn't refuse. He agreed to play Professor Higgins again on stage in a twenty-fifth anniversary presentation of *My Fair Lady* for two Californian impresarios in a deal reputed to have been worth a million pounds a year. There was some risk. The last New York revival hadn't been a success. By now, Harrison was too old for the part (although even in close-up he didn't look his years when wearing his toupee). But other stars – Yul Brynner with *The King and I*, Richard Burton with *Camelot* – had revived their stage hits, and Harrison was given the final word on the director, casting, and other details such as decor. He chose Patrick Garland to direct, having worked with him rewardingly on *Monsieur Perrichon's Travels* and *Our Theatre in the Nineties*.

In Harrison's mind were definite changes of approach. He felt the play could be done better than it had been in 1956. 'I didn't think Shaw was done total justice. We engaged singers rather than actors.' He wanted to tip the balance towards actors who could sing. In the autumn of

161

1979 he and Patrick Garland started searching for a new Eliza Doolittle in London. 'This time we'd like her to be a real London girl, a Cockney, perhaps, and much tougher than the other Elizas,' he said. 'That way it'll make it more difficult for Higgins to turn her into a lady, and pose more of a challenge for me. It's never been done that way before, and it should be much more interesting. The only problem, of course, is that it's going to be difficult getting permission for an English girl to do the show in America.'

It was not planned to start rehearsals before the following August and in the meantime Harrison undertook a tour of *The Kingfisher* across North America. With Patrick Garland, he settled on Cheryl Kennedy to be the new Eliza but, as he had anticipated, American Equity rejected a British actress and demanded that he chose a native performer. He and Garland obligingly auditioned a stream of performers without finding anyone they considered appropriate. 'All of them could sing like dickie birds,' commented Harrison, 'but none of them could do the Cockney accent which was vital.' Part of the problem was that Harrison had remained a British subject, as had 91-year-old Cathleen Nesbitt (playing Harrison's mother, Mrs Higgins) and American Equity baulked at conceding the case for another foreign artiste. Harrison flew from Florida (where *The Kingfisher* was playing) to argue the case before the Equity Council in New York, who still refused to allow Cheryl Kennedy to play Eliza. Harrison then decided not to proceed with the revival. The case went to arbitration and Ms Kennedy was at last accepted because of 'unique circumstances' (which meant that no precedent was being established).

Another decision Harrison made was that the revival should look more realistic. Out went a number of Cecil Beaton's costume designs in favour of ones with a more earthy colour to suit the grimy London of 1907. The revised production of *My Fair Lady* opened in New Orleans in September 1980 and was then somewhat wobbly in certain respects, according to *Variety*'s man on the spot ('Pope') who found fault with several of the performers and commented of Harrison: 'For most of the evening, he presents a delightful picture of irascibility, egotism and sexism, talk-singing his songs in the effective method he developed for the original production. Near the end, his effect on an audience is affecting as he sings "I've Grown Accustomed to Her Face". But there are several stretches when Harrison doesn't seem to have his heart in his work, resulting in an inconsistent performance that goes through rapturous peaks and uneasy valleys. On opening night, he made several flubs in his lines and in "I'm an Ordinary Man", the complex song in which Higgins spells out his credo.'

Harrison was aiming at a more profound, less eccentric portrayal of the Professor. 'My performance is a little less edgy than it was,' he remarked to W. J. Weatherby in Los Angeles in early 1981. 'It has just come out that way, perhaps because I'm personally less edgy, perhaps because I'm enjoying it so much. I don't know of anything more rewarding with an audience. The standing ovations we get for *My Fair Lady* make life very much easier than fighting audiences with plays that have material which is not always understandable, too light or too dark or whatever. It's a long show, longer than the average, and it's a very long part. But I love it.'

The actor found the part wasn't as exhausting as it had been. 'I think I'm finding this one easier because my life is organised at last and Mercia, my wife, is making sure that I eat properly. She is a keen nutritionist. Also, I'm pacing myself better. When I did the original show I seemed to spend my time running round the theatre like a rabbit. In those days I was always anxious to get back on stage. Now when someone else is on stage and I'm not, I'm delighted,' he told Roderick Mann.

After four months in Los Angeles, the production toured for a further eight months before reaching Broadway in August 1981 where it ran until the end of November, having been billed as a three-month limited run. *Variety*'s 'Humm' thought that 'some of the magic has faded, at least in the so-so current revival', and said of Harrison, 'Although at 73 he's clearly too mature for the role, Harrison's distinctive underplaying and patented talk-singing are as commanding and charming as ever. His performance is polished and seemingly effortless, but this Higgins is more avuncular than romantic, and there's little electricity in his scenes with the Cockney flower girl who melts his heart.' Although there had been talk of Harrison playing Higgins again in London, the highly successful revival of the musical in October 1979 with Tony Britton as Higgins, Liz Robertson as Eliza, and Anna Neagle as Mrs Higgins, had only just closed after a two-year run and had eaten into too much of the potential audience.

In 1982, Harrison accepted a suggestion that he re-do *The Kingfisher* for British television, this time co-starring with Wendy Hiller and Cyril Cusack. The production was opened out a bit and an appropriate manor house located in Norfolk to represent the home of Rex Harrison's titled writer who puts on evening dress and dispenses sidecars to the woman he wanted to run off with fifty years before and hopes he can marry now. Harrison's eyebrows arch expressively, his back freezes with immaculate timing at the mention of a belly dancer in his past, and the lines roll off his tongue only a little less crisply than before; Wendy Hiller fences with him ably; and for once Harrison is upstaged by the third side of the triangle, Cyril Cusack in a characteristically impish study of the gay manservant. For all its conversational gestures in the direction of modern explicitness, too much talk makes this love among the ruins exquisitely tedious.

Devotion to Shaw expressed itself again when Harrison was instrumental in dusting off another of his plays, the 1914 *Heartbreak House* which he had seen revived at the Liverpool Playhouse in his student days there. He appeared as the 88-year-old Captain Shotover, the rumbustious sea salt with a grey, shaggy beard in whose house a weekend party takes place. 'I've always thought Shotover was a marvellous part,' said Harrison. 'Shotover is a wise old bird with quite a lot of humour to him, though possibly slightly mad humour. But the play is really a team play. They are all damned fine parts and everyone has their scene.' Those who helped make up a stellar cast for the run at London's Theatre Royal, Haymarket, included Diana Rigg and Rosemary Harris as his daughters, although his recent Eliza, Cheryl Kennedy, was replaced at the last minute by Mel Martin. John Dexter directed the production.

Although Richard Findlater (in *Plays and Players*) suggested that 'it was hard to believe in Rex Harrison's muted Shotover as a wild, despairing and misanthropic master-mariner of 88 who is popularly believed to have sold his soul to the devil in Zanzibar, and who is planning his own means of universal destruction,' he added, 'there is enough humour and humanity in the role for Mr Harrison to feed on it, and for his admirers in the audience to feast on Mr Harrison: his performance was, within its limits, finely accomplished, and soared above the limits in some of the major speeches with surprising effect.'

Reviewing the year's male performances for *Plays* magazine, Sheridan Morley chose Harrison's Shotover as one of the six that had impressed him most. He described as 'shamefully grudging' the welcome other critics had afforded him, because of his long absence from the West End stage, and went on: '. . . so mesmeric was Harrison in his flamboyant and marvellously quirky theatricality that he managed to hover the play like some benign Prospero, neither coming or going but merely trying to make sense of a British isle that is still full of noises but no longer so very magical. All of that is of course a perfect role-description of Shotover himself, and when Harrison got himself into that last great speech about England ("The Captain is in his bunk drinking bottled ditchwater and crew is gambling in the forecastle; she will strike and splint. Do you think the laws of God will be suspended in favour of England because you were born in it?") it was to be reminded with a sudden shock of what an extraordinarily theatrical talent we have allowed to disappear over the Atlantic.'

By the time these words appeared, Harrison had disappeared to New York yet again, but this was only to repeat his performance as Captain Shotover. One other member of the British cast, Rosemary Harris, went with him, and she changed her part for the one Diana Rigg had played in London. The production was completely re-staged with another British director, Anthony Page, and its limited run at a small New York theatre was a huge success with standing room being occupied at many performances. 'Harrison is now well suited to the role of the crusty, sagacious old sea dog, Captain Shotover, the author's philosophical stand-in,' observed 'Humm' of *Variety*, adding, 'It's a slightly softer and less thundering Shotover than the usual interpretation, but Harrison's technique of underplaying emotion and cannily throwing away comedy lines is as impressively skilful as ever.'

After this desertion, Harrison hastened back to the West End for his next new performance, and even brought a bonus with him – his co-star of *The Kingfisher* on Broadway, Claudette Colbert, to make her first appearance on the London stage since a captivated Harrison had seen her perform in *The Barker* in 1928.

The play in which they were to appear was a curious choice, an obscure and trivial comedy by Frederick Lonsdale called *Aren't We All?*, originally written as *The Best People* in 1908, revised and first presented under its new title in New York in 1923, filmed on the cheap in 1932 (Gertrude Lawrence's first picture), and revived in the West End in 1954.

It brought Harrison full circle, back to the kind of drawing-room comedy on which he had cut his stage teeth. It was as though the actor was tired of quarrelling with the idea that he was only a master of light comedy and had said, 'All right, if that's how you want to regard me, I'll remind you of how deserved my reputation is.'

Much of the media attention focused on Miss Colbert returning to the stage at 81 years of age (Harrison, of course, was a mere stripling of 76). Looking miraculously thirty years younger and handling her not-too-demanding supporting role with sparkling command, Miss Colbert received most of the critics' plaudits on opening night (during a rare British heat-wave) while Harrison offered no surprises doing what was expected of him, except for fluffing many of his lines (but ploughing on regardless).

He played Lord Grenham, the ageing roué and widower who takes his young ladies to the British Museum to avoid being seen ('Only an air raid would drive his own class into it,' comments Colbert). His son Willie is caught kissing a vamp by his wife on her unexpected return from a rest cure in Egypt. Learning of this misconduct, Colbert enquires of Harrison, 'Is Willie being his father's son?', allowing Harrison to reply, 'No, the reverse – he's been found out.'

Aren't We All? carries on in this light-hearted, bantering way. Without the magnetism of its two veteran stars and the addition of stellar names like Nicola Pagett, Francis Matthews and Michael Gough, the play would waft away on its own insignificance. (Perhaps the biggest laugh of the show came when Nicola Pagett, as the wife, refers to her visit to Egypt and Claudette Colbert replied, 'Oh, darling, what memories you bring back to me!', evoking her Thirties screen appearance as Queen of the Nile.)

It is the Harrison character who discovers that his daughter-in-law compromised herself in Egypt, and organises a counter-attack on his son's behalf. From the first, Claudette Colbert has made no bones of the fact that she wants to marry Harrison, and the daughter-in-law has her revenge inserting a phoney marriage announcement in *The Times*, which Colbert assumes to have been placed by Harrison as his answer to her many proposals. The way Harrison absorbs the shock of learning about it and bluffs his way out of the situation, the way he reacts to Colbert's questioning (touching his forehead, walking around, coming up with the explanation that he has finally realised the need for companionship), the way his face lights up when he learns that Colbert will not only permit him to run over to Paris for a month while she handles all the nuptial arrangements but will allow him to keep on making trips after they're married – these have something of the old Harrison skill and sense of mischief.

Harrison's part had been the province of crusty old character actors like Hugh Wakefield (the 1932 film) and Ronald Squire. It had belonged to the kind of actor he had admired in his youth. The revival of *Aren't We All?* was valuable in one way, to theatre historians, as a chance to see an average, typical play of its period rather than the accepted classics that are normally revived. It could be viewed with the same interest as film buffs would flock to see the 1932 film version if that is ever found. This again was Harrison taking it easy, not fighting audiences with demanding material, basking in their ready applause. But the audience satisfaction was real enough: it was value for money. (Envious American playgoers were treated to the Harrison–Colbert combination in the summer of 1985 when *Aren't We All?* had a limited run on Broadway. The supporting cast was different, with Lynn Redgrave taking over from Nicola Pagett. The play delighted critics more than in London and drew good audiences. The Harrison charm was still working.)

As memories of the stage work fade, the film performances will be around to show just how good in his own particular way Harrison was. Not that we should even begin to think we've seen the last of him. As he has said: 'I should like to work until a spotlight falls on my head or my heart stops – maybe during a quarrel with a director.'*

*Harrison's granddaughter Cathryn looks set to keep alive the family acting tradition. His younger son, Carey, has written plays and has based himself in East Anglia. Older son Noel, besides being a member of the British Olympic ski team in 1952 and 1956, became a pop singer (with a hit, 'The Windmills of Your Mind', in 1969) and a TV star (in *The Girl from UNCLE*) before turning his back on show business and living on a farm in Nova Scotia for a few years; but he returned to stage acting, full time, from 1982. Noel's oldest daughter (by his first marriage), Cathryn, has not only acted for the Royal Shakespeare Company (she was in the acclaimed production of *Nicholas Nickleby*) but has worked for leading film directors Jacques Démy (in *The Pied Piper*, 1972, aged eleven), Robert Altman (*Images*, 1972), Louis Malle (*Black Moon*, 1975) and Peter Yates (*The Dresser*, 1983). She looks nothing like her famous grandfather and in 1976 declared that she hadn't seen him in five years. She is a talented actress, but it is hard as yet to tell if she has any of his screen charisma.

Theatre

The following is as full a record of Rex Harrison's stage appearances as possible, in the order in which they occurred. Cast lists are in order of appearance and do not reflect billing. Information about out-of-town openings and tours is listed when known and may be missing in some instances. The Rex Harrison profile in *The Great Movie Stars, The International Years* (1980 revised edition) by David Shipman suggests that Harrison played in a revival of Shaw's *The Devil's Disciple* in Los Angeles in 1978 but I have been unable to trace any details of this. Also included are plays which Harrison directed but in which he did not appear.

LIVERPOOL REPERTORY COMPANY (1924–27)

Rex Harrison is known to have appeared in *Thirty Minutes in a Street* (September 1924; as the Husband); *Old English* (by John Galsworthy; as a footman); *Links* (by Herman Heijermans; in September 1926); *Doctor Knock* (by Jules Romains); *Gold* (by Eugene O'Neill; opened 9 November 1926; as Jimmy Kanaka); *A Kiss for Cinderella* (by James M. Barrie); *Milestones*; and *Abraham Lincoln* (by John Drinkwater; 1927; as a messenger).

TOURING (1927–30)

Rex Harrison appeared in the following plays outside the West End: *Charley's Aunt* (by Brandon Thomas; 1927 in Hull and elsewhere; as Jack); *Potiphar's Wife* (by Edgar C. Middleton); *Alibi* (by Agatha Christie and Michael Morton); *The Chinese Bungalow* (by Marion Osmond and James Corbet); and *A Cup of Kindness* (by Ben Travers).

RICHARD III (1930)

Author: William Shakespeare. *Directors:* Caspar Middleton, John Counsell, Barbara Curtis. *Sets and costumes:* E. Werge Thomas. *Music composers: (original)* R. Vaughan Williams, *(other)* Gustav Holst.

Cast: Baliol Holloway (*Richard, Duke of Gloucester*), Norman Partiège (*George, Duke of Clarence*), Stanley Vine (*Sir Robert Brackenbury*), John Laurie (*Lord Hastings*), Madge Compton (*Lady Anne Nevill*), Doris Paul (*Elizabeth, Queen to Edward IV*), Atholl Fleming (*Lord Rivers*), Hubert Langley (*Lord Grey*), Alfred Harris (*Sir William Catesby*), John V. Trevor (*Sir Richard Ratcliff*), Gerald Lawrence (*Henry Stafford, Duke of Buckingham*), Henry Vibart (*Lord Stanley*), Harold Cox (*Marquess of Dorset*), Nancy Price (*Queen Margaret of Anjou*), Hubert Carter (*First murderer*), William J. Miller (*Second murderer*), Alan Napier (*Edward IV, King of England*), William A. MacLurg (*Sir Francis Lovel*), Mrs Tom Wise (*Duchess of York*), Gilbert Heron (*Archbishop of York*), Harold Reese (*Richard, the little Duke of York*), Roger Foster (*Edward, the little Prince of Wales*), A. Corney Grain (*Archbishop of Canterbury*), C. Haviland Burke (*Lord Mayor of London*), Richard Haines (*Messenger to Lord Hastings*), William J. Miller (*Bishop of Ely*), Denis Elliot-Watson

172

(*Sir James Tyrrel*), Tristan Lawson (*Henry Tudor, Earl of Richmond, later King Henry VII*), Arthur Stratton (*Earl of Oxford*), James E. Halsey (*Sir Walter Blunt*), Colin Poole (*Sir William Herbert*), Henry L. Paton (*Sir William Brandon*), A. Corney Grain (*Duke of Norfolk*), David King (*Earl of Surrey*), Dorinda Thorne, Lesley Braham, Stella Esdaile, Lesley Wareing, Joan Dunn, Sibell Dunn, Ernest Griffin, C. Dixon, A. N. Hilliard, D'Arcy Baker, T. Squire, Geoffrey Robinson, S. Butcher, Bernard Miles, Rex Harrison and others (*Halberdiers, priests, monks, nuns, acolytes, heralds, courtiers, aldermen, citizens and soldiers*).
Producer: Baliol Holloway.
First night: 1 September 1930 (New Theatre, London).

GETTING GEORGE MARRIED (1930)

Author: Florence Kilpatrick. *Director:* Malcolm Morley.

Cast: Isabel Wilford (*Marion Wynne*), Bruce Belfrage (*Hon. George Tremayne*), Louise Hampton (*Lady Thrippleton*), Vincent Murray (*Wetherby*), Rex Harrison (*Hon. Frederick Thrippleton*), Brember Wills (*Lord Thrippleton*), Clarence Bigge (*Jukes*), Marie Dainton (*Henrietta Loring*), Wilfred Babbage (*Captain Tony Loring*), Freda Lockhart (*Lady Avice Wilmer*), Roger Marley (*Prosser*), Diana Wyngate (*Mrs Lawson*), Marion Fawcett (*Mrs Burgess*), Lewis Allen (*Press photographer*).
First night: 26 November 1930 (Everyman Theatre, Hampstead, London).

THE NINTH MAN (1931)

Author: Frederick Jackson. *Director:* Campbell Gullan.

Cast: John Longden (*Costigan*), Nora Swinburne (*Laurel Prescott*), Edward Ashley-Cooper (*Ledgard Draper*), Diana Wilson (*Nadine Westley*), Philip Desborough (*Dr Sindor*), May Beamish (*Mrs Meadows*), Rex Harrison (*Rankin*), Leonard Brett (*An undertaker*), Frank Royde (*Hotsang*), John Ruddock (*A Chinese*).
Production company: Allfayre.
Pre-West End try-out: 19 January 1931 (Theatre Royal, Brighton).
First night: 11 February 1931 (Prince of Wales Theatre, London).

REPERTORY IN CARDIFF (May–September 1931)

TOURING (October 1931–1933)

Rex Harrison is known to have appeared in *After All* (by John Van Druten; October–December 1931; as Ralph); *Other Men's Wives* (1932); *For the Love of Mike* (by H. F. Maltby; 1932; as Conway Paton); *Mother of Pearl* (1933); and *The Road House* (by Walter Hacket; 1933).

NO WAY BACK (1934)

Author: Graham Hope. *Director:* A. R. Whatmore.

Cast: Mary Clare (*Caroline, Lady Beresford*), Esmé Church (*Janet Pleydell*), Sophie Stewart (*Patricia Beresford*), Douglas Jefferies (*Henry Pleydell*), Patrick Waddington (*Toni Silver*), Jack Allen (*Guy Pleydell*), Rex Harrison (*Peter Featherstone*), Frederick Piper (*Bill Littlejohn*), Jack Denton (*Saunders*), Peggy Chester (*Betty Hammond*), Joan Henley (*Dinah Showtallot*), Beatrice Boarer (*Queenie Ferraton*).
First night: 17 May 1934 (Whitehall Theatre, London). Closed 19 May 1934 after four performances.

OUR MUTUAL FATHER (1934)

Author: John Beanes. *Director:* Reginald Tate.

Cast: Joan White (*Nurse Caine*), Wilfred Caithness (*Rogers*), Basil Radford (*Donald Murdoch*), Lydia Sherwood (*Mrs Murdoch*), Julia Crawley (*Flora Murdoch*), Ronald Simpson (*Baillie Murdoch*), Joyce Barbour (*Guinevere Legree*), Fabia Drake (*Elaine Taunton*), Rex Harrison (*John Murdoch*), Eric Portman (*Carlo Monreale*), Helen Waring (*Nurse Budge*), Cecil Humphreys (*Joseph Murdoch*).
Production company: The Repertory Players.
First night: 4 November 1934 (Piccadilly Theatre, London, for a single performance only).

174

ANTHONY AND ANNA (1934)

Author: St John G. Ervine. *Director:* Jack Minster.

Cast: Charles Lefeaux (*Fred*), Herbert Lomas (*George*), Bruce Belfrage (*Hubert Dunwoody*), Rex Harrison (*Anthony Fair*), Edward Rigby (*Jacob Penn*), Carol Goodner (*Anna Penn*), Ann Codrington (*Lady Cynthia Speedwell*), Cameron Hall (*James Jago*).
Producer: John Y. Smart.
First night: 12 November 1934 (Shilling Theatre, Fulham, London).

MAN OF YESTERDAY (1935)

Author: Dion Titheradge (*from a French play by* Jean Bommart).
Director: Campbell Gullan.

Cast: Ann Todd (*Katherine Lindon*), Rex Harrison (*Paul Galloway*), Gipsy Raine (*A Nurse*), H. G. Stoker (*Mr Braham*), Eric Messiter (*Dr Trevor*), Leslie Banks (*James Brett*), C. V. France (*Sir George Rowland*), Allan Jeayes (*William Lawrence*), Gillian Lind (*Madeline Brett*), Bromley Davenport (*Robert Mason*), Winifred Evans (*Mrs Mason*), Frederick Piper (*Henry*).
Producer: Alec Rea.
First night: 19 February 1935 (St Martin's Theatre, London). Closed late May 1935.

TOURING (1935)

Rex Harrison appeared in *Not Quite a Lady*; and *The Wicked Flee* (circa September).

SHORT STORY (1935)

Author: Robert Morley. *Director:* Tyrone Guthrie.

Cast: A. E. Matthews (*Simon Leigh*), Una Venning (*Peacock*), Marie Tempest (*Georgina Leigh*), Margaret Rutherford (*Miss Flower*), Rex Harrison (*Mark Kurt*), Cyril Raymond (*Lord Bucktrout*), Ursula Jeans (*Penelope Marsh*), Sybil Thorndike (*Lady Bucktrout*).

175

Production companies: Moss Empires, Howard & Wyndham's Tours.
Pre-West End try-outs: 23 September 1935 (King's Theatre,
Edinburgh), then to Manchester, Birmingham and Leeds.
First night: 2 November 1935 (Queen's Theatre, London). A three
months' run was followed by a short tour.

CHARITY BEGINS (1936)

Author: Ireland Wood (from a story by Richmal Crompton). *Director:*
Henry Kendall.

Cast: Josephine Middleton (*Daker*), Wilfred Caithness (*Henry
Deveral*), Cathleen Cordell (*Judy Deveral*), Katie Johnson (*Emily
Deveral*), Beatrix Feilden-Kaye (*Agnes Deveral*), Rex Harrison (*Rodney
Walters*), Nigel Patrick (*Bobbie Forrester*), Rene Ritcher (*Miss Case*),
Ethel Griffies (*Mrs Deveral*), Iris Hoey (*Catherine Deveral*).
Production company: The Repertory Players.
First night: 12 January 1936 (Aldwych Theatre, London, for a single
performance only).

SWEET ALOES (1936)

Author: Jay Mallory [*i.e.* Joyce Carey]. *Director:* Tyrone Guthrie.

Cast: Elliot Mason (*Esther Warren*), Marjorie Martyn (*Rose*), Ruth
Vivian (*Miss Alice Dodd*), Evelyn Laye (*Belinda Warren*), Rex Harrison
(*Tubbs Barrow*), Nicholas Joy (*Lord Farrington*), Myra Hampton
(*Clara*), John Litel (*Jim Baker*), Henry Vincent (*Johnson*), Doris Dalton
(*Florence Cudahy*), Elizabeth Chase (*Maid*), Joyce Carey (*Lady
Farrington*), John Emery (*Hon Robert Melford*).
Producer: Lee Ephraim.
First night: 4 March 1936 (Booth Theatre, New York). Closed with
matinee on 25 March 1936 after 24 performances.

HEROES DON'T CARE (1936)

Author: Margot Neville. *Director:* Claud Gurney. *Sets:* Leon Davey.
Musical director: Carlton Mason.

176

Cast: Boris Ranevsky (*Trondsen*), Marguerite Allan (*Helga*), Henry Longhurst (*George Morris*), Felix Aylmer (*Sir Edward Pakenham*), Carol Goodner (*Lady Pakenham*), Herbert Cameron (*Dr McIlwaine*), Rex Harrison (*Tom Gregory*), Frederick Piper (*Leonard Woods*), Coral Browne (*Connie Crawford*).
First night: 10 June 1936 (St Martin's Theatre, London). Closed early October 1936.

FRENCH WITHOUT TEARS (1936)

Author: Terence Rattigan. *Director:* Harold French.

Cast: Trevor Howard (*Kenneth Lake*), Guy Middleton (*Brian Curtis*), Rex Harrison (*The Hon. Alan Howard*), Yvonne Andre (*Marianne*), Percy Walsh (*Monsieur Maingot*), Roland Culver (*Lieutenant-Commander Rogers*), Kay Hammond (*Diana Lake*), Robert Flemyng (*Kit Neilan*), Jessica Tandy (*Jacqueline Maingot*), William Dear (*Lord Heybrook*).
First night: 6 November 1936 (Criterion Theatre, London).

Harrison toured Europe with *French Without Tears*, entertaining the troops, in May–June 1945.

DESIGN FOR LIVING (1939)

Author: Noel Coward. *Director:* Harold French.

Cast: Diana Wynyard (*Gilda*), Alan Webb (*Ernest Friedman*), Anton Walbrook (*Otto*), Rex Harrison (*Leo*), Dorothy Hamilton (*Miss Hodge*), Cyril Wheeler (*Mr Mirbeck*), Everley Gregg (*Grace Totrence*), Cathleen Cordell (*Helen Carver*), Ross Landon (*Henry Carver*), James McIntyre (*Matthew*).
Producer: John C. Wilson.
First night: 25 January 1939 (Theatre Royal, Haymarket, London). Closed 2 September 1939 by outbreak of war. Provincial tour: 13 November 1939 & week (Prince of Wales, Birmingham), 20 November 1939 & week (Royal Court, Liverpool), 27 November 1939 & week (Lyceum, Edinburgh), 4 December 1939 & week (King's, Glasgow), 11 December 1939 & week (Theatre Royal, Newcastle).

NO TIME FOR COMEDY (1941)

Author: S. N. Behrman. *Director:* Harold French. *Set designer:* G. E. Calthrop.

Cast: Elisabeth Welch (*Clementine*), Diana Wynyard (*Linda Easterbrook*), Walter Fitzgerald (*Philo Smith*), Rex Harrison (*Gaylord Easterbrook*), Lilli Palmer (*Amanda 'Mandy' Smith*), Charles Peters (*Robert*), Arthur Macrae (*Makepeace Lovell*).
Production company: H. M. Tennent.
Pre-West End tour: from 23 December 1940 (Opera House, Blackpool), 13 January 1941 (Theatre Royal, Brighton), 20 January 1941 (King's, Glasgow), 27 January 1941 (Lyceum, Edinburgh), 3 February 1941 (New, Oxford), 17 February 1941 (Theatre Royal, Nottingham), 24 February 1941 (Opera House, Manchester), 3 March 1941 (Theatre Royal, Newcastle).
First night: 27 March 1941 (Theatre Royal, Haymarket, London). Closed 24 January 1942.

ANNE OF THE THOUSAND DAYS (1948)

Author: Maxwell Anderson. *Director:* H. C. Potter. *Setting and lighting:* Jo Mielziner. *Costumes:* Motley. *Music composer:* Lehman Engel.

Cast: Joyce Redman (*Anne Boleyn*), Rex Harrison (*Henry VIII*), Percy Waram (*Cardinal Wolsey*), Charles Francis (*Thomas Boleyn*), Ludlow Maury (*Servant*), Allan Stevenson (*Henry Norris*), John Merivale (*Mark Smeaton*), John Williams (*Duke of Norfolk*), Robert Duke (*Earl of Northumberland*), Viola Keats (*Elizabeth Boleyn*), Kathleen Bolton (*Serving woman*), Cecil Clovelly (*Servant*), Louise Platt (*Mary Boleyn*), Margaret Garland (*Madge Shelton*), Monica Lang (*Jane Seymour*), Russell Gaige (*Sir Thomas More*), Wendell K. Phillips (*Thomas Cromwell*), Harry Irvine (*Bishop Fisher*), George Collier (*Prior Houghton*), Harry Selby (*Messenger*), Fred Ayres Cotton (*Bailiff*), Harold McGee (*Bailiff*), Terence Anderson (*Clerk*). *Singers:* Richard Leone, Frank Myers, Donald Conrad. *Musicians:* Harold McGee, Malcolm Wells, Charles Ellis.
Producer: Leland Hayward. *Production company:* Playwrights' Company.

Pre-Broadway try-out: 9 to 27 November 1948 (Forrest Theatre, Philadelphia), 29 November to 4 December 1948 (Ford's Theatre, Baltimore).

First night: 8 December 1948 (Shubert Theatre, New York). Closed 8 October 1949 after 288 performances (with summer break from 25 June to 22 August 1949). Subsequently toured Midwest and Canada.

Footage of Rex Harrison in this play was included in a *March of Time* feature on New York theatre called 'On Stage' and issued to American movie houses in late February 1949.

ANTA ALBUM (1950)

The Dark Lady of the Sonnets

Author: George Bernard Shaw. *Director:* Sir Cedric Hardwicke. *Settings:* Paul Morrison.

Cast: Francis L. Sullivan (*The Beefeater*), Rex Harrison (*Shakespeare*), Peggy Wood (*Queen Elizabeth*), Lilli Palmer (*The Dark Lady*).

Other performers: Moss Hart and Clarence Derwent (*Masters of Ceremonies*); Yvonne Adair and choruses from *Kiss Me, Kate, Where's Charley?, Texas, Li'l Darling, South Pacific, Gentlemen Prefer Blondes* and *Miss Liberty* (number 'Another Op'nin', Another Show'); Will Mahoney ('Why Be Serious?' sketch); Fritzi Scheff (*songs 'Yesterdays' and 'Kiss Me Again'*); Philip Loeb, Murray Hamilton, Alexander Asro and Lionel Stander (*eating scene from* Room Service); Nancy Walker and Cris Alexander (*taxi cab scene from* On the Town); Ruth Gordon and Raymond Massey (*scene from* Ethan Frome); Burl Ives (*song* 'Foggy, Foggy Dew'); Francine Larrimore and Philip Bourneuf (*scene from* Let Us Be Gay); Mardi Bayne, Ethel Barrymore Colt, Jane Judge, Allyn McLerie, Candace Montgomery, Kate Murtah, Charles Bang, Maurice Kelly, Jay Murphy, Grehan Pearce, John Sheehan and Jack Whiting ('Tell Me, Pretty Maiden' from Floradora); Ethel Barrymore, Mildred Dunnock, Louis Hector and Philip Tonge (The Twelve Pound Look *by* James M. Barrie); Hall Johnson Choir ('Certainly Lord' and 'Pilate – Pilate – Pilate!'); Brenda Forbes (*song* 'And Why Not I?'); Burgess Meredith and Margo (*scene from* Winterset); Ethel Waters (*songs* 'Cabin in the Sky' and 'Takin' a Chance on Love'); John

Buckmaster, Arthur Margetson, Myron McCormick, Bert Lahr and Jack Benny (*'The Still Alarm' from* The Little Show); Bobby Clark (*song 'Robert the Roué from Reading PA'*); Celeste Holm and the choruses from *Lost in the Stars* and *Alive and Kicking* (*song 'There's No Business Like Show Business'*).
Producer: Robert Breen for the American National Theatre and Academy. *Music director:* Max Meth.
Special performance: Sunday, 29 January 1950 (Ziegfeld Theatre, New York).

THE COCKTAIL PARTY (1950)

Author: T. S. Eliot. *Director:* E. Martin Browne. *Decor:* Anthony Holland.

Cast: Robin Bailey (*Alexander MacColgie Gibbs*), Gladys Boot (*Julia – Mrs Shuttlethwaite*), Donald Houston (*Peter Quilpe*), Margaret Leighton (*Celia Coplestone*), Rex Harrison (*An unidentified guest*), Ian Hunter (*Edward Chamberlayne*), Alison Leggatt (*Lavinia Chamberlayne*), Freda Gaye (*A nurse-secretary*), John Richmond (*A caterer's man*).
Production company: Sherek Players in association with the Arts Council.
Pre-West End try-out: from 24 April 1950 (King's, Southsea).
First night: 3 May 1950 (New Theatre, London).

BELL, BOOK AND CANDLE (1950)

Author and director: John Van Druten. *Scenery and lighting:* George Jenkins. *Costumes:* (*for Lilli Palmer*) Valentina, (*others*) Anna Hill Johnstone.

Cast: Lilli Palmer (*Gillian Holroyd*), Rex Harrison (*Shepherd Henderson*), Jean Adair (*Miss Holroyd*), Scott McKay (*Nicky Holroyd*), Larry Gates (*Sidney Redlitch*).
Producer: Irene Mayer Selznick.
First night: 14 November 1950 (Ethel Barrymore Theatre, New York). Closed 2 June 1951 after 233 performances.

VENUS OBSERVED (1952)

Author: Christopher Fry. *Director:* Laurence Olivier. *Production designer:* Roger Furse. *Music composer:* Herbert Menges. *Costumes:* (*for Lilli Palmer*) Valentina, (*others*) Mildred Trebor.

Cast: Rex Harrison (*Hereward, Duke of Altair*), John Merivale (*Edgar, his son*), John Williams (*Herbert Reedbeck*), James Westerfield (*Captain Fox Reddleman*), Hurd Hatfield (*Dominic, Reedbeck's son*), Stuart Burge (*Bates, the footman*), Joan Haythorne (*Rosabel Fleming*), Claudia Morgan (*Jessie Dill*), Eileen Peel (*Hilda Taylor-Snell*), Lilli Palmer (*Perpetua*).
Production company: Theatre Guild.
First night: 13 February 1952 (Century Theatre, New York). Closed 26 April 1952 after 86 performances.

THE LOVE OF FOUR COLONELS (1953)

Author: Peter Ustinov. *Director:* Rex Harrison. *Settings and costumes:* Rolf Gerard.

Cast: Larry Gates (*Col. Wesley Breitenspiegel*), Robert Coote (*Col. Desmond De S Rinder-Sparrow*), George Voskovec (*Col. Aimé Frappot*), Stefan Schnabel (*Col. Alexander Ikonenko*), Reginald Mason (*Herzogenberg Mayor*), Rex Harrison (*Man*), Leueen McGrath (*Donovan*), Lilli Palmer (*Beauty*).
Production supervision: Lawrence Langner, Theresa Halburn.
Production company: Theatre Guild, Aldrich & Myers.
First night: 15 January 1953 (Shubert Theatre, New York). Closed 16 May 1953 after 141 performances. Subsequent tour: 2 to 4 October 1953 (Community Theatre, Hershey, Pennsylvania), 5 to 10 October 1953 (Nixon Theatre, Pittsburgh), 12 to 24 October 1953 (Shubert Theatre, Detroit), 26 to 31 October 1953 (Royal Alexandra Theatre, Toronto), 2 to 14 November 1953 (National Theatre, Washington).

BELL, BOOK AND CANDLE (1954)

Author: John Van Druten. *Director:* Rex Harrison. *Decor:* Alan Tagg.

Cast: Lilli Palmer (*Gillian Holroyd*), Rex Harrison (*Anthony Henderson*), Athene Seyler (*Miss Holroyd*), David Evans (*Nicholas Holroyd*), Wilfrid Lawson (*Sidney Redlitch*).
First night: 5 October 1954 (Phoenix Theatre, London).
Joan Greenwood replaced Lilli Palmer during the run; Harrison himself was replaced later on.

NINA (1955)

Author: André Roussin (translated by Arthur Macrae). *Director:* Rex Harrison. *Decor:* Arthur Barbosa.

Cast: Coral Browne (*Nina Tessier*), James Hayter (*Adolphe Tessier*), Michael Hordern (*Georges Chambery*), Lockwood West (*Agent de Police*), Raymond Young (*René Duvivier*).
Production company: Tennent Productions.
First night: 27 July 1955 (Theatre Royal, Haymarket, London).

MY FAIR LADY (1956 New York production)

Book: Alan Jay Lerner (*from the play* Pygmalion *by* George Bernard Shaw *and the 1938 film version*). *Director:* Moss Hart. *Music:* Frederick Loewe. *Lyrics:* Alan Jay Lerner. *Choreography and musical numbers:* Hanya Holm. *Scenery:* Oliver Smith. *Lighting:* Feder. *Costumes:* Cecil Beaton. *Musical conductor:* Franz Allers. *Songs performed by Rex Harrison:* 'Why Can't the English?', 'I'm an Ordinary Man', 'The Rain in Spain', 'You Did It', 'A Hymn to Him' and 'I've Grown Accustomed to Her Face'. *Other songs:* 'Wouldn't It Be Loverly?', 'With a Little Bit of Luck', 'Just You Wait', 'Ascot Gavotte', 'On the Street Where You Live', 'I Could Have Danced All Night', 'Show Me', 'Get Me to the Church on Time' and 'Without You'.

Cast: Imelda de Martin, Carl Jeffrey and Joe Rocco (*Buskers*), Viola Roache (*Mrs Eynsford-Hill*), Julie Andrews (*Eliza Doolittle*), John Michael King (*Freddy Eynsford-Hill*), Robert Coote (*Col. Pickering*), Christopher Hewitt and Rod McLennan (*Bystanders*), Rex Harrison (*Henry Higgins*), Gordon Dilworth (*Selsey man*), David Thomas (*Hoxton man*), Reid Shelton, Glenn Kezer, James Morris and Herb Surface (*Cockneys*), David Thomas (*Bartender*), Gordon Dilworth

Above:
Charlton Heston's Michelangelo visits Rex
Harrison's ailing warrior Pope in Carol Reed's
production of *The Agony and the Ecstasy*
(1965), the greatest epic ever made about the
painting of a ceiling.

Below:
Another bed, another movie… It's *The Honey
Pot* (1967), and this time Harrison's ailments
are faked, as nurse Maggie Smith will
eventually discover.

Right:
Rex Harrison shares a break with two of his co-stars, Chee-Chee the chimp and Polynesia the parrot, on the set of *Doctor Dolittle* (1967).

Below:
In *Doctor Dolittle* (1967), Rex Harrison tries to talk to goldfish in bubble language, watched by Anthony Newley and (rear) William Dix.

Right:
In the epic that almost sank a studio, *Cleopatra* (1963), Rex Harrison towered over Elizabeth Taylor who made a tartish Queen of the Nile.

Below:
Waiting, waiting, waiting for Elizabeth Taylor to appear in *Cleopatra* (1963). Part of the epic's huge Rome set with Rex Harrison flanked by Richard Burton (left) and Roddy McDowall.

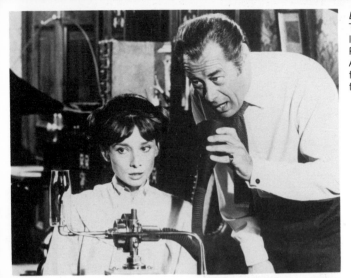

Left:
Teaching a guttersnipe to talk like a duchess: Rex Harrison as Professor Henry Higgins with Audrey Hepburn as Cockney flower girl Eliza Doolittle in the film of *My Fair Lady* (1964).

Right:
By Jove, she's got it! Rex Harrison, Audrey Hepburn and Wilfrid Hyde-White celebrate in 'The Rain in Spain' number from the 1964 film version of *My Fair Lady*.

Left:
The very end of *My Fair Lady* (1964 film): Rex's Professor realises that Audrey Hepburn's Eliza has returned.

Above:
The lady is a seal...and the cause of a murder charge against Rex Harrison in *Doctor Dolittle* (1967).

Below:
Actress Rachel Roberts, Harrison's fourth wife, made her only screen appearance with him in *A Flea in Her Ear* (1968).

Right:
The costumes at least were good: Rex Harrison as the Duke of Norfolk in the 1977 version of *The Prince and the Pauper* (shown in America as *Crossed Swords*).

Below:
On location in Paris for *A Flea in Her Ear* (1968), Rex Harrison receives a visit from his younger son Carey, who followed in his father's footsteps with a theatrical career.

Right:
Done on a dare, and since regretted: Rex Harrison and Richard Burton, formerly partnered in *Cleopatra*, played two ageing homosexuals in run-down Brixton for *Staircase* (1969).

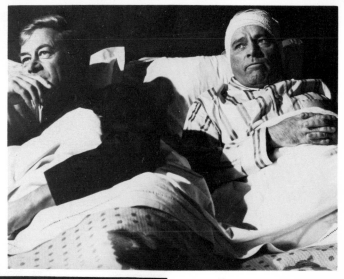

Left:
Harrison, as the cynical old sea salt, Captain Shotover, with Mel Martin aboard the sinking ship that is England in the 1983 London revival of Shaw's *Heartbreak House*.
[Photographed by Zoë Dominic.]

Right:
Broadway audiences saw Rex Harrison and Claudette Colbert together in *The Kingfisher* in 1978/9.

Right:
Rex Harrison at 76 exhibited his classic grasp of drawing room comedy in *Aren't We All?* (seen here with John Price).
[Photographed by Zoë Dominic.]

Below:
London playgoers had to wait until 1984 to see Harrison and Colbert together in the revival of Frederick Lonsdale's *Aren't We All?* (Also present: Francis Matthews, Madge Ryan and John Ingram.) [Photographed by Zoë Dominic.]

(*Bartender*), Rod McLennan (*Jamie*), Stanley Holloway (*Alfred P. Doolittle*), Philippa Bevans (*Mrs Pearce*), Olive Reeves-Smith (*Mrs Hopkins*), Reid Shelton (*Butler*), Rosemary Gaines, Colleen O'Connor, Muriel Shaw, Gloria Van Dorpe and Glenn Kezer (*Servants*), Cathleen Nesbitt (*Mrs Higgins*), Barton Mumaw (*Chauffeur*), Gordon Ewing and William Krach (*Footmen*), Gordon Dilworth (*Lord Boxington*), Olive Reeves-Smith (*Lady Boxington*), Barton Mumaw (*Constable*), Cathy Conklin (*Flower girl*), Christopher Hewett (*Zoltan Karpathy*), Maribel Hammer (*Queen of Transylvania*), Rod McLennan (*Ambassador*), Paul Brown (*Bartender*), Judith Williams (*Mrs Higgins' maid*).

Singers: Melilande Congdon, Lola Fisher, Rosemary Gaines, Maribel Hammer, Colleen O'Connor, Muriel Shaw, Patti Spangler, Gloria Van Dorpe, Paul Brown, Gordon Ewing, Glenn Kezer, William Krach, James Morris, Reid Shelton, Herb Surface, David Thomas.

Dancers: Estelle Aza, Cathy Conklin, Margaret Cuddy, Imelda de Martin, Pat Diamond, Pat Drylie, Barbara Heath, Vera Lee, Nancy Lynch, Judith Williams, Thatcher Clarke, Crandall Diehl, David Evans, Carl Jeffrey, Barton Mumaw, Gene Nettles, Paul Olson, Joe Rocco, Fernanda Schaffenburg, James White.

Producer: Herman Levin.

Pre-Broadway try-outs: 4 to 11 February 1956 (Shubert Theatre, New Haven), and 15 February 1956 for three weeks (Erlanger Theatre, Philadelphia).

First night: 15 March 1956 (Mark Hellinger Theatre, New York). Rex Harrison left the production after the performance on 28 November 1957.

MY FAIR LADY (1958 London production)

Book: Alan Jay Lerner (*from the play* Pygmalion *by* George Bernard Shaw *and the 1938 film version*). *Director:* Moss Hart. *Music:* Frederick Loewe. *Lyrics:* Alan Jay Lerner. *Choreography:* Hanya Holm. *Costumes:* Cecil Beaton. *Musical conductor:* Cyril Ornandel. *Songs performed by Rex Harrison and other songs:* as 1956 production.

Cast: Joan Elvin, Terry Williams and Willhelm Maurer (*Buskers*), Linda Gray (*Mrs Eynsford-Hill*), Julie Andrews (*Eliza Doolittle*), Leonard Wier (*Freddy Eynsford-Hill*), Robert Coote (*Col. Pickering*),

Max Oldaker and Bob Chisholm (*Bystanders*), Rex Harrison (*Henry Higgins*), Alan Dudley (*Selsey man*), Reg Templar (*Hoxton man*), Robert Crane, John Moore, Howard Davies and Robin Dunbell (*Cockneys*), Mostyn Evans (*Bartender*), Alan Dudley (*Harry*), Bob Chisholm (*Jamie*), Stanley Holloway (*Alfred P. Doolittle*), Betty Woolfe (*Mrs Pearce*), Elaine Garreau (*Mrs Hopkins*), John Moore (*Butler*), Howard Davies, Elaine Lovegrove, Mary Burgess, Freda Sessions and Brenda Gayl (*Servants*), Zena Dare (*Mrs Higgins*), Alan Burton (*Chauffeur*), Peter Newton and Lee Kenton (*Footmen*), Alan Dudley (*Lord Boxington*), Elaine Garreau (*Lady Boxington*), Alan Burton (*Constable*), Charmian Burn (*Flower girl*), Max Oldaker (*Zoltan Karpathy*), Wallace Stephenson and Lee Kenton (*Flunkeys*), Mostyn Evans (*Major Domo*), Margaret Halstan (*Queen of Transylvania*), Bob Chisholm (*Ambassador*), Robert Crane (*Bartender*), Willow Stockdale (*Mrs Higgins' maid*).
Singers: Mary Burgess, Muriel Cooke, Daphne Estelle, Brenda Gayl, Tonia Lee, Elaine Lovegrove, Anna Peters, Ann Pidgeon, Freda Sessions, Felicity Wilson, Robert Crane, Howard Davies, Robin Dunbell, Mostyn Evans, Roy Howell, Lee Kenton, John Moore, Peter Newton, Bernard Quinn, Wallace Stephenson. *Dancers:* Diana Beall, Doone Bingeman, Charmian Burn, Joyce Chapman, Joan Elvin, Helene Sprot, Willow Stockdale, Dorothy Walker, Ruth Walters, Richard Bennett, Alan Burton, Norman Caldas, Roy Carlton, Geoffrey Guy, Lionel Luyt, Willhelm Maurer, John Prescott, Reg Templar, Terry Williams, Fred Wisden, Ronald Yerrell.
Producer: Herman Levin. *Production company:* H. M. Tennent.
First night: 30 April 1958 (Theatre Royal, Drury Lane, London). Harrison left the production on 28 March 1959 to be succeeded by Alec Clunes.

THE BRIGHT ONE (1958)

Author: J. M. Fulton [*i.e.* Judy Campbell]. *Director:* Rex Harrison. *Settings:* Tanya Moiseiwitsch.

Cast: Kay Kendall (*Agatha Purvis*), Hugh McDermott (*Curtis*), Michael Gwynn (*Tom*), Kay Kendall (*Phaea–Echo*), Frederick Leister (*Prof. Christie*), Edgar Wreford (*Steward*), Gladys Cooper (*Dame Mildred*), A. J. Brown (*Old Swain*), Johanna Martin (*May*).

Producer: Jack Minster.
First night: 10 December 1958 (Winter Garden Theatre, London).
Closed after 12 performances.

THE FIGHTING COCK (1959)

Author: Jean Anouilh (*his French play* L'Hurluberlu, *adapted by*
Lucienne Hill). *Director:* Peter Brook. *Sets and costumes:* Rolf Gerard.
Lighting: Howard Bay.

Cast: Rex Harrison (*General*), Geoffrey Lumb (*Doctor*), Judy Sanford
(*Marie Christine*), Rhoden Streeter (*Milkman's son*), Claude Gersene
(*Toto*), Roger De Koven (*Milkman*), Michael Gough (*Father Gregory*),
Margo Anders (*Sophie*), Roddy McDowall (*Tarquin Edward
Mendigales*), Jane Lallig (*Bise*), Natasha Parry (*Aglae*), Arthur
Treacher (*Lebellue*), Gerald Hiken (*Michepain*), Alan MacNaughton
(*Baron Henri Belazor*).
Producer: Kermit Bloomgarden.
Pre-Broadway try-out: 16 to 28 November 1959 (Walnut Theatre,
Philadelphia).
First night: 8 December 1959 (ANTA Theatre, New York). Closed 20
February 1960 after 87 performances.

PLATONOV (1960)

Author: Anton Chekhov (*in an English version by* Dmitri Makaroff).
Directors: George Devine, John Blatchley. *Decor:* Richard Negri.
Lighting: Richard Pilbrow.

Cast: Rex Harrison (*Mikail Platonov*), Rachel Roberts (*Anna Petrovna*),
Ronald Barker (*Nikolai Triletski*), Graham Crowden (*Sergei Voinitsev*),
Norman Pitt (*Glagolyev*), Nicholas Selby (*Vengerovich*), Thomas
Hammerton (*Bugrov*), Mary Watson (*Sasha*), Frank Finlay (*Ivan
Triletski*), Peter Guguid (*Petrin*), Rosalind Knight (*Maria Grekova*),
Elvi Hale (*Sofya*), Jeremy Geidt (*Shcherbuk*), Morris Perry (*Vasili*),
George Murcell (*Osip*), James Bolam (*Yakov*), Peter Bowles (*Kirill*),
Susan Westerby (*Katya*), Murray Gilmore (*Village priest*), Peter
Duguid (*Marko*).
First night: 13 October 1960 (Royal Court Theatre, London). Closed
after a limited run of 44 performances.

AUGUST FOR THE PEOPLE (1961)

Author: Nigel Dennis. *Director:* George Devine. *Designer:* Stephen Doncaster.

Cast: Rex Harrison (*Sir Augustus Thwaites*), Rachel Roberts (*Mrs Fulton*), George Benson (*Mr Bolt*), Pauline Munro (*Angela*), Hugh Latimer (*Dr Swinburne*), John Junkin (*Toastmaster*), Elizabeth Bell (*Finola*), William Kendall (*Lord Woodham*), Cyril Raymond (*Mr Glumly*), Gordon Rollings (*Thompson*), Kate Lansbury (*Mrs Thompson*), Arthur Mullard (*Beamer*), Laura Graham (*Miss Willoughby*), Prior Pitt (*1st reporter*), Terrence Brook (*2nd reporter*), Kenneth McClellan (*3rd reporter*), Paulette Preney (*French lady reporter*), Constance Lorne (*Lady reporter*), Donald Sutherland (*American reporter*), Caroline John (*The Mother*), Douglas Ditta (*The Father*), Gwen Nelson (*Lady in red hat*), John Junkin (*Lichee of Tambucca*), Yemi Ajibade (*Aide to Lichee*).
Try-out: from 28 August 1961 (Theatre Royal, Newcastle).
First night: 4 September 1961 (Lyceum Theatre, Edinburgh, for one week).
London performance: from 12 September 1961 (Royal Court Theatre). Withdrawn after 11 performances in London.

THE LIONEL TOUCH (1969)

Author: George Hulme. *Director:* John Gorrie. *Settings:* John Bury. *Lighting:* Michael Northen.

Cast: Rex Harrison (*Lionel Fairleigh*), Joyce Redman (*Vivian Fairleigh*), Christopher Witty (*Tony*), Sharon Gurney (*Melanie*), Christopher Reynalds (*Stanley*), John Leslie (*Bailiff*), Michael Fleming (*School Inspector*), Charles Carson (*Vicar*), Christopher Cazenove (*Courtenay*), Dixon Adams (*Policeman*).
Producer: John Gale. *Production company:* Volcano.
First night: 5 November 1969 (Lyric Theatre, Shaftesbury Avenue, London).

186

EMPEROR HENRY IV (1973 New York production)

Author: Luigi Pirandello (translation by Stephen Rich). *Director:* Clifford Williams. *Scenery and costumes:* Abd'al Farrah. *Lighting design:* Neil Peter Jampolis.

Cast: Michael Diamond and Thom Christopher (*Guards*), Stephen D. Newman, Reno Roop, Michael Durrell and George Taylor (*Secret counsellors*), Douglas Seale (*Butler*), Eileen Herlie (*Countess Matilda*), Paul Hecht (*Baron Tito*), David Hurst (*Dr Genoni*), Linda De Coff (*Frida*), Rudolph Willrich (*Marquis Carlo*), Rex Harrison (*Henry IV*). *Producer:* Elliot Martin. *A* Sol Hurok *presentation. Associate producer:* Herbert Wasserman.
Pre-New York tour: dates unknown (Toronto, Washington), 30 January to 17 February 1973 (Shubert Theatre, Los Angeles). *First night* (following three previews): 28 March 1973 (Ethel Barrymore Theatre, New York). Closed 28 April 1973 after 37 performances.

HENRY IV (1974 London production)

Author: Luigi Pirandello (translation by Stephen Rich). *Director:* Clifford Williams. *Production designer:* Farrah. *Lighting:* Robert Ornbo.

Cast: James Beckett and Sean Roantree (*Two guards*), Peter Cellier (*Landolph*), John Watts (*Harold*), Gregory De Polnay (*Ordulph*), Robin Sachs (*Berthold*), Tony Sympson (*Giovanni*), Yvonne Mitchell (*Matilde Spina*), James Villiers (*Tito Belcredi*), Carolyn Courage (*Frida*), James Faulkner (*Carlo Di Nolli*), Paul Bacon (*Dr Dionisio Genoni*), Rex Harrison (*Henry IV*).
Producers: Bernard Delfont, Richard M. Mills. *Production company:* Delfont Organisation.
First night: 20 February 1974 (Her Majesty's Theatre, Haymarket, London). Limited season ended 18 May 1974.

IN PRAISE OF LOVE (1974)

Author: Terence Rattigan. *Director:* Fred Coe. *Settings and lighting:* Jo Mielziner. *Costumes:* Theoni V. Aldredge.

Cast: Julie Harris (*Lydia Cruttwell*), Rex Harrison (*Sebastian Cruttwell*), Martin Gabel (*Mark Walters*), Peter Burnell (*Joey Cruttwell*).
Producer: Arthur Cantor.
Pre-New York try-outs: 2 to 9 November 1974 (Playhouse, Wilmington, Delaware), 11 to 30 November 1974 (Opera House at the Kennedy Center, Washington DC).
First night (following previews): 10 December 1974 (Morosco Theatre, New York). Closed late May 1975.

MONSIEUR PERRICHON'S TRAVELS (1976)

Authors: Eugene Labiche and Martin (*translated by* R. H. Ward). *Director:* Patrick Garland. *Sets:* Eileen Diss. *Lighting:* Jim Parker, Mick Hughes. *Costumes:* Robin Fraser Paye.

Cast: Rex Harrison (*Monsieur Perrichon*), Keith Michell (*Mathieu*), Tony Robinson (*Majorin*), Clive Francis (*Armand*), Andrew Sachs (*Daniel*), Christopher Selbie (*Joseph*), Michael Cotterill (*Jean*), Vivian Pickles (*Madame Perrichon*), Deborah Grant (*Henriette*), Julian Somers (*The Hotel Keeper*), Charles Baillie (*The Alpine Guide*), Bill Fraser (*The Booking Office Clerk*), Eliza Hunt (*The Bookstall Attendant*), Martin Chamberlain, Carl Oatley and Kevin Williams (*Porters*), Lee Hudson, Adam Kurakin, Karen Lewis and Desmond Maurer (*Travellers*), Emilio and Jo Rosen (*Musicians*).
Production company: Chichester Festival Theatre.
First night: 3 August 1976 (Chichester Festival Theatre, West Sussex).

CAESAR AND CLEOPATRA (1977)

Author: George Bernard Shaw. *Director:* Ellis Rabb. *Scenery:* Ming Cho Lee. *Lighting:* Thomas Skelton. *Costumes:* Jane Greenwood.

Cast: Rex Harrison (*Julius Caesar*), Elizabeth Ashley (*Cleopatra*), Novella Nelson (*Ftatateeta*), Paul Hecht (*Rufio*), Patrick Hines (*Pothinus*), William Robertson (*Theodotus*), Roger Campo (*Ptolemy*), Mike Dantuono (*Achillas*), James Valentine (*Brittanus*), John Bergstrom (*Lucius Septimius*), Edwin Owens (*Roman Sentinel*), Thom Christopher (*Apollodorus*), Charles Turner (*Musician, Nubian*), Fiddle

188

Viracola (*Iras*), Linda Lartin (*Charmian*), Pawnee Sills (*Court lady*), Cain Richards, Joseph Scalzo and Eric Booth (*Slaves*), Paul Rosson (*Major Domo*), Ian Stuart and Cain Richards (*Priests*).
Producers/production companies: Elliot Martin and Gladys Rachmil, John F. Kennedy Center for the Performing Arts, in association with James Nederlander.
First night: 24 February 1977 (Palace Theatre, New York). Closed after 12 performances.

OUR THEATRES IN THE NINETIES (1977)

Author: George Bernard Shaw (extracts from his theatre criticisms for the British *Saturday Review* 1895–98). *Director/deviser:* Patrick Garland. *Historical design (slide illustrations):* Raymond Mander and Joe Mitchenson.

Cast: Rex Harrison.
First performance: 30 August 1977 (St Cecilia's Hall, Cowgate, Niddry Street, Edinburgh). Limited run of five afternoon readings ending 3 September 1977, as part of Edinburgh Festival.

THE KINGFISHER (1978)

Author: William Douglas Home. *Director:* Lindsay Anderson. *Setting:* Alan Tagg. *Lighting:* Thomas Skelton. *Costumes:* Jane Greenwood.

Cast: George Rose (*Hawkins*), Rex Harrison (*Cecil*), Claudette Colbert (*Evelyn*).
Producers: Elliot Martin, with Hinks Shimberg, in association with John Gale.
First night: 6 December 1978 (Biltmore Theatre, New York). Closed 13 May 1979.
Harrison took the play on an American tour in late 1979 and made a film of it for British television in 1982.

MY FAIR LADY (1980)

Book: Alan Jay Lerner (*from the play* Pygmalion *by* George Bernard Shaw). *Director:* Patrick Garland. *Music:* Frederick Loewe. *Lyrics:* Alan Jay Lerner. *Musical staging and choreography:* Crandall Diehl. *Settings:* Oliver Smith. *Lighting:* Ken Billington. *Costumes:* Cecil Beaton. *Musical director:* Franz Allers. *Musical conductor:* Robert Kreis. *Songs performed by Rex Harrison and other songs:* as 1956 production.

Cast: Eric Alderfer, Alan Guilbert and Lisa Guignard (*Buskers*), Harriet Medin (*Mrs Eynsford-Hill*), Cheryl Kennedy (*Eliza Doolittle*), Nicholas Wyman (*Freddy Eynsford-Hill*), Jack Gwillim (*Col. Pickering*), Rex Harrison (*Henry Higgins*), Ben Wrigley (*Selsey man*), Clifford Fearl (*Hoxton man*), Joseph Billone and Ned Coulter (*Bystanders*), John Caleb, Ned Coulter, Jeffrey Calder and Ned Peterson (*Cockneys*), David Cale Johnson (*Bartender*), Ben Wrigley (*Harry*), Clifford Fearl (*Jamie*), Milo O'Shea (*Alfred P. Doolittle*), Marian Baer (*Mrs Pearce*), Mary O'Brien (*Mrs Hopkins*), Frank Bouley (*Butler*), Jeralyn Glass, David Miles, Ellen McLain and Judith Thiergaard (*Servants*), Cathleen Nesbitt (*Mrs Higgins*), Alan Gilbert (*Chauffeur*), John Caleb and Ned Peterson (*Footmen*), Richard Ammon (*Lord Boxington*), Mary O'Brien (*Lady Boxington*), Alan Gilbert (*Constable*), Karen Toto (*Flower girl*), Jack Sevier (*Zoltan Karpathy*), David Cale Johnson (*Major Domo*), Svetlana McLee Grody (*Queen of Transylvania*), Ben Wrigley (*Ambassador*), Ned Peterson (*Bartender*), Elizabeth Worthington (*Mrs Higgins' maid*).
Singers: Frank Bouley, Jeffrey Calder, John Caleb, Ned Coulter, Diana Lynne Drew, Julie Ann Fogt, Terri Gervais, Jeralyn Glass, David Cale Johnson, Michael McGifford, Ellen McLain, David Miles, Mary O'Brien, Ned Peterson, Nancy Ringham and Judith Thiergaard. *Dancers:* Eric Alderfer, Richard Ammon, Joseph Billone, Arlene Columbo, Ron Crofoot, Raul Gallyot, Alan Gilbert, Svetlana McLee Grody, Lisa Guignard, Scott Harris, Lynn Keeton, Gail Lohla, James Boyd Parker, Karen Paskow, Karen Toto and Elizabeth Worthington.
Producers: Don Gregory, Mike Merrick.
First night: 23 September 1980 (Saenger Performing Arts Center, New Orleans). Then on tour: 9 October to 22 November 1980 (Golden Gate Theatre, San Francisco), 27 November 1980 to 8 March 1981 (Pantages Theatre, Los Angeles), 12 March to 26 April 1981

(Arie Crown Theatre, Chicago), 30 April to 17 May 1981 (Kiel Theatre, St. Louis), 21 May to 14 June 1981 (Theatre of the Performing Arts, Miami Beach), 18 June to 19 July 1981 (Metropolitan Center, Boston), 14 August (start of previews)/18 August (official opening) to 29 November 1981 (Uris Theatre, New York).

HEARTBREAK HOUSE (1983 London production)

Author: George Bernard Shaw. *Director:* John Dexter. *Designer:* Jocelyn Herbert. *Lighting:* Andy Phillips.

Cast: Mel Martin (*Ellie Dunn*), Doris Hare (*Nurse Guinness*), Rex Harrison (*Captain Shotover*), Rosemary Harris (*Ariadne Utterword*), Diana Rigg (*Hesione Hushabye*), Paul Curran (*Mazzini Dunn*), Paxton Whitehead (*Hector Hushabye*), Frank Middlemass (*Boss Mangan*), Simon Ward (*Randall Utterword*), Charles Rea (*Billy Dunn*).
Production company: Triumph Apollo.
First night (following two previews from 8 March 1983): 10 March 1983 (Theatre Royal, Haymarket, London). Limited run ended 11 June 1983.

HEARTBREAK HOUSE (1983 New York production)

Author: George Bernard Shaw. *Director:* Anthony Page. *Settings:* Marjorie Bradley Kellogg. *Costumes:* Jane Greenwood. *Lighting:* Paul Gallo.

Cast: Amy Irving (*Ellie Dunn*), Jan Miner (*Nurse Guinness*), Rex Harrison (*Captain Shotover*), Dana Ivey (*Ariadne Utterword*), Rosemary Harris (*Hesione Hushabye*), William Prince (*Mazzini Dunn*), Stephen McHattie (*Hector Hushabye*), Philip Bosco (*Boss Mangan*), Bill Moor (*Randall Utterword*).
First night (following previews from 18 November 1983): 7 December 1983 (Circle in the Square Theatre, New York). Limited run ended after 66 performances on 5 February 1984.
Taped for cable TV transmission and shown on *Broadway on Showtime* in the United States in April 1985.

191

AREN'T WE ALL? (1984 London production)

Author: Frederick Lonsdale. *Director:* Clifford Williams. *Set designer:* Finlay James. *Lighting:* Mark Pritchard. *Costume designer:* Judith Bland. *Music composer:* David Firman.

Cast: Robert Gladwell (*Morton*), Francis Matthews (*Hon. Willie Tatham*), Claudette Colbert (*Lady Frinton*), Timothy Peters (*Arthur Wells*), Ben Bazell (*Martin Steele*), Annie Lambert (*Kitty Lake*), Rex Harrison (*Lord Grenham*), Nicola Pagett (*Hon. Mrs W. Tatham*), John Ingram (*Roberts*), Madge Ryan (*Angela Lynton*), Michael Gough (*Reverend Ernest Lynton*), John Price (*John Willocks*).
Producer: Duncan C. Weldon with Paul Gregg and Lionel Becker in association with Jerome Minskoff. *Production companies:* Triumph Apollo, Birmingham Repertory Theatre.
Pre-West End try-out: from 14 May 1984 (Birmingham Repertory Theatre).
First night (following nine previews from 12 June 1984): 20 June 1984 (Theatre Royal, Haymarket, London). Limited run ended 3 November 1984 after 134 performances.

AREN'T WE ALL? (1985 New York production)

Author: Frederick Lonsdale. *Director:* Clifford Williams. *Set designer:* Finlay James. *Lighting:* Natasha Katz. *Costume designer:* Judith Bland.

Cast: Peter Pagan (*Mortan*), Jeremy Brett (*Hon. William Tatham*), Claudette Colbert (*Lady Frinton*), Steven Sutherland (*Arthur Wells*), John Patrick Hurley (*Martin Steele*), Leslie O'Hara (*Kitty Lake*), Rex Harrison (*Lord Grenham*), Lynn Redgrave (*Hon. Mrs W. Tatham*), George Ede (*Roberts*), Brenda Forbes (*Angela Lynton*), George Rose (*Reverend Ernest Lynton*), Ned Schmidtke (*John Willocks*).
Producers: Douglas Urbanski, Karl Allison, Bryan Bantry and James M. Nederlander in association with Duncan C. Weldon, Paul Gregg, Lionel Becker and Jerome Minskoff. *Associate producers:* Robert Michael Geisler, John Roberdeau.
First night (following previews from 16 April 1985): 29 April 1985 (Brooks Atkinson Theatre). Limited run ended 21 July 1985. Tour announced from 23 September 1985 (Curran Theatre, San Francisco).

Cinema and Television

The following is a record of all Rex Harrison's known work in films and television, excepting personal appearances on chat shows and possibly some work on variety programmes. Cast lists are, as far as possible, in order of billing. Work is listed in order of release (whereas in the text it is discussed in the order it was made, which is sometimes different). The name of the distributor is usually the one for the country which made the film, and running times are normally also those in the country of origin.

In addition, I am grateful to *Film Dope* for the snippets that Rex Harrison can be seen as himself in the French *Festival Flashes* (1965) and the Chaplin history *The Gentleman Tramp* (1975) and that he narrated two shorts, *The Charm of Life* (English version of *Les Charmes de l'Existence*, 1949) and *This Is London* (1956). He was also seen in an edition of *March of Time* – see footnote to *Anne of the Thousand Days* (1948) in preceding Theatre section.

THE GREAT GAME (1931)

Director: Jack Raymond. *Writers:* W. P. Lipscomb, Ralph Gilbert Bettinson (*from a story by* William Hunter *and* John Lees). *Photographer:* Percy Strong.

Cast: Randle Ayrton (*Mr Henderson*), Neil Kenyon (*Mr Jackson*), Renee Clama (*Peggy Jackson*), Kenneth Kove (*Mr Bultitude*), A. G. Poulton (*Mr Franks*), John Batten (*Dicky Brown*), Jack Cock [of Milwall FC] (*Jim Blake*), Billy Blyth [of Birmingham FC] (*Billy*), Lew Lake (*Tubby*), Walter [Wally] Patch (*Joe Miller – Trainer*), Harry Bagge (*Harry*), Rex Harrison (*George*), and with the following professional football players: John, Seddon and Butler [of Arsenal]; Andy Wilson, Ferguson, Mills, Millington, Smith and Thain [of Chelsea]; Penn [of Fulham]; Pike [of Birmingham]; Cook, Dimmock, Forster, Lowdell, O'Callaghan, Osborne, Bann and Crompton [of Tottenham Hotspur]; Hufton, Earle, Cox and Ruffell [of West Ham]; and Cutmore [unattached].
Producer: L'Estrange Fawcett. *Distributor:* Gaumont–British.
Running time: 79 minutes.
Filmed in April and late May 1930 at Shepherd's Bush studios with location work at Wembley and Stamford Bridge (Chelsea FC) grounds, Harrods' private sports ground at Barnes, and St George's Hill golf course at Weybridge.
Generally released: 23 February 1931.

THE SCHOOL FOR SCANDAL (1931)

Director: Maurice Elvey. *Writer:* Jean Jay (*from the play by* Richard Brinsley Sheridan). *Photographed in* Raycolcolor.

Cast: Basil Gill (*Sir Peter Teazle*), Madeleine Carroll (*Lady Teazle*), Ian Fleming (*Joseph Surface*), Henry Hewitt (*Charles Surface*), Edgar K. Bruce (*Sir Oliver Surface*), Hayden Coffin (*Sir Harry Bumper*), Hector Abbas (*Moses*), Dodo Watts (*Maria*), Anne Grey (*Lady Sneerwell*), John Charlton (*Benjamin Backbite*), Stanley Lathbury (*Crabtree*), Henry Vibart (*Squire Hunter*), May Agate (*Mrs Candour*), Maurice Braddell (*Careless*), Gibb McLaughlin (*William – the servant*), William [Wallace?] Bosco (*Rawley*), Edward O'Neil, Irene Tripod, Prunella Norman Page. [Rex Harrison's part is unidentified.]

Production company: Albion. *Distributor:* Paramount. *Running time:* 76 minutes.
Filmed at Elstree studios from 2 June 1930 and completed in approximately three weeks.
Generally released: 8 June 1931.

GET YOUR MAN (1935)

Director: George King. *Writer:* George Dewhurst *(from the play* Tu M'Epouseras *by* Louis Verneuil).

Cast: Dorothy Boyd *(Nancy McAlpine)*, Helen Ferrers *(Agatha McAlpine)*, Sebastian Shaw *(Robert Halbeam)*, Clifford Heatherley *(Parker Halbeam)*, Hugh E. Wright *(Rev. John Vivien)*, Kay Walsh *(Mary Vivien)*, Rex Harrison *(Tom Jakes)*, Charles Barrett *(Butler)*.
Production company: British & Dominions. *Distributor:* Paramount.
Running time: 68 minutes.
Filmed at Elstree Studios.
Generally released: 25 February 1935.

LEAVE IT TO BLANCHE (1935)

Director: Harold M. Young. *Writer:* Brock Williams *(from a screen story by* Rowland Brown).

Cast: Henry Kendall *(Peter Manners)*, Olive Blakeney *(Blanche Wetherby)*, Miki Hood *(Doris Manners)*, Griffith Jones *(Philip Amesbury)*, Hamilton Keene *(Brewster)*, Rex Harrison *(Ronnie)*, Julian Royce *(Patteridge)*, Elizabeth Jenns *(Blossom)*, Molly Clifford *(Mrs Mumsey)*, Phyllis Stanley *(Blues Singer)*, Harold Warrender *(Guardee)*, Denise Sylvester, Margaret Gunn, Kenneth Kove, Hermione Hannen.
Producer: Irving Asher. *Production company:* Warner Bros.–First National. *Distributor:* First National. *Running time:* 51 minutes.
Filmed from the end of May 1934 at Teddington Studios under the title *February 29th*.
Generally released: 25 March 1935.

ALL AT SEA (1936)

Director: Anthony Kimmins. *Writers:* Charles Bennett, Anthony Kimmins (*from the novel* Ocean Air *by* Ian Hay). *Photographer:* Alex Bryce. *Art director:* W. Ralph Brinton. *Editor:* Sam Simmonds.

Cast: Tyrrell Davis (*Joe Finch*), Googie Withers (*Daphne Tomkins*), James Carew (*Julius Mablethorpe*), Rex Harrison (*Aubrey Bellingham*), Cecily Byrne (*Mary Maggs*), James Harcourt (*Mr Humphrey*), Dorothy Vernon (*Mrs Humphrey*), Colin Lesslie (*Tony Lambert*), Dorothy Hammond (*Lady Thorncliffe*), Charles Delph (*Parson*), Georgina Esmond (*Parson's wife*).
Production company/distributor: Fox British. *Running time:* 60 minutes.
Filmed at Fox British studios at Wembley under the title *Mr Faintheart* from 21 January 1935 and completed in approximately one month.
Generally released: 10 February 1936.

MEN ARE NOT GODS (1936)

Director: Walter Reisch. *Writers:* Walter Reisch, (*scenario and dialogue*) G. B. Stern and Iris Wright. *Photographer:* Charles Roscher [Rosher]. *Art director:* Vincent Korda. *Editors:* Henry Cornelius, (*supervision*) William Hornbeck. *Music:* (*uncredited*) Geoffrey Toye (*based on themes from Samuel Coleridge-Taylor's* Othello Suite).

Cast: Miriam Hopkins (*Ann Williams*), Gertrude Lawrence (*Barbara Halford*), Sebastian Shaw (*Edmond Davey*), Rex Harrison (*Tommy – Thomas Newbiggin Stapleton*), A. E. Matthews (*Frederick T. H. Skeates*), Val Gielgud (*The Producer*), Laura Smithson (*Katherine*), Laurence Grossmith (*Stanley*), Sybil Grove (*Painter*), Winifred Willard (*Mrs Williams*), Wally Patch (*Gallery attendant*), James Harcourt (*Porter*), Rosamund Greenwood (*Pianist*), Noel Howlett (*Cashier*), Paddy Morgan (*Kitty*), Nicholas Nadejin (*Iago*), Michael Hogarth (*Cassio*).
Producer: Alexander Korda. *Production company:* London Films.
Distributor: United Artists. *Running time:* 90 minutes.
Filmed from early August 1936 at Denham Studios under the title *Triangle*, with theatre interiors shot at the Alhambra, Leicester Square on 8 October 1936.
First shown: 14 December 1936 (London Pavilion).

196

STORM IN A TEACUP (1937)

Directors: Victor Saville, Ian Dalrymple. *Writers:* Ian Dalrymple, Donald Bull (*from the German play* Sturm im Wasserglas *by* Bruno Frank *and the Anglo-Scottish version* Storm in a Teacup *by* James Bridie). *Photographer:* Mutz Greenbaum. *Art director:* André Andrejew. *Editors:* Hugh Stewart, Cyril Randell, (*supervision*) William Hornbeck. *Music composer:* Frederic Lewis.

Cast: Vivien Leigh (*Victoria Gow*), Rex Harrison (*Frank Burdon*), Cecil Parker (*Provost William Gow*), Sara Allgood (*Mrs Honoria Hegarty*), Ursula Jeans (*Lisbet Skirving*), Gus McNaughton (*Horace Skirving*), Edgar K. Bruce (*McKellar*), Robert Hale (*Lord Skerryvore*), Quinton MacPherson (*Baillie Callender*), Arthur Wontner (*Fiscal*), Eliot Makeham (*Sheriff*), George Pughe (*Menzies*), Arthur Seaton (*Police Sergeant*), Cecil Mannering (*Police Constable*), Ivor Barnard (*Watkins*), Cyril Smith (*Councillor*), W. G. Fay (*Cassidy*), Mervyn Johns (*Court official*), Stuart Hibberd (*Newsreader*), Scruffy (*Patsy, the dog*). *Producer:* Victor Saville. *Associate producer:* Stanley Haynes. *Production company:* London Films. *Distributor:* United Artists. *Running time:* 86 minutes. *Filmed* at Denham Studios from November 1936. *First shown:* 7 June 1937 (Leicester Square Theatre, London).

SCHOOL FOR HUSBANDS (1937)

Director: Andrew Marton. *Writers:* (*scenario*) Austin Melford, (*dialogue*) Frederick Jackson, Austin Melford and Gordon Sherry (*from the play by* Frederick Jackson). *Photographer:* Phil Tannura. *Art director:* D. W. Daniels. *Editor:* E. M. Hunter. *Music composer:* Allan Gray.

Cast: Rex Harrison (*Leonard Drummond*), Diana Churchill (*Marion Carter*), June Clyde (*Diana Cheswick*), Henry Kendall (*Geoffrey Carter*), Romney Brent (*Morgan Cheswick*), Roxie Russell (*Kate*), Richard Goolden (*Whittaker*), Phil Thomas (*Walker, the chauffeur*), Judith Gick (*Joan*), Joan Kemp Welsh. *Producer:* Richard Wainwright. *Production company:* A Wainwright production. *Distributor:* General Film Distributors. *Running time:* 72 minutes.

Filmed at Universal–Wainwright Studios, Sound City, Shepperton.
First shown: 26 December 1937 (New Gallery, London).

ST MARTIN'S LANE (1938)

Director: Tim Whelan. *Writer:* Clemence Dane. *Photographer:* Jules
Kruger. *Art director:* Tom Morahan. *Editors:* Hugh Stewart, Robert
Hamer. *Music composer:* Arthur Johnston. *Lyricist:* Eddie Pola.

Cast: Charles Laughton (*Charlie Saggers*), Vivien Leigh (*Liberty,
known as Libby*), Rex Harrison (*Harley Prentiss*), Larry Adler (*Dan
Constantine*), Tyrone Guthrie (*Gentry*), Maire O'Neill (*Mrs Such*), Gus
McNaughton (*Arthur Smith*), Polly Ward (*Frankie*), Basil Gill
(*Magistrate*), Helen Haye (*Lady Selena*), David Burns (*Hackett*),
Phyllis Stanley (*Della Fordingbridge*), Edward Lexy (*Mr Such*), Clare
Greet (*Old Maud*), Alf Goddard (*Doggie*), Cyril Smith (*Blackface*),
Romilly Lunge (*Jan Duchesi*), Ronald Ward (*Jack Temperley*), Bart
Cormack (*American newspaperman*), Carroll Gibbons and His
Orchestra, The Luna Boys, Jerry Verno, and London street
entertainers.
Producer: Erich Pommer. *Production company:* Mayflower Pictures. *A
Pommer Laughton production. Distributor:* Associated British.
Running time: 85 minutes.
Filming started around the beginning of February 1938 at Elstree
Studios and was completed in May 1938.
First shown: 19 October 1938 (Carlton, Haymarket, London).
American release title: Sidewalks of London.

THE CITADEL (1938)

Director: King Vidor. *Writers:* Ian Dalrymple, Frank Wead, Elizabeth
Hill, (*additional dialogue*) Emlyn Williams (*from the novel by* A. J.
Cronin). *Photographer:* Harry Stradling. *Art directors:* Lazare
Meerson, Alfred Junge. *Editor:* Charles Frend. *Music composer:* Louis
Levy.

Cast: Robert Donat (*Andrew Manson*), Rosalind Russell (*Christine*),
Ralph Richardson (*Denny*), Rex Harrison (*Dr Freddie Lawford*), Emlyn
Williams (*Owen*), Penelope Dudley-Ward (*Toppy Leroy*), Francis

198

Sullivan (*Ben Chenkin*), Mary Clare (*Mrs Orlando*), Cecil Parker
(*Charles Every*), Nora Swinburne (*Mrs Thornton*), Edward Chapman
(*Joe Morgan*), Athene Seyler (*Lady Raeburn*), Felix Aylmer (*Mr Boon*),
Joyce Bland (*Nurse Sharp*), Percy Parsons (*Mr Stillman*), Dilys Davis
(*Mrs Page*), Basil Gill (*Dr Page*), Joss Ambler (*Dr A. H. Llewellyn*).
Producer: Victor Saville. *Production company and distributor:*
Metro-Goldwyn-Mayer. *Running time:* 112 minutes.
Filming started 9 June 1938 at Denham Studios and was completed
towards the end of August 1938.
First shown: 28 October 1938 (various American cities). *British
premiere:* 22 December 1938 (Empire, Leicester Square, London).

THE SILENT BATTLE (1939)

Director: Herbert Mason. *Writers:* Wolfgang Wilhelm, Rodney
Ackland (*from the novel* Le Poisson Chinois *by* Jean Bommart *and,
uncredited, the 1937 French film version,* La Bataille Silencieuse,
dialogued by Jacques Natanson). *Photographer:* Bernard Browne. *Art
director:* Wilfred Arnold. *Editor:* Philip Charlot. *Music composer:* Louis
Beydts.

Cast: Rex Harrison (*Jacques Sauvin*), Valerie Hobson (*Draguisha
Montescu*), John Loder (*René Bordier*), Muriel Aked (*Mme Duvivier*),
George Devine (*Sonnemann*), John Salew (*Ernest*), Kaye Seeley
(*Bartoff*), Carl Jaffe (*Rykoff*), Megs Jenkins (*Louise*), Arthur Maude
(*The Editor*), David Keir (*Editor's assistant*), Joan Gibson (*Editor's
secretary*).
Producer: Anthony Havelock-Allan. *Production company:* Pinebrook.
Distributor: Paramount. *Running time:* 70 minutes.
Filmed at Denham Studios from 3 February 1939 to mid-March 1939,
then tentatively titled *Peace In Our Time*.
First shown: 14 April 1939 (Plaza, Piccadilly Circus, London).
American release title: Continental Express.

OVER THE MOON (1939)

Directors: Thornton Freeland, (*uncredited*) William K. Howard.
Writers: Anthony Pelissier, Alec Coppel, (*dialogue*) Arthur Wimperis
(*from a story by* Robert Sherwood *and* Lajos Biro). *Photographer*

(Technicolor): Harry Stradling. *Art director:* Vincent Korda. *Editors:* Pat Woolley, *(supervision)* William Hornbeck. *Music composer:* Michael [Mischa] Spoliansky. *Lyrics:* Desmond Carter.

Cast: Merle Oberon *(Jane Benson)*, Rex Harrison *(Dr Freddie Jarvis)*, Ursula Jeans *(Lady Millie Parsmill)*, Robert Douglas *(The Unknown Man – John Flight)*, Louis Borrell *(Marquis Pietro d'Altamura)*, Zena Dare *(Julie Deethorpe)*, Peter Haddon *(Lord Petcliffe)*, David Tree *(Journalist)*, Mackenzie Ward *(Lord Guy Carstairs)*, Elizabeth Welch *(Cabaret singer)*, Carl Jaffe *(Michel)*, Herbert Lomas *(Ladbrooke)*, Wilfred Shine *(Frude)*, Gerald Nodin *(Cartwright)*, Bruce Winston *(Director of clinic)*, Wilfrid Hyde-White *(Dwight)*, Lewis Gilbert, Evelyn Ankers.
Producer: Alexander Korda. *Production company:* London Films.
Distributor: United Artists. *Running time:* 78 minutes.
Filmed at Denham Studios from 1 November 1937 to late January 1938.
First shown: 14 November 1939 (Odeon, Leicester Square, London).

TEN DAYS IN PARIS (1940)

Director: Tim Whelan. *Writers:* John Meehan Jr, James Curtis *(from the novel* The Disappearance of Roger Tremayne *by* Bruce Graeme).
Photographer: Otto Kanturek. *Art director:* Frederick Pusey. *Editor:* Hugh Stewart. *Music composer:* Miklos Rozsa.

Cast: Rex Harrison *(Robert Stevens)*, Karen Verne *(Diane de Guermantes)*, C. V. France *(General de Guermantes)*, Joan Marion *(Denise)*, Leo Genn *(Lanson)*, Anthony Holles *(François)*, Robert Rendel *(Sir James Stevens)*, Andre Morell *(Victor)*, John Abbott *(André)*, Mavis Clair *(Marie)*, Hay Petrie *(Benoit)*, Frank Atkinson *(Pierre)*, Mai Bacon *(Clarice)*, Donald McLeod *(Jean)*, Percy Walsh *(Inspector)*.
Producer: Irving Asher. *Associate producer:* Jerome J. Jackson.
Production company: Irving Asher Productions. *Distributor:* Columbia. *Running time:* 82 minutes.
Filmed at Denham Studios, from 30 May 1939.
First shown: 18 April 1940 (Regal, Marble Arch, London).
American release title: Missing Ten Days.

NIGHT TRAIN TO MUNICH (1940)

Director: Carol Reed. *Writers:* Sidney Gilliat, Frank Launder *(from an original story,* Report on a Fugitive, *by* Gordon Wellesley). *Photographer:* Otto Kanturek. *Art director:* Vetchinsky. *Editor:* R. E. Dearing. *Cutting:* Michael Gordon. *Music director:* Louis Levy. *Songs performed by Rex Harrison:* 'Our Love Can Lead the Way', 'It's True'.

Cast: Margaret Lockwood *(Anna Bomasch),* Rex Harrison *(Dickie Randall, also known as Gus Bennett),* Paul von Hernreid [later Paul Henreid] *(Karl Marsen),* Basil Radford *(Charters),* Naunton Wayne *(Caldicott),* James Harcourt *(Axel Bomasch),* Felix Aylmer *(Dr John Fredericks),* Wyndham Goldie *(Dryton),* Roland Culver *(Roberts),* Eliot Makeham *(Schwab),* Raymond Huntley *(Kampenfeldt),* Austin Trevor *(Capt. Prada),* Keneth Kent *(Controller),* C. V. France *(Admiral Hassinger),* Fritz [later Frederick] Valk *(Gestapo officer),* Morland Graham *(Teleferic assistant),* Irene Handl *(Station mistress),* Billy Russell *(Hitler),* Torin Thatcher, Pardoe Woodman, Albert Lieven, Edward Baxter, J. H. Roberts, David Horne, G. H. Mulcaster, Ian Fleming, Wilfred Walter, Jane Cobb, Charles Oliver, Pat Williams, Winifred Oughton.
Producer: Edward Black. *Production company:* Twentieth Century Productions. *Distributor:* Metro-Goldwyn-Mayer. *Running time:* 95 minutes.
Filmed from 20 December 1939 to mid-February 1940 at Gaumont–British Studios, Lime Grove, Shepherd's Bush, under the title *Gestapo.*
First shown: 25 July 1940 (Empire, Leicester Square, London).
American release title: Night Train.

MAJOR BARBARA (1941)

Director: Gabriel Pascal. *Assistants in direction: (dialogue supervision)* Harold French, *(technical adviser)* David Lean. *Writer:* George Bernard Shaw *(from his play). Photographer:* Ronald Neame, *(uncredited, Devon locations)* Freddie Young, *(also uncredited)* Osmond Borradaile. *Art directors:* Vincent Korda, John Bryan. *Editor:* Charles Frend. *Montage:* David Lean. *Music composer:* William Walton.

Cast: Wendy Hiller *(Major Barbara Undershaft),* Rex Harrison

(*Adolphus 'Dolly' Cusins*), Robert Morley (*Andrew Undershaft*), Robert Newton (*Bill Walker*), Emlyn Williams (*Snobby Price*), Sybil Thorndike (*The General*), Deborah Kerr (*Jenny Hill*), David Tree (*Charles 'Cholly' Lomax*), Penelope Dudley-Ward (*Sarah Undershaft*), Marie Lohr (*Lady Britomart*), Walter Hudd (*Stephen Undershaft*), Marie Ault (*Rummy Mitchens*), Donald Calthrop (*Peter Shirley*), Cathleen Cordell (*Mog Habbijam*), Torin Thatcher (*Todger Fairmile*), Miles Malleson (*Morrison*), Felix Aylmer (*James*), Stanley Holloway (*Policeman*), S. I. Hsiung (*Ling, the laundryman*), Kathleen Harrison (*Mrs Price*), Mary Morris (*A girl*), Finlay Currie, Jack Watling, Ronald Shiner, O. B. Clarence.
Producer: Gabriel Pascal. *Assistant in production:* Stanley Haynes. *Production company:* Pascal Film Productions. *Distributor:* General Film Distributors. *Running time:* 121 minutes. (A longer version, kept by Pascal and running 137 minutes, survives.)
Filming began 26 May 1940 on location with studio work commencing at Denham on 17 June 1940 and completed by the end of November 1940.
First shown: 7 April 1941 (Odeon, Leicester Square, London).

BLITHE SPIRIT (1945)

Director: David Lean. *Writer:* Noel Coward (*from his play adapted for the screen by* David Lean, Ronald Neame *and* Anthony Havelock-Allan). *Photographer* (Technicolor): Ronald Neame. *Art director:* C. P. Norman. *Art supervisor to Noel Coward:* G. E. Calthrop. *Editor:* Jack Harris. *Special effects:* Tom Howard. *Music composer:* Richard Addinsell.

Cast: Rex Harrison (*Charles Condomine*), Constance Cummings (*Ruth Condomine*), Kay Hammond (*Elvira*), Margaret Rutherford (*Madame Arcati*), Hugh Wakefield (*Dr George Bradman*), Joyce Carey (*Mrs Violet Bradman*), Jacqueline Clarke (*Edith*).
In charge of production: Anthony Havelock-Allan. *Production company:* Two Cities/Cineguild. *Distributor:* General Film Distributors. *Running time:* 96 minutes.
Filmed in early 1944 at Denham Studios.
First shown: 5 April 1945 (Odeon, Leicester Square, London).

I LIVE IN GROSVENOR SQUARE (1945)

Director: Herbert Wilcox. *Writers:* Nicholas Phipps, William D. Bayles (*additional dialogue by* Arvid O. Dahl) (*from a screen story by* Maurice Cowan). *Photographer:* Otto Heller. *Production designer:* William C. Andrews. *Editor:* Vera Campbell. *Music composer:* Anthony Collins.

Cast: Anna Neagle (*Lady Patricia Fairfax*), Rex Harrison (*Major David Bruce*), Dean Jagger (*Sgt John Patterson*), Robert Morley (*Duke of Exmoor*), Jane Darwell (*John's mother*), Nancy Price (*Mrs Wilson*), Dame Irene Vanbrugh (*Mrs Catchpole*), Edward Rigby (*Devonshire innkeeper*), Walter Hudd (*Vicar*), Elliott Arluck (*Sgt Benn Greenburgh, US Army*), Irene Manning (*Herself*), Carrol Gibbons and his Savoy Orchestra (*Themselves*), Cecil Ramage (*Trewhewy*), Percy Walsh (*Merridew*), H. R. Hignett (*Parker*), Brenda Bruce (*1st girl in guard's van*), Sheilagh Frazer (*2nd girl in guard's van*), Helen Lowry (*Miss Borrow*), Aubrey Mallalieu (*Bates*), Michael Shepley (*Lieut Lutyens*), Charles Victor (*Taxi driver*), Francis Pierlot (*Postman*), Peter Hobbes (*Paratroop Colonel*), Frank Webster (*Devon farmer*), David Horne (*War Office Major*), William Murton (*'Dakota' pilot*), Ronald Shiner, John Slater, Neville Mapp and Norman Williams (*Paratroopers*), Alvar Liddell (*Announcer*), Cyril Baker (*American pianist*). *Narration spoken by:* Gerry Wilmot.
Producer: Herbert Wilcox. *Associate producer:* Max Greene. *Production:* George Maynard. *Production company:* Associated British.
Distributor: Pathe. *Running time:* 113 minutes.
Filmed from September 1944 to January 1945 at Welwyn Studios and at Devon locations including Totnes and Dartington Hall. John's mother's sequence filmed by Warner Bros. in Hollywood.
First shown: 19 July 1945 (Empire, Leicester Square, and Warner, Leicester Square, London).
American release title: A Yank in London.

JOURNEY TOGETHER (1945)

Director: John Boulting. *Writers:* (*story*) Terence Rattigan, (*adaptation*) John Boulting, (*research*) Hugh Gray. *Photographers:* Harry Waxman, Gilbert Taylor. *Production designer:* John Howell. *Editors:* Reginald Beck, Michael Del Campo, (*chief cutter*) Cliff Boote. *Music composer:* Gordon Jacob.

Cast: Richard Attenborough (*David Wilton*), Jack Watling (*John Aynesworth*), David Tomlinson (*Smith*), Sid Rider (*A Fitter*), Stuart Latham (*A Flight Sergeant Fitter*), Hugh Wakefield (*An Adjutant*), Bromley Challenor (*AC2 Jay*), Z. Porzanowski (*An Anson Pilot*). *Aircrew Interview Board* – Ronald Squire (*A Group Captain*), Derek Twist (*A Wing Commander*). *Aircrew Reception Centre* – Leslie Nixon (*The Group Captain*), Ian Reeve (*A Corporal*), W. Busby (*A Squadron Leader*). *Initial Training Wing* – Arthur Macrae (*Flight Commander*), Reginald Tate (*The Commanding Officer*), Elwyn Price (*An Instructor*), Tommy Duggan (*Air Gunner Cadet*). *Flying Grading School* – John Justin (*A Flying Instructor*), Anthony Hulme (*The Chief Flying Instructor*), Michael Harroway (*The Commanding Officer*). *Aircrew Distribution Centre* – Edward Rutherford (*A Wing Commander*). *Falcon Field, Arizona* – Sebastian Shaw (*Squadron Leader Marshall*), Ronald Adam (*The Commanding Officer*), Edward G. Robinson (*Dean McWilliams*), Bessie Love (*Mary McWilliams*), Norvell Crutcher (*A Driver*). *Canadian Navigation School* – Arthur Bolton (*Airfield Controller*), Fletcher Markle (*A Staff Pilot*), Jack Baker (*A Flight Commander*), Stuart Dick (*A Wireless Instructor*), Peter Baylis (*Cadet Wireless Operator*), Nick Stuart (*A Met Officer*). *An English Bomber Station* – Patrick Waddington (*Flight Lieutenant Mander*), Tommy Tomlinson (*Briefing Officer*), Michael McNeile (*Fred*), Jerry Fitzgerald (*Jeff*), Eric Worth (*Mutt*), George Cole (*Curly*), Hamish Nicol (*Angus*), Murray Matheson (*Pete*), Rex Harrison [*See note*].
Production companies: RAF Film Unit/Ministry of Information. *Distributor:* RKO Radio. *Running time:* 95 minutes.
In production: July 1944 at Pinewood Studios.
First shown: 5 October 1945 (Odeon, Leicester Square, London, in support of *Where Do We Go from Here?*).
Note: Although Rex Harrison did participate in the film, his name does not appear in the lengthy cast list issued at the time of release and reproduced here; this suggests that he may have had a cameo part which was subsequently deleted. The film has not been in circulation in recent years.

THE RAKE'S PROGRESS (1945)

Director: Sidney Gilliat. *Writers:* Sidney Gilliat. Frank Launder (*from a screen story by* Val Valentine). *Photographer:* Wilkie Cooper. *Production designer:* David Rawnsley. *Art director:* Norman Arnold.

Editor: Thelma Myers. *Music composer:* William Alwyn.

Cast: Rex Harrison (*Vivian R. Kenway*), Lilli Palmer (*Erika [Rikki] Krausner*), Godfrey Tearle (*Colonel Kenway*), Griffith Jones (*Sandy Duncan*), Margaret Johnston (*Jennifer Calthrop*), Guy Middleton (*Fogroy*), Jean Kent (*Jill Duncan*), Marie Lohr (*Lady Angela Parks*), Garry Marsh (*Sir Hubert Parks*), David Horne (*Sir John Brockley*), Alan Wheatley (*Edwards*), Brefni O'Rorke (*Bromhead*), John Salew (*Burgess*), Charles Victor (*Old Sweat*), Jan van Loewen, Patrick Curwen (*The Major*), Joan Hickson (*Miss Barker*), Joan Maude (*Alice Duncan*), Olga Lindo (*Woman in Palais de Danse*), Patricia Laffan (*Miss Fernandez*), Howard Marion Crawford (*Coldstream guardsman*), David Wallbridge (*Vivian Kenway as a boy*), John Dodsworth (*Team manager*), Emrys Jones (*Bateson*), Jack Vyvyan (*Fred, mechanic*), Frederick Burtwell (*Magistrate*), George Cross (*Policeman*), Frank Ling (*The Corporal*), Kynaston Reeves (*The Dean*), Howard Douglas, Joy Frankau, Sheila Huntington, Maureen MacDermot, Jack Melford, David Ward, Frank Phillips (*Voice on radio*), Sidney Gilliat (*Voice of Pedro the barman*).
Producers: Sidney Gilliat, Frank Launder. *Production company:* Individual. *Distributor:* Eagle-Lion. *Running time:* 124 minutes.
Principal filming started late January 1945 at Shepherd's Bush Studios (location scenes were shot in the autumn of 1944).
First shown: 7 December 1945 (Odeon, Leicester Square, London).
American release title: The Notorious Gentleman.

ANNA AND THE KING OF SIAM (1946)

Director: John Cromwell. *Writers:* Talbot Jennings, Sally Benson (*from the biography by* Margaret Landon). *Photographer:* Arthur Miller. *Art directors:* Lyle Wheeler, William Darling. *Editor:* Harmon Jones. *Music composer:* Bernard Herrmann.

Cast: Irene Dunne (*Anna Owens*), Rex Harrison (*King Mongkut*), Linda Darnell (*Tuptim*), Lee J. Cobb (*Kralahome*), Gale Sondergaard (*Lady Thiang*), Mikhail Rasumny (*Alak*), Dennis Hoey (*Sir Edward Ramsay*), Tito Renaldo (*Prince Chulalongkorn*), Richard Lyon (*Louis Owens*), William Edmunds (*Moonshee*), John Abbott (*Phya Phrom*), Leonard Strong (*Interpreter*), Mickey Roth (*Prince Chulalongkorn as a boy*), Diana van den Ecker (*Princess Fa-Ying*), Connie Leon (*Beebe*),

Si-lan Chen (*Dancer*), Marjorie Eaton (*Miss MacFarlane*), Helena Grant (*Mrs Cortwright*), Stanley Mann (*Mr Cortwright*), Addison Richards (*Captain Orton*), Neyle Morrow (*Phra Palat*), Yvonne Rob (*Lady Sno Kim*), Julian Rivero (*Government clerk*), Oie Chan (*Old woman*), Ted Hecht and Ben Welden (*Judges*), Pedro Regas (*Guide*), Laurette Luez, Chabing, Marianne Quon, Lillian Molieri, Buff Cobb and Sydney Logan (*King's wives*), Aram Katcher and Rico DeMontes (*Guards*), Joe Garcio and Constantine Romanoff (*Whippers*).
Producer: Louis D. Lighton. *Production company and distributor:* 20th Century-Fox. *Running time:* 128 minutes.
Filmed from late November 1945 to mid-February 1946.
First shown: 20 June 1946 (Radio City Music Hall, New York). *British premiere:* 11 August 1946 (New Gallery, and Tivoli, Strand, London).

Scenes were filmed but subsequently deleted featuring Sir C. Aubrey Smith as Sir John Lawford and Margaret Bannerman as Mrs Hillary.

THE GHOST AND MRS MUIR (1947)

Director: Joseph L. Mankiewicz. *Writer:* Philip Dunne (*from the novel* The Ghost of Captain Gregg and Mrs Muir *by* R. A. Dick).
Photographer: Charles Lang Jr. *Art directors:* Richard Day, George Davis. *Editor:* Dorothy Spencer. *Special photographic effects:* Fred Sersen. *Music composer:* Bernard Herrmann.

Cast: Gene Tierney (*Lucy Muir*), Rex Harrison (*Ghost of Captain Daniel Gregg*), George Sanders (*Miles Fairley*), Edna Best (*Martha*), Vanessa Brown (*Anna grown up*), Anna Lee (*Mrs Miles Fairley*), Robert Coote (*Coombe*), Natalie Wood (*Anna as a child*), Isobel Elsom (*Angelica*), Victoria Horne (*Eva*), Whitford Kane (*Sproule*).
Producer: Fred Kohlmar. *Production company and distributor:* 20th Century-Fox. *Running time:* 104 minutes.
Production: began on 29 November 1946 and was completed on 13 February 1947.
First shown: 25 May 1947 (New Gallery, London).
American premiere: 26 June 1947 (Radio City Music Hall, New York).

THE FOXES OF HARROW (1947)

Director: John M. Stahl. *Writer:* Wanda Tuchock (*from the novel by*

Frank Yerby). *Photographer:* Joe La Shelle. *Art directors:* Lyle Wheeler, Maurice Ransford. *Editor:* James B. Clark. *Music composer:* David Buttolph.

Cast: Rex Harrison (*Stephen Fox*), Maureen O'Hara (*Odalie D'Arceneaux*), Richard Haydn (*André Le Blanc*), Victor McLaglen (*Mike Farrel*), Vanessa Brown (*Aurore*), Patricia Medina (*Desirée*), Gene Lockhart (*The Vicomte*), Charles Irwin (*Sean Fox*), Hugo Haas (*Otto Ludenbach*), Dennis Hoey (*Master of Harrow*), Roy Roberts (*Tom Warren*), Marcel Journet (*St Ange*), Kenneth Washington (*Achille*), Helene Crozier (*Zerline*), Sam McDaniel (*Josh*), Libby Taylor (*Angelina*), Renee Beard (*Little Inch – aged 6*), A. C. Bilbrew (*Tante Caleen*), Suzette Harbin (*Belle*), Perry William (Bill) Ward (*Etienne Fox – aged 6*), William (Bill) Walker (*Ty Demon*), Mary Currier (*Mrs Warren*), Clear Nelson Jr (*Little Inch – aged 3*), James Lagano (*Etienne – aged 3*), Henri Letondal (*Maspero*), Jean Del Val (*Dr Le Fevre*), Dorothy Adams (*Mrs Fox*), Andre Charlot (*Dr Terrebone*), Georges Renavent (*Priest*), Jasper Weldon (*Jode*), Celia Lovsky (*Minna Ludenbach*), Napoleon Simpson (*Georges*), Eugene Borden (*French auctioneer*), Joseph Crehan (*Captain of River Boat*), Ralph Faulkner (*Fencing Instructor*), Randy Stuart (*Stephen Fox's mother*), Gordon Clark (*Fop*), Frederick Burton (*Creole gentleman*), Robert Emmett Keane (*Auctioneer*), Bernard DeRoux (*Creole waiter*), Wee Willie Davis (*Sailor*).
Producer: William A. Bacher. *Production company and distributor:* 20th Century-Fox. *Running time:* 117 minutes.
Filmed from mid-April 1947 to late July 1947.
First shown: 20 September 1947 (Saenger Theatre, New Orleans).
British premiere: 14 October 1948 (New Gallery, and Tivoli, Strand, London).

ESCAPE (1948)

Director: Joseph L. Mankiewicz. *Writer:* Philip Dunne (*from the play by* John Galsworthy). *Photographer:* Frederick A. Young. *Art director:* Vetchinsky. *Editor:* Alan L. Jaggs. *Music composer:* William Alwyn.

Cast: Rex Harrison (*Matthew Denant*), Peggy Cummins (*Dora Winton*), William Hartnell (*Inspector Harris*), Norman Wooland (*Parson*), Jill Esmond (*Grace Winton*), Frederick Piper (*Brownie*),

Marjorie Rhodes (*Mrs Pinkem*), Betty Ann Davies (*Girl in park*), Cyril Cusack (*Rodgers*), John Slater (*Car salesman*), Frank Pettingell (*Village constable*), Michael Golden (*Detective Penter, the plain clothes man*), Maurice Denham (*Crown counsel*), Frederick Leister (*Judge*), Walter Hudd (*Defence counsel*), Jacqueline Clarke (*Phyllis*), Frank Tickle (*Mr Pinkem*), Peter Croft (*Titch*), George Woodbridge (*Farmer Browning*), Stuart Lindsel (*Sir James*), Ian Russell (*Car driver*), Patrick Troughton (*Shepherd*), Cyril Smith (*Policeman*).
Producer: William Perlberg. *Personal assistants to producer:* Freddie Fox, R. E. Dearing. *Production company:* Twentieth Century Productions. *Distributor:* 20th Century-Fox. *Running time:* 79 minutes.
Filming started 15 September 1947 and finished on 18 December 1947. Locations on Dartmoor, Devon; studio work at Denham.
First shown: 28 March 1948 (Gaumont, Haymarket, and Marble Arch Pavilion, London).

UNFAITHFULLY YOURS (1948)

Director and writer: Preston Sturges. *Photographer:* Victor Milner. *Art directors:* Lyle Wheeler, Joseph C. Wright. *Editor:* Robert Fritch. *Special photographic effects:* Fred Sersen. *Music:* from *Semiramide* by Gioacchino Rossini, *Tannhäuser* by Richard Wagner, and *Francesca da Rimini* by Peter Ilich Tchaikovsky. *Music director:* Alfred Newman. *Conducting instructor for Rex Harrison:* Robin Sanders-Clark.

Cast: Rex Harrison (*Sir Alfred de Carter*), Linda Darnell (*Daphne de Carter*), Rudy Vallee (*August Henschler*), Barbara Lawrence (*Barbara*), Kurt Kreuger (*Tony*), Lionel Stander (*Hugo Standoff*), Edgar Kennedy (*Sweeney*), Alan Bridge (*House detective*), Julius Tannen (*Tailor*), Torben Meyer (*Dr Schultz*), Robert Greig (*Jules*), Evelyn Beresford (*Mme Pompadour*), Harry Seymour (*Musician*), Isabel Jewell and Marion Marshall (*Telephone operators*), Charles Tannen (*Airline clerk*), Frank Moran (*Fire chief*), J. Farrell MacDonald (*Concert hall doorman*).
Producer: Preston Sturges. *Production assistant:* Stephen Brooks. *Production company and distributor:* 20th Century-Fox. *Running time:* 105 minutes.
Filmed from 18 February 1948 under title *The Symphony Story*.
First shown: 6 November 1948 (Roxy, New York). *British premiere:* 17 February 1949 (New Gallery, and Tivoli, Strand, London).

THE WALKING STICK (1950) (for American TV)

Cast: Rex Harrison, Dennis Hoey, Una O'Connor, Elizabeth Eustis, Eileen Peel.
Running time: 60 minutes (with breaks).
First transmission: 20 March 1950 (NBC TV Chevrolet Tele-Theatre).

THE LONG DARK HALL (1951)

Directors: Anthony Bushell, Reginald Beck. *Writers:* Nunnally Johnson, (*additional scenes and dialogue*) W. E. C. Fairchild (*from the novel* A Case to Answer *by* Edgar Lustgarten). *Photographer:* Wilkie Cooper. *Art director:* George Patterson. *Editor:* Tom Simpson. *Music composer:* Benjamin Frankel.

Cast: Rex Harrison (*Arthur Groome*), Lilli Palmer (*Mary Groome*), Denis O'Dea (*Sir Charles Morton*), Raymond Huntley (*Chief Inspector Sullivan*), Patricia Wayne [Patricia Cutts] (*Rose Mallory*), Anthony Dawson (*The Man*), Anthony Bushell (*Clive Bedford*), Meriel Forbes (*Marjorie Danns*), Brenda De Banzie (*Mrs Rogers*), William Squires (*Sergeant Cochran*), Michael Medwin (*Leslie Scott*), Colin Gordon (*Pound*), Eric Pohlmann (*Polaris*), Tania Heald (*Sheila Groome*), Henrietta Barry (*Rosemary Groome*), Dora Sevening (*Mary's mother*), Ronald Simpson (*Mary's father*), Ballard Berkeley (*Superintendent Maxey*), Henry Longhurst (*Judge*), Douglas Jefferies (*Dr Conway*), Fletcher Lightfoot (*Jury foreman*), Anthony Shaw (*Clerk of the Court*), Lional Murton (*Jefferson*), Lilly Molnar (*Mrs Polaris*), Frank Tickle (*Mr Tripp*), Tom Macaulay (*Ironworks manager*), Richard Littledale (*Mr Sims*), Jenny Laird (*Mrs Sims*), Tony Quinn (*Joe*), Jill Bennett (*First murdered girl*).
Producer: Anthony Bushell. *Production arranged by:* Peter Cusick. *Associate producer:* Ronald Kinnoch. *Production company:* Five Oceans. *A* Cusick International *presentation. Distributor:* British Lion.
Running time: 86 minutes.
Filmed at Nettlefold Studios, Walton-on-Thames, from 10 July 1950.
First shown: 9 February 1951 (Leicester Square Theatre, London).

THE FOUR POSTER (1952)

Director: Irving Reis. *Writer:* Allan Scott (*from the play by* Jan de

209

Hartog). *Photographer:* Hal Mohr. *Production design:* Rudolf Sternad. *Art director:* Carl Anderson. *Editors:* Henry Batista, (*supervision*) Harry Gerstad. *Music composer:* Dimitri Tiomkin.

Interscenes. Director: John Hubley. *Animators:* Paul Julian, Art Babbitt, Lew Keller. *Producer:* Stephen Bosustow. *Production company:* UPA.

Cast: Rex Harrison (*John Edwards*), Lilli Palmer (*Abby Edwards*). *Associate producer:* Allan Scott. *Production company:* Stanley Kramer Company. *Distributor:* Columbia. *Running time:* 103 minutes.
In production from 17 September 1951 for twenty-one days.
First shown: 15 October 1952 (Sutton and Victoria Theatres, New York).
British premiere: 21 November 1952 (Carlton, Haymarket, London).

OMNIBUS (1952) (for American TV)

Director: Andrew McCullough. *Writer:* Alistair Cooke.
Presenter: Alistair Cooke.

Trial of Anne Boleyn
Director: Alex Segal. *Writer:* Maxwell Anderson. *Music composer:* Suzanne Bloch.
Cast: Lilli Palmer (*Anne Boleyn*), Rex Harrison (*Henry VIII*), Edwin Jerome, Jonathan Harris, Richard Kylie [Kiley?], Robert Pastene.
Producer: Alan Anderson.

Also included:

The Mikado
Conductor: Lehman Engel.
Cast: Martyn Green, Ella Halman.

The Bad Men
Writer: William Saroyan.
Cast: Russell Collins, Joshua Shelley, Harry Bellaver, Malcolm Broderick, James Westerfield, Mary Stuart, Sidney Poitier, Sharon Porter.

Witch Doctor
Dancers: Jean Leon Destine, Jeanne Ramon, Alphonse Cimber.

Production companies: Ritter-Lerner-Young Associates, Unity Films. Producer: William Spier. Executive producer: Robert Saudek. Running time: 90 minutes (with breaks).

First transmission: 9 November 1952 (CBS TV).

MAIN STREET TO BROADWAY (1953)

Director: Tay Garnett. Writer: Samson Raphaelson (from a story by Robert E. Sherwood). Photographer: James Wong Howe. Art director: Perry Ferguson. Editors: Gene Fowler Jr, (assistant) Robert Lawrence. Music composer: Ann Ronell. Song: Richard Rodgers, Oscar Hammerstein II.

Cast: Tom Morton (Tony Monaco), Mary Murphy (Mary Craig), Agnes Moorehead (Mildred Waterbury), Herb Shriner (Frank Johnson), Rosemary De Camp (Mrs Craig), Clinton Sundberg (Mr Craig), Gertrude Berg (Landlady); and in the fantasy scenes: Florence Bates, Madge Kennedy, Carl Benton Reid, Frank Ferguson and Robert Bray; and making guest appearances as themselves: Tallulah Bankhead, Ethel Barrymore, Lionel Barrymore, Vivian Blaine, Joan Blondell, Shirley Booth, Louis Calhern, June Collyer, Chris Durocher, Leo Durocher, Faye Emerson, Stuart Erwin, Oscar Hammerstein II, Rex Harrison, Joshua Logan, Mary Martin, Lilli Palmer, Bill Rigney, Richard Rodgers, Arthur Shields, John Van Druten, Cornel Wilde and Peggy Wood.
Producer: Lester Cowan. Co-ordinator for The Council of the Living Theatre: Jean Dalrymple. Distributor: Metro-Goldwyn-Mayer. Running time: 97 minutes.
Filmed from mid-October 1952 in Hollywood; New York location work done in November and December 1952.
First shown: 13 October 1953 (Astor Theatre, New York). Generally released in Britain: 11 January 1957.

MAN IN POSSESSION (1953) (for American TV)

Director: Alex Segal. Writer: Arthur Arent (from the play by H. M. Harwood). Costumes for Lilli Palmer: Gene Coffin. Music composer: Bernard Green.

Cast: Rex Harrison (*Raymond Dabney*), Lilli Palmer (*Mrs Chrystal Weatherby*), Anthony Kemble Cooper (*Binkie Bellairs*), Francis Compton (*Paul Dabney*), Robert Coote (*Claude Dabney*), Jack Raine (*Sir Charles Cartwright*), William Podmore (*Bailiff*), Brenda Forbes (*Clara, the maid*), Betty Sinclair (*Mrs Dabney*).
Production company: Theatre Guild. *Running time:* 60 minutes (with breaks).
First transmission: 8 December 1953 (ABC TV US Steel Hour).

KING RICHARD AND THE CRUSADERS (1954)

Director: David Butler. *2nd unit director:* Yakima Canutt. *Writer:* John Twist (*from the novel* The Talisman *by* Sir Walter Scott). *Photographer* (WarnerColor, CinemaScope)*:* J. Peverell Marley. *Art director:* Bertram Tuttle. *Editor:* Irene Morra. *Music composer:* Max Steiner.

Cast: Rex Harrison (*Emir Ilderim/Sultan Saladin*), Virginia Mayo (*Lady Edith*), George Sanders (*King Richard I*), Laurence Harvey (*Sir Kenneth*), Robert Douglas (*Sir Giles Amaury*), Michael Pate (*Conrad, Marquis of Montferrat*), Paula Raymond (*Queen Berengaria*), Lester Matthews (*Archbishop of Tyre*), Anthony Eustrel (*Baron de Vaux*), Henry Corden (*King Philip of France*), Wilton Graff (*Duke Leopold of Austria*), Nejla Ates (*A dance speciality*), Nick Cravat (*Nectobanus*), Leslie Bradley (*Castelain Captain*), Bruce Lester (*1st Castelain*), Mark Dana (*2nd Castelain*), Peter Ortiz (*3rd Castelain*), Larry Chance (*Castelain bowman*), Robin Hughes (*King's guard*), Leonard Penn, Lumsden Hare and Leonard Mudie (*Physicians*), Erik Blythe (*Drillmaster*), John Alderson (*Mob leader*), Harry Cording (*Castelain spokesman*), Paul Marion (*Arab falconer*), Abdullah Abbas (*Arab*), John Epper (*Wounded Castelain*).
Producer: Henry Blanke. *Production company and distributor:* Warner Bros. *Running time:* 114 minutes.
Filmed from 8 December 1953, under the title *The Talisman*, to late February 1954.
Generally released: August 1954. *British premiere:* 21 October 1954 (Warner, Leicester Square, London).

THE CONSTANT HUSBAND (1955)

Director: Sidney Gilliat. *Writers:* Sidney Gilliat, Val Valentine.

Photographer (Technicolor): Ted Scaife. *Art director:* Wilfrid Shingleton. *Editor:* Gerald Turney-Smith. *Music composer:* Malcolm Arnold.

Cast: Rex Harrison (*Charles Hathaway, a man who has lost his memory*), Margaret Leighton (*Miss Chesterman, Counsel for the Defence*), Kay Kendall (*Monica, fashion photographer*), Cecil Parker (*Llewellyn, Professor of Psychological Medicine*), Nicole Maurey (*Lola Sopranelli*), George Cole (*Luigi Sopranelli*), Raymond Huntley (*J. F. Hassett, a Senior Civil Servant*), Michael Hordern (*The Judge*), Robert Coote (*Jack Carter*), Eric Pohlmann (*Papa Sopranelli*), Marie Burke (*Moma Sopranelli*), Eric Berry (*Counsel for the Prosecution*), Arthur Howard (*Clerk of the Court*), Charles Lloyd Pack (*Mr Daniels, solicitor*), Derek Sydney (*Giorgio Sopranelli*), Guy Deghy (*Stromboli*), Valerie French (*Bridget*), Jill Adams (*Joanna Brewer*), Ursula Howells (*Ann Pargiter*), Roma Dumville (*Elizabeth, sixth wife*), Stephen Vercoe (*Dr Thomson*), Sally Lahee (*Nurse*), Nora Gordon (*Housekeeper*), Muriel Young (*Clara*), Noel Hood (*Gladys*), Pat Kenyon (*1st model*), Doreen Dawn (*2nd model*), Myrette Morven (*Miss Prosser*), John Robinson (*Club Secretary*), Sam Kydd (*Barman – Adelphi Hotel*), Paul Connell (*Barman – Cardiff Hotel*), Nicholas Tannar (*Usher*), Graham Stuart (*Government messenger*), Jill Melford (*Monica's golf partner*), Enid McCall (*Welsh chambermaid*), Janette Richer (*Typist – Ministry of Munitions*), Michael Ripper (*Left Luggage attendant*), Alfred Burke (*Porter*), David Yates (*1st detective*), Robert Sydney (*2nd detective*), Monica Stevenson (*Olwen*), Stuart Saunders (*Police Sergeant*), George Woodbridge (*1st warder – Old Bailey*), Joe Clark (*2nd warder – Old Bailey*), Frank Webster (*3rd warder – Old Bailey*), Arthur Cortez (*Luigi's car driver*), Peter Edwards (*1st fisherman*), Evie Lloyd (*2nd fisherman*), Paul Whitsun Jones (*Welsh farmer*), Arnold Diamond (*Manager – Car Loan Ltd*), Olive Kirby (*Car Loan assistant*), Geoffrey Lovat (*Commissionaire – Ministry of Munitions*), Leslie Weston (*Prison jailer*), George Thorne (*Horrocks*). *Producers:* Sidney Gilliat, Frank Launder. *Associate producer:* M. Smedley Aston. *Production company:* Individual/London Films. *Distributor:* British Lion. *Running time:* 88 minutes.
Filming started 1 April 1954 at Shepperton Studios.
First shown: 22 April 1955 (London Pavilion, Piccadilly Circus). Opening night selection at Berlin Film Festival, 24 June 1955.

CRESCENDO (1957) (for American TV)

Director: Bill Colleran. *Writers:* Peter Ustinov, Leslie Stevens.

Cast: Rex Harrison (*Mr Sir*) with (*guest artists*) Julie Andrews, Stanley Holloway, Louis Armstrong, Eddy Arnold, Diahann Carroll, Carol Channing, Benny Goodman, Peggy Lee, Dinah Washington and others.
Producer: Paul Gregory. *Running time:* 90 minutes (with breaks).
First transmission: 29 September 1957 (CBS TV DuPont Show of the Month).

THE RELUCTANT DEBUTANTE (1958)

Director: Vincente Minnelli. *Writer:* William Douglas Home (*from his play*). *Photographer* (Metrocolor, CinemaScope)*:* Joseph Ruttenberg. *Art director:* Jean d'Eaubonne. *Editor:* Adrienne Fazan. *Dance and music arrangements:* Eddie Warner.

Cast: Rex Harrison (*Jimmy Broadbent*), Kay Kendall (*Sheila Broadbent*), John Saxon (*David Parkson*), Sandra Dee (*Jane Broadbent*), Angela Lansbury (*Mabel Claremont*), Peter Myers (*David Fenner*), Diane Clare (*Clarissa Claremont*), Sheila Raynor (*Maid*), Ambrosine Phillpotts (*Secretary*), Charles Cullum (*English Colonel*), Darryl Carey.
Producer: Pandro S. Berman. *Production company:* Avon. *Distributor:* Metro-Goldwyn-Mayer. *Running time:* 95 minutes.
Filmed from 10 February 1958 to late March 1958, initially in London, then in Paris.
First shown: 14 August 1958 (Radio City Music Hall, New York).
British premiere: 26 December 1958 (Empire, Leicester Square, London).

THE FABULOUS FIFTIES (1960) (for American TV)

Director: Norman Jewison. *Writers:* Max Wilk, A. J. Russell. *Musical director:* Alfredo Antonini. *Conductor for* My Fair Lady *numbers:* Franz Allers. *Choreography:* Danny Daniels. Live, tape and film.

Rex Harrison and Julie Andrews presented songs from *My Fair Lady* (Rex: 'I'm an Ordinary Man', Julie: 'Just You Wait').

Also featured: Henry Fonda (*host*), Jackie Gleason, Shelley Berman, Mike Nichols and Elaine May, Betty Comden and Adolph Green,

Dick Van Dyke and Maria Karnilova, Suzy Parker (*in film sequence by* Richard Avedon), voices of Arthur Godfrey, Roy Campanella, Roger Bannister, Kurt Carlsen, Edmund Hillary and (*commentary*) Eric Sevareid. Clips from outstanding television shows and films, plus excerpts from 1950s records.
Producer: Leland Hayward. *Running time:* 120 minutes (with breaks).
First transmission: 31 January 1960 (CBS TV from New York).

DEAR ARTHUR (1960) (for American TV)

Director: Bretaigne Windust. *Writer:* Gore Vidal (*from* Arthur *by* P. G. Wodehouse *based on the play* Jemand *by* Ferenc Molnar). In colour.

Cast: Rex Harrison (*Fred Cortin*), Sarah Marshall (*Edith Brooks*), Hermione Baddeley (*Emerald Dane*), Nicholas Pryor (*Robert Griffiths*), Olga Fabian (*Julie*), John Garson (*Ribaud*), Robert Dryden (*Lawyer*), Gaby Rodgers (*Woman*), Guy Repp (*Secretary of State*).
Producer: Bretaigne Windust. *Running time:* 60 minutes (with breaks).
First transmission: 22 March 1960 (NBC TV Ford Startime).

THE DATCHET DIAMONDS (1960) (for American TV)

Director: Gower Champion. *Writer:* Walter Kerr (*from a novel by* Richard Marsh). Tape.

Cast: Rex Harrison (*Cyril Paxton*), Tammy Grimes (*Daisy Strong*), Robert Flemyng (*Lawrence*), David Hurst (*Baron*), Alice Ghostley (*Charlotte*), Reginald Denny (*Inspector Ireland*), Melville Cooper (*Franklyn*), George Turner (*Hotel manager*), Laurie Main (*Connors*), Hedlie Rainie (*Skittles*), Joseph Welch (*Host*).
Producer: Robert Saudek. *Running time:* 60 minutes (with breaks).
First transmission: 20 September 1960 (NBC TV Dow Hour of Great Mysteries).

MIDNIGHT LACE (1960)

Director: David Miller. *Writers:* Ivan Goff, Ben Roberts (*from the play*

Matilda Shouted Fire *by* Janet Green). *Photographer* (Eastman Color): Russell Metty. *Art directors:* Alexander Golitzen, Robert Clatworthy. *Editors:* Russell F. Schoengarth, Leon Barsha, *(uncredited)* Milton Carruth and William Lyon. *Music composer:* Frank Skinner.

Cast: Doris Day *(Kit Preston)*, Rex Harrison *(Tony Preston)*, John Gavin *(Brian Younger)*, Myrna Loy *(Aunt Bea)*, Natasha Parry *(Peggy Thompson)*, Herbert Marshall *(Charles Manning)*, Roddy McDowall *(Malcolm Stanley)*, John Williams *(Inspector Byrnes)*, Hermione Baddeley *(Dora Hammer)*, Doris Lloyd *(Nora)*, Richard Lupino *(Simon Foster)*, Anthony Dawson *(Roy Thompson)*, Richard Ney *(Daniel)*, Rhys Williams *(Victor Elliott)*, Rex Evans *(Basil Stafford)*, Hayden Rorke *(Doctor)*, Anthony Eustrel *(Salesman)*, Elspeth March.
Producers: Ross Hunter, Martin Melcher. *Production companies:* Ross Hunter, Arwin. *Distributor:* Universal. *Running time:* 108 minutes.
Filmed in Hollywood from mid-March 1960 to late May 1960.
First shown: 13 October 1960 (Radio City Music Hall, New York).
British premiere: 19 January 1961 (Leicester Square Theatre, London).

THE HAPPY THIEVES (1961)

Director: George Marshall. *Writer:* John Gay *(from the novel* The Oldest Confession *by* Richard Condon). *Photographer:* Paul Beeson. *Art director:* Ramiro Gómez. *Editor:* Oswald Hafenrichter. *Music composer:* Mario Nascimbene.

Cast: Rex Harrison *(Jim Bourne)*, Rita Hayworth *(Eve Lewis)*, Joseph Wiseman *(Jean Marie Calbert)*, Grégoire Aslan *(Dr Muñoz)*, Alida Valli *(Duchess Blanca)*, Virgilio Texeira *(Cayetano)*, Peter Illing *(Pickett)*, Brita Ekman *(Mrs Pickett)*, Julio Peña *(Señor Elek)*, Gérard Tichy *(Antonio)*, Lou Weber and Antonio Fuentes *(Guards)*, Georges Rigaud *(Inspector)*, Barta Barri *(Chern)*, Karl-Heinz Schwerdtfeger *(Police official)*, Yasmin Khan *(Small girl)*.
Executive producers: James Hill, Rita Hayworth. *Production company:* Hillworth. *Distributor:* United Artists. *Running time:* 89 minutes.
Filmed from 21 February 1961 to April 1961 in Madrid under the title *Once a Thief.*
First shown: 20 December 1961 (Woods Theatre, Chicago). *British premiere:* 23 February 1962 (London Pavilion, Piccadilly Circus).

CLEOPATRA (1963)

Director: Joseph L. Mankiewicz. *2nd unit directors:* Ray Kellogg, Andrew Marton. *Writers:* Joseph L. Mankiewicz, Ranald MacDougall, Sidney Buchman (*from histories by* Plutarch, Suetonius, Appian *and other ancient sources and* The Life and Times of Cleopatra *by* C. M. Franzero). *Photographers* (colour by DeLuxe, Todd-AO)*:* Leon Shamroy, (*2nd unit*) Claude Renoir and Piero Portalupi. *Production designer:* John De Cuir. *Art directors:* Jack Martin Smith, Hilyard Brown, Herman Blumenthal, Elven Webb, Maurice Pelling, Boris Juraga. *Music composer:* Alex North.

Cast: Elizabeth Taylor (*Cleopatra*), Richard Burton (*Mark Antony*), Rex Harrison (*Julius Caesar*), Pamela Brown (*High Priestess*), George Cole (*Flavius*), Hume Cronyn (*Sosigenes*), Cesare Danova (*Apollodorus*), Kenneth Haigh (*Brutus*), Andrew Keir (*Agrippa*), Martin Landau (*Rufio*), Roddy McDowall (*Octavian*), Robert Stephens (*Germanicus*), Francesca Annis (*Eiras*), Grégoire Aslan (*Pothinos*), Martin Benson (*Ramos*), Herbert Berghof (*Theodotus*), John Cairney (*Phoebus*), Jacqui Chan (*Lotos*), Isabelle Cooley (*Charmian*), John Doucette (*Achillas*), Andrew Faulds (*Canidius*), Michael Gwynn (*Cimber*), Michael Hordern (*Cicero*), John Hoyt (*Cassius*), Marne Maitland (*Euphranor*), Carroll O'Connor (*Casca*), Richard O'Sullivan (*Ptolemy*), Gwen Watford (*Calpurnia*), Douglas Wilmer (*Decimus*), Marina Berti (*Queen at Tarsus*), John Karlsen (*High Priest*), Loris Loddi (*Caesarion, aged 4*), Jean Marsh (*Octavia*), Gin Mart (*Marcellus*), Furio Meniconi (*Mithridates*), Kenneth Nash (*Caesarion, aged 12*), Del Russell (*Caesarion, aged 7*), John Valva (*Valvus*), Finlay Currie (*Titus*), Laurence Naismith (*Archesilius*), John Alderson, Maria Badmajev, Michèle Bally, Marie Devereux, Peter Forster, John Gayford, Maureen Lane, Kathy Martin, Gesa Meiken, Simon Mizrahi. *Producer:* Walter Wanger. *Production companies:* Walwa, MCL, 20th Century-Fox. *Distributor:* 20th Century-Fox. *Running time:* 243 minutes (later cut).
Filmed from 20 or 25 September 1961 to 28 July 1962 at Cinecittà Studios in Rome with locations in Italy (Torre Astura, Anzio, Ischia and Lanuvio) and Egypt (Alexandria, Edkou and desert areas) and with additional shooting on 14 February 1963 at Almeria, Spain, and at Pinewood Studios, England (finishing 2 March 1963).
First shown: 12 June 1963 (Rivoli Theatre, New York). *British premiere:* 31 July 1963 (Dominion, Tottenham Court Road, London).

217

MY FAIR LADY (1964)

Director: George Cukor. *Writer:* Alan Jay Lerner (*from his book for the Broadway musical of the same name based on the play* Pygmalion *by* George Bernard Shaw *and the film version, also called* Pygmalion *with a screenplay by* George Bernard Shaw *and adaptation by* Ian Dalrymple, Cecil Lewis *and* W. P. Lipscomb). *Photographer* (Technicolor, Super Panavision 70)*:* Harry Stradling. *Production designer and costume designer:* Cecil Beaton. *Art director:* Gene Allen. *Editor:* William Ziegler. *Music composer:* Frederick Loewe. *Music director:* Andre Previn. *Lyricist:* Alan Jay Lerner. *Songs performed by Rex Harrison:* 'Why Can't the English?', 'I'm an Ordinary Man', 'The Rain in Spain', 'You Did It', 'A Hymn to Him' and 'I've Grown Accustomed to Her Face'. *Other songs:* 'Wouldn't It Be Loverly?', 'With a Little Bit of Luck', 'Just You Wait', 'Ascot Gavotte', 'On the Street Where You Live', 'I Could Have Danced All Night', 'Show Me', 'Get Me to the Church On Time' and 'Without You'. *Choreographer:* Hermes Pan.

Cast: Audrey Hepburn (*Eliza Doolittle*), Rex Harrison (*Henry Higgins*), Stanley Holloway (*Alfred P. Doolittle*), Wilfrid Hyde-White (*Colonel Hugh Pickering*), Gladys Cooper (*Mrs Higgins*), Jeremy Brett (*Freddy Eynsford-Hill*), Theodore Bikel (*Zoltan Karpathy*), Mona Washbourne (*Mrs Pearce*), Isobel Elsom (*Mrs Eynsford-Hill*), John Holland (*Butler*), Roy Dean (*Footman*), John Alderson (*Jamie*), John McLiam (*Harry*), Baroness Veronica Rothschild (*Queen of Transylvania*), Marjorie Bennett (*Cockney with pipe*), Barbara Pepper (*Doolittle's dancing partner*), Owen McGiveney (*Man at coffee stand*), Betty Blythe (*Ad lib at ball*), Henry Daniell (*Prince of Transylvania*), Alan Napier (*Ambassador*), Jack Greening (*George*), Ron Whelan (*Algernon/bartender*), Dinah Anne Rogers and Lois Battle (*Maids*), Jacqueline Squire (*Parlour maid*), Gwendolyn Watts (*Cook*), Charles Fredericks (*King*), Lily Kemble-Cooper (*Lady Ambassador*), Moyna MacGill (*Lady Boxington*), Ben Wright (*Footman at ball*), Oscar Beregi (*Greek Ambassador*), Buddy Bryan (*Prince*), Jennifer Crier (*Mrs Higgins' maid*), Olive Reeves-Smith (*Mrs Hopkins*), Grady Sutton (*Ascot extra/guest at ball*), Major Sam Harris (*Guest at ball*), Ben Wrigley, Clive Halliday, Richard Peel, Eric Heath and James O'Hara (*Costermongers*), Kendrick Huxham (*Elegant bystander*), Britannia Beatey (*Daughter of elegant bystander*), Walter Burke (*Main bystander*), Queenie Leonard (*Cockney bystander*), Laurie Main (*Hoxton man*), Maurice Dallimore (*Selsey man*), Beatrice Greenough (*Grand lady*),

Hilda Plowright (*2nd bystander*), Eugene Hoffman and Kai Farrelli (*Jugglers*), Iris Bristol, Alma Lawton and Jennifer Raine (*Flower girls*), Raymond Foster, Joe Evans, Marie Busch, Mary Alexander, William Linkie, Henry Sweetman, Andrew Brown, Samuel Holmes, Thomas Dick, William Taylor, James Wood, Goldie Kleban, Elizabeth Aimers, Joy Tierney, Lenore Miller, Donna Day, Corinne Ross, Phyllis Kennedy and Dave Robel (*Ad lib Cockneys*), Gigi Michel, Sandy Steffens, Sandy Edmundson, Merlene Marrow, Carol Merrill, Sue Bronson and Lea Genovese (*Ad lib toffs*), Orville Sherman, Harvey Dunn, Barbara Morrison, Natalie Core, Helen Albrecht, Marjorie Hawtrey, Paulle Clark, Allison Daniell and Diana Bourbon (*Ad libs at Ascot*), Colin Campbell (*Man at Ascot*), Nick Navarro (*Dancer*), Tom Cound and William Beckley (*Footmen*), Geoffrey Steele (*Taxi driver*), Victor Rogers (*Policeman*), Michael St Clair (*Bartender*), Miriam Schiller (*Landlady*), Ayllene Gibbons (*Fat woman at pub*), Brendan Dillon (*Leaning man*), Elzada Wilson, Jeanne Gerson, Buddy Shaw, Jack Goldie, Sid Marion, Stanley Fraser, George Pelling, Colin Kenny, Phyllis Kennedy, LaWana Backer, Monika Henreid, Anne Dore, Pauline Drake, Shirley Melline, Wendy Russell, Meg Brown, Clyde Howdy, Nicholas Wolcuff, Martin Eric and John Mitchum (*Ad libs in pub for 'Get Me to the Church On Time' number*), Jack Raine, Frank Baker, Pat O'Moore.
Singing voice for Audrey Hepburn: Marni Nixon. *Singing voice for Jeremy Brett:* Bill Shirley.
Producer: Jack L. Warner. *Production company and distributor:* Warner Bros. *Running time:* 170 minutes.
Filming started on 13 August 1963 and finished mid-December 1963.
First shown: 22 October 1964 (Criterion, New York). *British premiere:* 21 January 1965 (Warner, Leicester Square, London).

THE YELLOW ROLLS-ROYCE (1964)

Director: Anthony Asquith. *Writer:* Terence Rattigan. *Photographer* (Metrocolor, Panavision): Jack Hildyard. *Production designer:* Vincent Korda. *Art directors:* (*first episode*) Elliot Scott, (*other episodes*) William Kellner. *Editor:* Frank Clarke. *Music composer:* Riz Ortolani.

Casts:
First episode: Rex Harrison (*Marquess of Frinton*), Jeanne Moreau (*Marchioness of Frinton*), Edmund Purdom (*John Fane*), Michael

219

Hordern (*Harmsworth*), Moira Lister (*Lady St Simeon*), Roland Culver (*Norwood*), Lance Percival (*assistant car salesman*), Harold Scott (*Taylor*), Grégoire Aslan (*Albanian Ambassador*), Isa Miranda (*Duchesse d'Angoulême*), Jacques Brunius (*Duc d'Angoulême*), Richard Pearson (*Osborn, the chauffeur*), Richard Vernon, Reginald Beckwith, Tom Gill, Dermot Kelly.
Second episode: Shirley MacLaine (*Mae Jenkins*), George C. Scott (*Paolo Maltese*), Alain Delon (*Stefano*), Art Carney (*Joey Friedlander*), Riccardo Garrone (*Bomba*).
Third episode: Ingrid Bergman (*Mrs Gerda Millett*), Omar Sharif (*Davich*), Joyce Grenfell (*Miss Hortense Astor*), Wally Cox (*Ferguson*), Guy Deghy (*Mayor*), Carlo Groccolo (*Chauffeur*), Martin Miller (*Waiter*), Andreas Malandrinos (*Hotel manager*).
Producer: Anatole de Grunwald. *Associate producer:* Roy Parkinson. *Production company and distributor:* Metro-Goldwyn-Mayer. *Running time:* 122 minutes.
Filming started in London on 6 April 1964 with location work for second and third episodes in Italy and Austria.
First shown: 31 December 1964 (Empire, Leicester Square, London). *American premiere:* 13 May 1965 (Radio City Music Hall, New York).

GOLDEN DRAMA (1965) (for British TV)

Director (for TV): Bill Ward. *Settings:* Tom Lingwood. *Music:* John Lanchbery. *Orchestra conductor (for Rex Harrison's number):* Cyril Ornandel.

Cast: Laurence Olivier, Celia Johnson, Maggie Smith and Frank Cellier (*extract from* The Master Builder); Peggy Ashcroft and Peter Finch (*extract from* The Seagull); John Clements, Julian Holloway and Daniel Massey (*extract from* The Rivals); Peter O'Toole (*three soliloquies from* Hamlet); Edith Evans, Judi Dench and Rachel Kempson (*extract from* Romeo and Juliet); John Mills and Mark Dignam (*extract from* Ross); Paul Schofield, Megs Jenkins, Leo McKern, Anna Massey and John Carson (*extract from* A Man for All Seasons); Rex Harrison (*number 'I've Grown Accustomed to Her Face' from* My Fair Lady); Laurence Olivier, Maggie Smith, Jeanne Hepple, Sarah Miles, Colin Blakely, Derek Jacobi and Robert Stephens (*extract from* The Recruiting Officer). Noel Coward, Robert Morley and Anthony Quayle (*Introducers*).

220

Producer: Cecil Clarke. Production company: ATV. Running time: 115 minutes (with breaks).
First transmission (live): 31 January 1965 (from Queen's Theatre, London).

THE AGONY AND THE ECSTASY (1965)

Director: Carol Reed. 2nd unit director: Robert D. Webb. Writer: Philip Dunne (from the novel by Irving Stone). Photographer (colour by DeLuxe, 70mm Todd-AO): Leon Shamroy. 2nd unit photographer: Piero Portalupi. Production designer: John De Cuir. Art director: Jack Martin Smith. Editor: Samuel E. Beetley. Music composer: Alex North.

Cast: Charlton Heston (Michelangelo), Rex Harrison (Pope Julius II), Diane Cilento (Contessina de' Medici), Harry Andrews (Bramante), Alberto Lupo (Duke of Urbino), Adolfo Celi (Giovanni de' Medici), Venantino Venantini (Paris de Grassis), John Stacy (Sangallo), Fausto Tozzi (Foreman), Maxine Audley (Woman), Tomas Milian (Raphael).
Producer: Carol Reed. Production company: International Classics.
Distributor: 20th Century-Fox. Running time: 139 minutes.
Filmed from 1 June 1964 to mid-September 1964 in Rome and at locations including Canale de Monterano (for battle sequences) and Todi (for St Peter's Square).
First shown: 7 October 1965 (Loew's State, New York). British premiere: 27 October 1965 (Astoria, Charing Cross Road, London).

THE HONEY POT (1967)

Director and writer: Joseph L. Mankiewicz (from the play Mr Fox of Venice by Frederick Knott, based on the novel The Evil of the Day by Thomas L. Sterling, inspired by the play Volpone by Ben Jonson). Photographers (Technicolor): Gianni Di Venanzo, (uncredited) Pasqualino De Santis. Production designer: John De Cuir. Art director: Boris Juraga. Editor: David Bretherton. Music composer: John Addison.

Cast: Rex Harrison (Cecil Fox), Susan Hayward (Mrs Lone-Star Crockett Sheridan), Cliff Robertson (William McFly), Capucine (Princess Dominique), Edie Adams (Merle McGill), Maggie Smith

221

(*Sarah Watkins*), Adolfo Celi (*Inspector Rizzi*), Herschel Bernardi (*Oscar Ludwig*), Hugh Manning (*'Volpone'*), David Dodimead (*'Mosca'*), Cy Grant and Frank Latimore (*Revenue agents*), Luigi Scavran (*Massimo*), Mimmo Poli (*cook*), Antonio Corevi (*tailor*), Carlos Valles (*assistant tailor*).
Producers: Charles K. Feldman, Joseph L. Mankiewicz. *Production company:* Famous Artists. *Distributor:* United Artists. *Running time:* 150 minutes (premiere in Britain) (cut to 131 minutes for American release).
Filmed in Italy at Cinecittà Studios and on location in Venice from 20 September 1965 to 26 February 1966 under the title *Anyone for Venice . . . ?*
First shown: 21 March 1967 (Odeon, Marble Arch, London). *American premiere:* 21 May 1967 (Trans-Lux West, New York).

DOCTOR DOLITTLE (1967)

Director: Richard Fleischer. *Writer:* Leslie Bricusse (*from the* Dr Dolittle *stories by* Hugh Lofting). *Photographer* (colour by DeLuxe, 70mm Todd-AO)*:* Robert Surtees. *Production designer:* Mario Chiari. *Art directors:* Jack Martin Smith, Ed Graves. *Editors:* Samuel E. Beetley, Marjorie Fowler. *Music composers:* Lionel Newman, Alexander Courage. *Songs:* Leslie Bricusse. *Director of musical numbers:* Herbert Ross. *Songs performed by Rex Harrison:* 'The Vegetarian', 'Talk to the Animals', 'I've Never Seen Anything Like It', 'When I Look Into Your Eyes', 'Like Animals', 'I Think I Like You', 'Something in Your Smile'. *Other songs:* 'My Friend the Doctor', 'At the Crossroads', 'After Today', 'Fabulous Places', 'Doctor Dolittle'. *Supplier and trainer of animals and birds:* Jungleland of Thousand Oaks (California). *Special photographic effects:* L. B. Abbott, Art Cruickshank, Emil Kosa Jr, Howard Lydecker.

Cast: Rex Harrison (*Doctor John Dolittle*), Samantha Eggar (*Emma Fairfax*), Anthony Newley (*Matthew Mugg*), Richard Attenborough (*Albert Blossom*), Peter Bull (*General Bellowes*), Muriel Landers (*Mrs Blossom*), William Dix (*Tommy Stubbins*), Geoffrey Holder (*Willie Shakespeare*), Portia Nelson (*Sarah Dolittle*), Norma Varden (*Lady Petherington*).
Producer: Arthur P. Jacobs. *Associate producer:* Mort Abrahams. *Production company:* Apjac. *Distributor:* 20th Century-Fox. *Running time:* 152 minutes.

Filmed from late June 1966 to mid-February 1967 with location work at Castle Combe, Wiltshire, England, and Santa Lucia, British West Indies.
First shown: 12 December 1967 (Odeon, Marble Arch, London).
American premiere: 19 December 1967 (Loew's State, New York).

A FLEA IN HER EAR (1968)

Director: Jacques Charon. *2nd unit director:* Noel Howard. *Writer:* John Mortimer *(from his English stage adaptation of the French play* La Puce à l'Oreille *by* Georges Feydeau). *Photographer* (colour by DeLuxe, Panavision): Charles Lang. *2nd unit photographer:* Walter Wottitz. *Production designer:* Alexandre Trauner. *Art director:* Auguste Capelier. *Editor:* Walter Thompson. *Music composer:* Bronislau Kaper.

Cast: Rex Harrison (*Victor Chandebisse/Poche*), Rosemary Harris (*Gabrielle Chandebisse*), Louis Jourdan (*Henri Tournel*), Rachel Roberts (*Suzanne de Castilian*), John Williams (*Dr Finache*), Grégoire Aslan (*Max*), Edward Hardwicke (*Pierre*), Georges Descrières (*Don Carlos de Castilian*), Isla Blair (*Antoinette*), Frank Thornton (*Charles*), Victor Sen-Yung (*Oke Saki*), Laurence Badie (*Eugénie*), Dominique Davray (*Olympe*), Olivier Hussenot (*Uncle Louis*), Estella Blain (*Defendant*), Moustache (*Fat man*), David Horne (*Prosecutor*), Roger Carel (*Taxi driver*).
Producer: Fred Kohlmar. *Production company and distributor:* 20th Century-Fox. *Running time:* 94 minutes.
Filmed in Paris from 17 July 1967 to the end of October 1967.
First shown: October 1968 (various cinemas in Paris). *British premiere:* 14 November 1968 (Carlton, Haymarket, London). *American release:* November 1968.

STAIRCASE (1969)

Director: Stanley Donen. *Writer:* Charles Dyer (*from his play*).
Photographer (colour by DeLuxe, Panavision): Christopher Challis.
Art director: Willy Holt. *Editor:* Richard Marden. *Music composer:* Dudley Moore.

Cast: Richard Burton (*Harry Leeds*), Rex Harrison (*Charlie Dyer*), Cathleen Nesbitt (*Harry's mother*), Beatrix Lehmann (*Charlie's mother*), Stephen Lewis (*Jack*), Neil Wilson (*Policeman*), Gordon Heath (*Postman*), Avril Angers (*Miss Ricard*), Shelagh Fraser (*Cub mistress*), Gwen Nelson (*Matron*), Pat Heywood (*Nurse*), Dermot Kelly (*Gravedigger*), Jake Kavanagh (*Choirboy*), Rogers and Starr (*Drag singers*).
Producer: Stanley Donen. *Production company:* Stanley Donen Films. *Distributor:* 20th Century-Fox. *Running time:* 98 minutes.
Filmed in Paris (interiors at the Billancourt Studios) from 3 September 1968 to mid-December 1968.
First shown: 20 August 1969 (various theatres, New York). *British premiere:* 22 October 1969 (Carlton, Haymarket, London).

PLATONOV (1971)

Author: Anton Chekhov (*translated by* Dmitri Makaroff *and adapted for television by* John Elliot). *Director:* Christopher Morahan. In colour. *Designer:* Eileen Diss. *Lighting:* Sam Barclay. *Music composer:* Norman Kay.

Cast: Rex Harrison (*Mikhail Platonov, a schoolmaster*), Patsy Byrne (*Sasha, his wife*), Sian Phillips (*Anna Voinitseva, a widow*), Clive Revill (*Nicolai Triletski, Sasha's brother*), Donald Eccles (*Count Glagolyev, Anna's suitor*), Geoffrey Bayldon (*Sergei Voinitsev, Anna's stepson*), Willoughby Goddard (*Bugrov, a merchant*), Trevor Kent (*Yakov, a servant*), Stacey Tendeter (*Katya, a maid*), John Gill (*Col. Triletski, Sasha's father*), Kevin Stoney (*Vengerovich, a rich Jew*), Joanna Dunham (*Sofia, Voinitsev's wife*), Bridget Armstrong (*Maria Grekova, a student of chemistry*), Neil McCarthy (*Osip, a bandit*), Peter Eyre (*Kiril, Glagolyev's son*), Joe Gladwin (*Marko, a messenger*).
Producer: Cedric Messina. *Production company:* BBC TV. *Running time:* 115 minutes (approximately).
In production circa February 1971.
First shown: 23 May 1971 (BBC 1 Play of the Month).

THE BURT BACHARACH SHOW (1972) (for American TV)

[In March 1972, Rex Harrison recorded the number 'If I Could Go

224

Back' from the musical version of *Lost Horizon* at Elstree for transmission at a subsequent date not known.]

THE ADVENTURES OF DON QUIXOTE (1973) (for TV)

Director: Alvin Rakoff. *Writer:* Hugh Whitemore (*from the novel by* Miguel Cervantes *as translated by* J. M. Cohen). *Photographer* (colour)*:* Peter Bartlett. *Production designer:* Austen Spriggs. *Editor:* Dave King. *Music composer:* Michel Legrand.

Cast: Rex Harrison (*Don Quixote*), Frank Finlay (*Sancho Panza*), Rosemary Leach (*Dulcinea*), Bernard Hepton (*The Priest*), Ronald Lacey (*The Barber*), Roger Delgado (*The Monk*), Robert Eddison (*The Duke*), Gwen Nelson (*The Housekeeper*), Murray Melvin (*Travelling barber*), Paul Whitsun Jones (*First landlord*), Brian Coburn (*First muleteer*), Athol Coats (*Second muleteer*), John Hollis (*First prisoner*), Walter Sparrow (*Second prisoner*), Brian Spink (*Death*), Michael Golden (*Second landlord*), Françoise Pascal (*Harlot*), Jon C. P. Mattocks (*Goatherd*).
Producer: Gerald Savory. *Production companies:* BBC Television, Universal. *Running time:* 115 minutes (approximately).
Filmed on the plains of La Mancha in Spain during the summer of 1972.
First shown: 7 January 1973 (BBC 1, Great Britain), 23 April 1973 (CBS, United States).

SHORT STORIES OF LOVE (1974) (for American TV)

Presenter: Rex Harrison. *Music:* David Shire.

Epicac
Director: John Badham. *Writer:* Liam O'Brien (*from the story by* Kurt Vonnegut Jr). *Photographer* (colour)*:* Jacques R. Marquette. *Art director:* Raymond Beal. *Editor:* Henry Batista.
Cast: Julie Sommars (*Patricia*), Bill Bixby (*William*), Roscoe Lee Brown (*Mr Secretary*), David Scheiner (*Ed*).

Kiss Me Again, Stranger
Director: Arnold Laven. *Writer:* Arthur Dales (*from the story by*

Daphne du Maurier). *Photographer* (colour): Harry Wolf. *Art director:* Robert Luthardt. *Editor:* Jean J. Berthelot.
Cast: Leonard Nimoy (*Mick*), Juliet Mills (*Usherette*), Donald Moffat (*Fred*), Diana Webster (*Doris*).

The Fortunate Painter
Director: Jeannot Szwarc. *Writer:* John T. Kelly (*from the story by* W. Somerset Maugham). *Photographer* (colour): Ralph Woolsey. *Art director:* Alexander Mayer. *Editor:* George O. Hanian.
Cast: Lorne Green (*Hercule*), Agnes Moorehead (*Hercule's wife*), Lloyd Bochner (*David*), Alan Hale Jr (*Walter*), Jess Walton (*Angelique*), Lawrence Casey (*Charlie*).
Producer: Herbert Hirschman. *Executive producer:* William Sackheim. *Production company:* Universal Television.
First transmission: 1 May 1974 (NBC).

THE PRINCE AND THE PAUPER (1977)
American release title: **Crossed Swords**

Director: Richard Fleischer. *Writer:* George MacDonald Fraser (*from an original screenplay by* Berta Dominguez *and* Pierre Spengler *based on the story* The Prince and the Pauper *by* Mark Twain). *Photographer* (Technicolor, Panavision): Jack Cardiff. *Production designer:* Anthony Pratt. *Art directors:* Jack Stephens, Maurice Fowler, John Hoesli. *Editor:* Ernest Walter. *Music composer:* Maurice Jarre.

Cast: Oliver Reed (*Miles Hendon*), Raquel Welch (*Edith*), Mark Lester (*Tom Canty/Prince Edward*), Ernest Borgnine (*John Canty*), George C. Scott (*The Ruffler*), Rex Harrison (*Duke of Norfolk*), David Hemmings (*Hugh Hendon*), Charlton Heston (*King Henry VIII*), Harry Andrews (*Hertford*), Murray Melvin (*De Brie*), Sybil Danning (*Mother Canty*), Felicity Dean (*Lady Jane*), Lalla Ward (*Princess Elizabeth*), Julian Orchard (*St John*), Graham Stark (*Jester*), Preston Lockwood (*Father Andrew*), Arthur Hewlett (*Fat man*), Tommy Wright (*Constable*), Harry Fowler (*Nipper*), Richard Hurndall (*Archbishop Cranmer*), Dan Meaden (*First guard*), Tyrone Cassidy (*Second guard*), Don Henderson (*Burly ruffian*), Sydney Bromley (*Peasant*), Ruth Madoc (*Moll*), Dudley Sutton (*Hodge*), Roy Evans (*Night owl*), William Lawford (*Mandrake*), Peter O'Farrell (*Linklight*), Anthony Sharp (*Dr Buttes*), Peter Cellier (*Mean man*), Andrew Lodge (*Captain of the*

Guard), Igor De Savitch (*Master of Music*), Dervis Ward (*Forester*),
Michael Ripper (*Edith's servant*), Jacques Le Carpentier (*Giant*).
Producer: Pierre Spengler. *Executive producers:* Ilya Salkind,
Alexander Salkind. *Production company:* International, for Film
Trust. *Distributor:* 20th Century-Fox. *Running time:* 121 minutes.
Filming started 17 May 1976 at Penshurst, Kent, and continued in
Budapest, Hungary, until August 1976.
First shown: 2 June 1977 (Carlton, Haymarket, London). *American
premiere:* 2 March 1978 (Radio City Music Hall, New York).

SHALIMAR (1978)

Director and writer: Krishna Shah (*from a screen story by* Stanford
Sherman *and* Krishna Shah) (*dialogue of Hindi version by* Kadar Khan).
Photographer (Technicolor, Panavision): Harvey Genkins. *2nd unit
director and photographer:* Ernest Day. *Director of video sequences:*
Kumar Vasudev. *Additional photography:* K. Ramanlal. *Art director:*
Ram Yedekar. *Editors:* Teddy Darvas, (*Hindi version*) Amit Bose.
Music composer: R. D. Burman. *Costumes:* Bhanu Athaiya.

Cast: Rex Harrison (*Sir John Locksley*), Sylvia Miles (*Countess
Rasmussen*), John Saxon (*Col. Columbus*), Dharmendra (*Captain S. S.
Kumar*), Zeenat Aman (*Sheila Enders*), O. P. Ralhan (*Romeo K. P. W.
Ayyangar*), Shammi Kapoor (*Dr Bukhari*), Dr Shriram Lagoo
(*Tolaram*), Aruna Irani (*Dance teacher*), Clyde Chai-Fa (*Dogro*), M. B.
Shetty (*Tribal chief*), Jaya Malini and Anita (*Tribal dancers*), Premnath
(*Raja Bahadur Singh*).
Producer: Suresh Shah. *Executive producer:* Ranveer Singh. *Associate
producer:* Bhupendra Shah. *Production companies:* Laxmi (Bombay),
Judson (New York). *Running time (English version):* 85 minutes
(approximately).
Filming started mid-September 1977 on locations in the states of
Karnataka (including the Maharajah's Palace at Bangalore),
Tamilnadu and Maharashtra, and continued at Chamundeswari
Studios in Bangalore and at Mehboob Studios in Bombay, finishing
in late November 1977.
First shown (Hindi version): circa December 1978 (India).

227

ASHANTI (1979)

Director: Richard Fleischer. *Writer:* Stephen Geller (*from the novel* Ebano *by* Alberto Vasquez-Figueroa). *Photographer* (Technicolor, Panavision): Aldo Tonti. *Production designers:* Mario Chiari, Aurelio Crugnola, Kuli Sander. *Editor:* Ernest Walter. *Music composer:* Michael Melvoin.

Cast: Michael Caine (*Dr David Linderby*), Omar Sharif (*Prince Hassan*), Peter Ustinov (*Suleiman*), Rex Harrison (*Brian Walker*), Beverly Johnson (*Dr Anansa Linderby*), Kabir Bedi (*Malik*), William Holden (*Jim Sandell*), Zia Mohyeddin (*Djamil*), Winston Ntshona (*Ansok*), Tariq Yunus (*Faid*), Tyrone Jackson (*Dongoro*), Akosua Busia (*Senoufo girl*), Jean-Luc Bideau (*Marcel*), Olu Jacobs (*Commissioner Batak*), Johnny Sekka (*Captain Bradford*), Marne Maitland (*Touareg Chief*), Eric Pohlmann (*Zeda El-Kabir*), Harry Araten (*Slave dealer*), Jack Cohen (*German at slave market*), Jay Koller (*Buyer at slave market*), Enzo Patti (*Pearl dealer*), Ori Levi (*Hotel attendant*).
Producer: Georges-Alain Vuille. *Executive producer:* Luciano Sacripanti. *Associate producer:* John C. Vuille. *Production companies:* Beverly/GAV. *Distributor:* Columbia. *Running time:* 117 minutes. *Filmed* in Kenya and Israel.
First shown: 25 January 1979 (Odeon, Leicester Square, London). *American release* (through Warner Bros.): April 1979.

THE 5TH MUSKETEER (1979)

Director: Ken Annakin. *Writer:* David Ambrose (*from the screenplay for the 1939 production of* The Man in the Iron Mask *by* George Bruce *based on the novel by* Alexandre Dumas). *Photographer* (Eastmancolor): Jack Cardiff. *Production designer:* Elliot Scott. *Art director:* Theo Harisch. *Editor:* Malcolm Cooke. *Music composer:* Riz Ortolani.

Cast: Beau Bridges (*King Louis XIV/Philippe*), Sylvia Kristel (*Marie-Thérèse*), Ursula Andress (*Madame de la Vallière*), Cornel Wilde (*D'Artagnan*), Ian McShane (*Fouquet*), Lloyd Bridges (*Aramis*), Alan Hale Jr (*Porthos*), Jose Ferrer (*Athos*), Helmut Dantine (*Spanish Ambassador*), Rex Harrison (*Colbert*), Olivia de Havilland (*Queen Anne*), Roman Ariznavarreta, Bernard Bresslaw, Stephen Bastian, Victor Couzin, Karl Ferth, Fritz V. Friedl, Christine Glasner, Fritz

Goblirsch, Erhart Hartmann, Bill Horrigan, Michael Janisch, Cissy
Kraner, Elizabeth Neumann-Viertel, Heinz Nick, Ingrid Olofson,
Stephan Paryla, Albert Reuprecht, Ute Rumm, Tony Smart, Robert
Werner, Heinz Winter.
Producer: Ted Richmond. *Executive producer:* Heinz Lazek. *Production
companies:* Sascha/Wien Films, Ted Richmond Productions.
Distributor (United States): Columbia. *Running time:* 103 minutes.
Filmed from 20 October 1976 under the title *Behind the Iron Mask* in
and around Vienna.
Generally released (United States): September 1979.

THE KINGFISHER (1982) (for British TV)

Director: James Cellan Jones. *Writer:* William Douglas Home (*from his
stage play*). *Photographer* (colour): Richard Crafter. *Designer:* Spencer
Chapman. *Editor:* Keith Judge.

Cast: Rex Harrison (*Sir Cecil*), Wendy Hiller (*Lady Evelyn Thornton*),
Cyril Cusack (*Hawkins*), Gary Owen (*Chauffeur*).
Producer: John Rosenberg. *Executive producer:* John Woolf. *Production
company:* Anglia Television. *Running time:* 90 minutes (with breaks).
Filmed at Hunworth, Norfolk.
First shown: 23 December 1982 (ITV network).

A TIME TO DIE (1983)

Directors: Matt Cimber [Matteo Ottaviano], (*additional scenes and
action sequences*) Joe Tornatore. *Writers:* John Goff, Matt Cimber,
William Russell (*from a story by* Mario Puzo). *Photographers* (CFI
colour): Eddy van der Enden, Tom Denove, (*2nd unit*) Nicholas von
Sternberg. *Art directors:* Frank Rosen, John G. Thompson. *Editors:*
Byron 'Buzz' Brandt, Fred Chulack. *Music composers:* Robert O.
Ragland, Ennio Morricone.

Cast: Rex Harrison (*Klaus von Osten*), Rod Taylor (*Jack Bailey*),
Edward Albert Jr (*Michael Rogan*), Raf Vallone (*Genco Bari*), Linn
Stokke (*Dora*), Cor Van Rijn (*Vrost*), Herbert Mittendorf (*Sandor
Lakatosh*), Tom Van Beek (*John Schmidt*), Tim Beekman (*Hans
Friesling*), Rijk De Gooyer (*Karl*), Ferd Hugas (*Eric Friesling*), Lucie

229

Visser (*Charlene Rogan*), Charles Brown (*Herman*), Johan Hobo (*Schmidt's bodyguard*), Marlies Van Alcmaer (*Marci Von Osten*), Dorothy Puzo (*Prostitute*), Joe Dante and Red Horton (*Bodyguards*). *Producer:* Charles Lee. *Associate producers:* Edward Albert Jr, Su Mi Lee, Alexander Tabrizi. *Production company:* Carnation International Pictures. *Distributor (United States):* Almi. *Running time:* 91 minutes. *Filmed* from 1 September 1979 in Holland and Italy as *Mario Puzo's Seven Graves for Rogan*.
Generally released (United States): circa September 1983.

230

Bibliography

Agee, James, *Agee On Film* (New York, McDowell, Obolensky, 1958).

Aherne, Brian, *A Proper Job* (Boston, Houghton Mifflin, 1969).

Behlmer, Rudy, 'Rex Harrison' (*Films in Review*, December 1965).

Brown, Geoff, *Launder and Gilliat* (London, British Film Institute, 1977).

Clarens, Carlos, *George Cukor* (London, Secker and Warburg in association with the British Film Institute).

Coveney, Michael, 'Harrison Rex' (*Plays and Players*, March 1974).

Curtis, James, *Between Flops: A Biography of Preston Sturges* (New York and London, Harcourt Brace Jovanovich, 1982).

Dunne, John Gregory, *The Studio* (London, Jonathan Cape, 1969).

Harrison, Elizabeth, *Love, Honour and Dismay* (London, Weidenfeld and Nicolson, 1976).

Harrison, Rex, 'Why I Left Hollywood' (*Picturegoer*, 5 and 12 August 1950).

Harrison, Rex, *Rex* (London, Macmillan, 1974).

Harrison, Rex, *If Love Be Love, Poems and Prose Chosen by Rex Harrison* (London, W.H. Allen, 1979).

Heston, Charlton, *The Actor's Life, Journals 1956–1976* (Harmondsworth, Middlesex, Penguin Books, 1980).

Hodson, Gillian, and Darlow, Michael, *Terence Rattigan: The Man and His Work* (Quartet Books, 1979).

Hotchner, A. E., *Doris Day: Her Own Story* (London, W.H. Allen, 1976).

Kendall, Henry, *I Remember Romano's* (London, MacDonald, 1960).

Lambert, Gavin, *On Cukor* (London, W.H. Allen, 1973).

Lerner, Alan Jay, *The Street Where I Live* (New York and London, W. W. Norton & Company, 1978).

Lockhart, Freda Bruce, 'Success Comes to Rex Harrison' (*Film Weekly*, 25 December 1937).

McVay, Douglas, *The Musical Film* (London, A. Zwemmer, 1979).

Palmer, Lilli, *Change Lobsters and Dance* (London, W.H. Allen, 1976).

Parish, James Robert, and Stanke, Don E., *The Debonairs* (New Rochelle, New York, Arlington House, 1975).

Rosenberg, Bernard, and Silverstein, Harry, *The Real Tinsel* (New York, The Macmillan Company, 1970).

Sheppard, Dick, *Elizabeth: The Life and Career of Elizabeth Taylor* (London, W.H. Allen, 1975).

Walker, Alexander, *No Bells on Sunday: The Journals of Rachel Roberts* (London, Pavilion Books/Michael Joseph, 1984).

Wanger, Walter, and Hyams, Joe, *My Life with Cleopatra* (London, Corgi, 1963).

Windeler, Robert, *Julie Andrews* (London, W.H. Allen, 1982).

Index

Abraham Lincoln 13, 172
Adams, Edie 133
Adventures of Don Quixote, The
   148–9, 225
After All 15, 174
Agate, James 14
Agee, James 51
Agony and the Ecstasy, The 130–2,
   221
Aherne, Brian 97, 126
Albery, Bronson 23
Albert, Edward, Jr 159
Alibi 172
All About Eve 111, 113
All at Sea 16–17, 196
Allen, Gene 126
Allers, Franz 94, 121
Allgood, Sara 24, 25
Aman, Zeenat 156
Anderson, Lindsay 158
Anderson, Maxwell 73, 77
Andress, Ursula 154
Andrews, Dana 61
Andrews, Julie 91, 93, 96, 97, 99,
   100, 119, 121, 126, 138
Androcles and the Lion 82
Anna and the King of Siam 55–8, 65,
   72, 114, 205
Anne of the Thousand Days 73, 75,
   77–8, 85, 145, 178

Another Language 15
Anouilh, Jean 102
Anthony and Anna 16, 175
Aren't We All? 167–9, 192
Armstrong, Louis 97
Armstrong, William 12, 13
Ashanti 157–8, 228
Ashley, Elizabeth 155
Asquith, Anthony 33, 41, 129
Attenborough, Richard 107, 136
August for the People 107, 109, 110,
   186
Aylmer, Felix 18, 64

Banks, Leslie 17, 38, 87
Barker, The 167
Barker, Ronald 89
Barker, Vere 37
Barnes, Barry K. 26
Barrie, J. M. 13, 82
Barry, John 148
Bataille Silencieuse, La 34
Beaton, Cecil 126, 162
Beecham, Sir Thomas 65
Behlmer, Rudy 96
Behrman, S. N. 44
Bell, Book and Candle 2, 81–2, 89–90,
   93, 180, 181
Bergen, Edgar 67
Blithe Spirit 46–7, 60, 74, 202

Bogart, Humphrey 64
Boyd, Dorothy 15
Boyd, Stephen 109
Boy Friend, The 92
Bracken, Eddie 67
Bradley-Dyne, Michael 144
Brahms, Caryl 105
Brandon-Thomas, Jevan 13
Brass Monkey, The 73
Brent, Romney 27, 28
Bricusse, Leslie 134, 137, 146
Bridges, Beau 154
Bridges, Lloyd 154
Brighouse, Harold 13
Bright One, The 101, 184
Britannia Mews 61
Britton, Tony 164
Brogger, Frederick 151
Brook, Peter 102, 103
Browne, Coral 18, 90
Browne, E. Martin 79
Bruce Lockhart, Freda 18, 22, 25
Brynner, Yul 101, 161
Bujold, Genevieve 78
Burt Bacharach Show, The 224
Burton, Richard 78, 110, 111, 112, 113, 117, 126, 140, 142, 161

Caesar and Cleopatra 78, 114, 155, 188
Cagney, James 58, 118
Caine, Michael 157, 158
Camelot 110, 138, 161
Campbell, Judy 101
Capra, Frank 24
Capucine 133
Carey, Joyce 18
Carey, Olive 46
Casanova's Homecoming 143–4
Cervantes, Miguel 148
Champion, Gower 139
Charity Begins 17, 176
Charley's Aunt 13, 172
Charon, Jacques 139
Chekhov, Anton 86, 105, 147
Chinese Bungalow, The 13, 172
Christmas Carol, A 143
Churchill, Diana 27, 28
Citadel, The 31–2, 198

Clements, John 38
Cleopatra 109–15, 117, 119, 130, 217
Clyde, June 27, 28
Cocktail Party, The 79–80, 180
Colbert, Claudette 104, 158, 167, 168, 169
Colman, Ronald 21
Compton, Fay 47
Condon, Richard 106
Constant Husband, The 88–9, 97, 212
Cooper, Gary 32
Cooper, Gladys 101
Coote, Robert 87, 94, 99
Cordell, Cathleen 17
Cormack, Bartlett 30
Cornell, Katharine 44
Coveney, Michael 85
Coward, Noel 32, 46, 47, 92
Crawford, Joan 104
Crescendo 96–7, 213
Cromwell, John 56, 57
Cronin, A. J. 32
Cronyn, Hume 82
Cukor, George 118, 119, 120, 124, 125, 126, 143, 144
Culver, Roland 23, 33, 54, 73
Cummings, Constance 46, 47
Cummins, Peggy 55, 62, 63, 64
Cup of Kindness, A 13, 172
Cusack, Cyril 164

Dane, Clemence 30
Dantine, Helmut 154
Dare, Zena 99
da Rimini, Francesca 67, 68
Dark Lady of the Sonnets, The 78–80, 179
Dark Passage 64
Dark Waters 104
Darling Lili 138
Darnell, Linda 67
Datchet Diamonds, The 103, 215
Davis, Bette 142
Davis, Tyrell 16
Dawson, Anthony 80
Day, Doris 103, 104, 105
Dear Arthur 103, 215
Dee, Sandra 99
De Hartog, Jan 82

234

De Havilland, Olivia 154
de Nagy, Kate 34
Dennis, Nigel 107, 110, 111
Design for Living 32–3, 37, 177
Devine, George 34, 105, 110
Dexter, John 165
Dharmendra 156, 157
Dick, Mrs R. A. 58
Dickens, Charles 143, 146
Doctor Dolittle 134–8, 143, 153, 222
Doctor Knock 172
Donat, Robert 32
Donen, Stanley 101, 142
Donlevy, Brian 67
Double Life, A 21
Douglas, Robert 29
Drew, Ellen 33
Dumas, Alexandre 154
du Maurier, Sir Gerald 2, 3, 61
Dunne, Irene 56, 57
Dunne, John Gregory 134
Dunne, Philip 58, 61, 130
Dyer, Charles 140, 141

Eggar, Samantha 107, 136, 137
Eliot, T. S. 79, 80, 85
Emperor Henry IV 149–51, 187
Enrico IV 149–52
Ervine, St John G. 16
Escape 61–4, 73, 81, 111, 207
Evans, Dame Edith 90
Evans, Maurice 90

Fabulous Fifties, The 103, 214
Ferrer, Jose 154
Feydeau, Jacques 139
Fiddick, Peter 147, 148
5th Musketeer, The 154, 228
Fighting Cock, The 102–3, 185
Finch, Peter 109
Findlater, Richard 165
Finney, Albert 139, 146
Flea in Her Ear, A 139–40, 143, 223
Fleischer, Richard 134, 157
Flemyng, Robert 23, 103
Fonda, Henry 67, 146
Fonda, Peter 146
Fontanne, Lynn 32, 81
Forbidden Street 61

For the Love of Mike 15, 174
Four Poster, The 82–4, 209
Fox, Edward 151
Foxes of Harrow, The 60–1, 73, 206
Francis, Kay 18
Franken, Rose 15
Freed, Arthur 117, 121
Freeland, Thornton 27, 29
French, Harold 23, 32, 41, 44
French Without Tears 23, 30, 32, 33, 46, 54, 73, 78, 129, 177
Fresnay, Pierre 34
Fry, Christopher 84, 85

Gable, Clark 26, 60
Galsworthy, John 13, 61, 62, 64
Garfield, John 48
Garland, Patrick 154, 155, 161, 162
Gavin, John 104
Genevieve 97
Genn, Leo 35
Gestapo 38
Getting George Married 14, 173
Get Your Man 15, 195
Ghost and Mrs Muir, The 58–60, 61, 84, 97, 111, 206
Gielgud, Sir John 3, 107
Gilliat, Sidney 38, 39, 50, 51, 88, 89
Give Me Your Heart 18
Godfather, The 159
Gold 13, 172
Golden Drama 220
Goldman, William 130
Goodbye Mr Chips 38, 138–9
Gone with the Wind 26, 60
Goodner, Carol 16, 18
Gough, Michael 168
Graeme, Bruce 34
Grant, Cary 118, 119
Great Game, The 14, 194
Great McGinty, The 67
Greene, Graham 106, 107
Greene, Richard 55
Greenwood, Joan 152
Grimes, Tammy 103
Guinness, Alec 79
Gullan, Campbell 14, 17
Gun Crazy 63
Guthrie, Tyrone 17

Gwynne, Michael 101

Hail the Conquering Hero 71
Half a Sixpence 138
Hammerstein II, Oscar 58, 91
Hammond, Kay 23, 46, 47
Hans le Marin 77
Hale, Alan, Jr 154
Happy Thieves, The 106, 216
Hardwicke, Sir Cedric 78
Harley, Francis 55
Harris (Harrison), Elizabeth 7, 146,
    149, 150, 152–3
Harris, Julie 152
Harris, Richard 146
Harris, Rosemary 139, 165, 166
Harrison, Carey 46, 169
Harrison, Cathryn 169
Harrison, Noel 16, 169
Harrison, William Reginald 11
Hart, Moss 94
Hartnell, William 64
Harvey, Laurence 87, 88
Harwood, H. M. 87
Hawtrey, Sir Charles 2
Hayward, Susan 133, 134
Hayworth, Rita 106
Heartbreak House 165–6, 191
Henreid, Paul 38, 40
Hepburn, Audrey 121, 123, 124,
    125, 126
Heroes Don't Care 18–19, 176
Heston, Charlton 130, 131, 132, 153
Hicks, Sir Seymour 2
Hiller, Wendy 41, 42, 44, 91, 151,
    164
Hitchcock, Alfred 21, 38
Hobson, Valerie 34
Holden, William 158
Holloway, Baliol 14
Holloway, Stanley 94, 97, 99, 119
Home, William Douglas 97, 158
Honey Pot, The 132–4, 156, 221
Hopkins, George James 126
Hopkins, Miriam 21, 22, 32
Hopper, Hedda 72, 74, 78, 97
Hordern, Michael 90
Howard, Leslie 26, 41, 92, 125
Howard, Trevor 23, 109

Howard, William K. 29
Howes, Bobby 15
Hughes, Howard 82
Hulbert, Jack 27
Hulme, George 145
Hunter, Ian 79
Hurleberlu, L' 102–3
Huth, Angela 146
Hyde-White, Wilfrid 120

Ibsen, Henrik 4
Ides of March, The 111
I Live in Grosvenor Square 48–9, 203
In Praise of Love 152, 187
I Remember Romano's 17
Irma La Douce 140

Jacobs, Arthur P. 134, 138, 139
Jagger, Dean 48
Jayston, Michael 146
Jenkins, Roy 144
Johnson, Celia 158
Johnson, Nunnally 80
Johnston, Arthur 31
Johnston, Margaret 50, 51, 52
Jonson, Ben 4, 5, 132
Journey Together 203
Julius Caesar 111

Kapoor, Shammi 156
Kean, Edmund 11
Kendall, Kay 5, 6, 8, 88, 97–8,
    101–2, 106, 152
Kendall, Henry 15, 17, 27, 28
Kennedy, Cheryl 162, 165
Kerr, Deborah 3, 58, 77
Killing of Sister George, The 142
King and I, The 58, 161
Kingfisher, The 158, 162, 164–5, 166,
    189, 229
King Lear 152
King Richard and the Crusaders 87–8,
    118, 212
Kingsford, Walter 154
Kinski, Nastassja 72
Kiss for Cinderella, A 172
Kiss Me Goodnight 27
Korda, Alexander 19, 21, 26, 27, 28,
    73

236

Kramer, Stanley 82
Kreuger, Kurt 68
Kristel, Sylvia 154
Kutz, Irma 3

Lady Liza 91
Lady Vanishes, The 38
Landis, Carole 7, 72–4
Landon, Margaret 55
Lange, Hope 60
Laughton, Charles 30, 31, 78
Launder, Frank 38, 39, 50, 51, 89
Lawrence, Gertrude 21, 167
Lawrence of Arabia 119
Laye, Evelyn 17
Lean, David 42, 46
Leave It to Blanche 15, 195
Leggatt, Alison 79
Leigh, Vivien 23, 25, 26, 30, 31, 114
Leighton, Margaret 79, 89
Lerner, Alan Jay 5, 6, 7, 79, 91, 92, 94, 95, 110, 119, 121, 122, 134, 136, 148
Lester, Mark 153
Lewin, David 6
Links 172
Lionel Touch, The 145–6, 150, 186
Living Room, The 107
Lockwood, Margaret 39, 40
Loder, John 34
Loewe, Frederick 6, 91, 92, 93, 94, 95, 110
Lofting, Hugh 134, 136, 138
Lom, Herbert 55
Long Dark Hall, The 80–1, 209
Lonsdale, Frederick 167
Love of Four Colonels, The 86–7, 181
Low, Bill 93
Lubitsch, Ernst 32
Lunt, Alfred 32, 81
Lynn, Ralph 2
Lyon, Ben 55

MacLaine, Shirley 146
MacMurray, Fred 67
Macrae, Arthur 90
Magee, Patrick 140
Main Street to Broadway 85–6, 211
Major Barbara 41–4, 151, 201

Mamoulian, Rouben 109
Man from UNCLE, The 157
Man in Possession 87, 211
Man in the Iron Mask, The 154
Mankiewicz, Joseph L. 5, 58, 61, 63, 109, 110, 111, 113, 115, 132
Mann, Roderick 6, 164
Man of La Mancha 148
Man of Yesterday 17, 175
Man Who Knew Too Much, The 21
March, Fredric 32
Mario Puzo's Seven Graves for Rogan 159
Marriott, R. B. 155
Marshall, George 106
Marshall, Herbert 15
Marshall, Sarah 103
Martin, Mel 165
Mary Poppins 119, 120
Mason, James 55, 56, 58, 65, 74, 148
Masquerade 130
Matthews, A. E. 17, 22
Matthews, Francis 168
Maurey, Nicole 88
Mayo, Virginia 87
Men Are Not Gods 21–2, 25, 30, 31, 196
Merivale, John 84
McDowall, Roddy 104
McShane, Ian 154
McVay, Douglas 126
Michell, Keith 155
Middleton, Guy 23, 33
Midnight Lace 103–5, 215
Midsummer Night's Dream, A 12
Mielziner, Jo 77
Miles, Sarah 147
Milestones 172
Miles, Sylvia 156, 157
Milland, Ray 33, 92
Miller, David 104
Minnelli, Vincente 6
Miracle of Morgan's Creek, The 67, 71
Molière (Jean-Baptiste Poquelin) 4, 5
Molnar, Ferenc 103
Montgomery, Robert 26
Moore, Dudley 71

Monsieur Perrichon's Travels 154–5, 161, 188
Moreau, Jeanne 129, 130
Morley, Robert 17, 41, 42, 44, 48
Morley, Sheridan 165
Mortimer, John 139, 151
Most Dangerous Game, The 157
Mother of Pearl 15, 174
Mrs Miniver 49
Mr Smith Goes to Washington 25
Mulhare, Edward 60, 97, 103
My Fair Lady 1, 5, 6, 31, 91–7, 99–101, 102, 117–27, 132, 134, 136, 137, 143, 150, 161, 163, 182, 183, 190, 218

Nabokov, Vladimir 148
Nathan, George Jean 81
Neagle, Anna 48, 49, 54, 164
Neal, Patricia 115
Nesbitt, Cathleen 162
Nicholas and Alexandra 146
Night Train to Munich 38–41, 50, 58, 201
Nina 90, 182
Ninth Man, The 14, 21, 173
Norman, Barry 4
No Time for Comedy 44–5, 178
Notorious Gentleman, The 56
Not Quite A Lady 17, 175
Novak, Kim 90
No Way Back 15, 16, 174
Nowhere Girl 146, 147

Oberon, Merle 28, 104
O'Hara, Maureen 61
Old English 13, 172
Oldest Confession, The 106
Olivier, Laurence 44, 84, 151
Omnibus 85
Once A Thief 106
Once More With Feeling 101
O'Neill, Eugene 13
Only Game in Town, The 140, 141
Osborn, Andrew 41
Osborne, John 144
O'Shea, Milo 140
Other Men's Wives 15, 174
O'Toole, Peter 119, 126, 139, 148

Our Mutual Father 15, 174
Our Theatres in the Nineties 155–6, 161, 189
Over the Moon 28–9, 32, 199

Page, Anthony 166
Pagett, Nicola 168, 169
Palmer, Lilli 7, 8, 38, 45, 52, 55, 56, 73, 74, 78, 80, 81, 82, 83, 84, 85, 86, 87, 89, 97, 152
Paradise for Two 27
Parker, Cecil 13, 24, 25, 32, 47
Parry, Natasha 103, 104
Parsons, Louella 72, 74, 82
Pascal, Gabriel 41, 44, 82, 91
Patrick, Nigel 17
Peace In Our Time 33
Phillips, Sian 147
Pimpernel Smith 41
Pirandello, Luigi 149
Platonov 105, 106, 147–8, 185, 224
Playboy, The 27
Plummer, Christopher 135
Poitier, Sidney 115
Pola, Eddie 31
Pommer, Erich 30
Portman, Eric 107
Portrait of Jennie 60
Potiphar's Wife 13, 172
Potter, H. C. 77
Powell, Michael 107
Power, Tyrone 16
Previn, Andre 121, 126
Price, Stanley 145
Pride of Lions 46
Prince and the Pauper, The 153–4, 226
Purdom, Edmund 129
Pursall, David 146
Pygmalion 5, 41, 91, 92, 125

Quayle, Anthony 144, 145
Quinn, Anthony 126

Rabb, Ellis 155
Radford, Basil 15, 38
Rainer, Luise 26
Rake's Progress, The 18, 49–54, 55, 89, 152, 204
Rakoff, Alvin 148, 151

238

Ramsden, Frances 67
Random Harvest 49
Rank, J. Arthur 74
Rattigan, Terence 23, 129, 152
Real Tinsel, The 110
Redgrave, Lynn 169
Redgrave, Michael 92
Redgrave, Vanessa 146
Redman, Joyce 77, 78, 145
Reed, Carol 38, 39, 130
Reisch, Walter 21
Reluctant Debutante, The 6, 97–9, 214
Remember the Night 67
Return of the Scarlet Pimpernel, The 26
Richard III 14, 172
Richardson, Ralph 158
Rigg, Diana 165, 166
Right Honourable Gentleman, The 144
Riscoe, Arthur 15, 27
Road House, The 15, 174
Roberts, Rachel 5, 8, 105–6, 107, 115, 119, 133, 139, 143, 145, 146, 147
Robertson, Cliff 130, 133
Robertson, Liz 7, 164
Robinson, Edward G. 80
Robson, Flora 107
Rodgers, Richard 58, 91
Rogell, Sid 111
Rose, George 158
Ross, Herbert 139
Rossini, Gioacchino 67, 68
Roussin, André 90
Rutherford, Margaret 46, 47

Sanders, George 87
Sanders-Clark, Robin 66, 67
Saroyan, William 85
Saturday Night Revue 79
Saville, Victor 23, 26, 32
Saxon, John 99, 156, 157
Scarlet Pimpernel, The 26
Scofield, Paul 140, 142
School for Scandal, The 14, 56, 194
School for Husbands 27–8, 197
Scott, Sir Walter 87
Scrooge 146
Secret Fury, The 104

Seddon, Jack 146
Sellers, Peter 71, 126
Selznick, David O. 60
Semiramide 66, 67, 68
Shaffer, Anthony 145
Shah, Krishna 157
Shakespeare, William 4, 5, 14, 86, 102
Shalimar 156–7, 160, 227
Shamroy, Leon 130
Shaw, George Bernard 5, 13, 41, 42, 78, 79, 82, 91, 92, 94, 122, 125, 155, 156, 161, 165
Shaw, Sebastian 13, 15, 21, 22
Sheridan, Richard Brinsley 14
Short Stories of Love 225
Short Story 17, 175
Sim, Alastair 151
Simon, Michel 34
Silent Battle, The 33–4, 199
Simpson, Ronald 15
Sinden, Donald 152
Skouras, Spyros 110, 113
Sleep My Love 104
Smilin' Through 60
Smith, Maggie 133
Something About Anne 144
Sound of Music, The 120, 135
Staircase 140–2, 143, 223
Star! 138
Star is Born, A 118
Stewart, James 45, 90
St Martins Lane 30–1, 66, 198
Storey, Anthony 144
Storm in a Teacup 23–6, 30, 197
Stott, Catherine 141
Stradling, Harry 126
Sturges, Preston 65, 67, 68, 69, 70, 71
Sudden Fear 104
Sutherland, Donald 147, 148
Suzman, Janet 146
Swanson, Gloria 90
Sweet Aloes 17–18, 176

Tagg, Alan 158
Talisman, The 87
Taming of the Shrew, The 102
Tandy, Jessica 82

Tannhäuser-Venusberg 67, 68
Taylor, Elizabeth 109, 110, 111, 113, 114, 118, 155
Tchaikovsky, Peter Ilich 67, 68
Tearle, Godfrey 50
Tempest, Marie 17
Ten Days in Paris 34–5, 200
13 Rue Madeleine 58
Thirty Minutes in a Street 12–13, 172
This Sporting Life 115
Thomas, Collette 8, 15
Thorndyke, Sybil 17
Threepenny Opera, The 79
Tierney, Gene 6, 59, 60, 67, 72
Time to Die, A 159–60, 229
Tinker, Mercia 8, 158, 162
Topper 60
Trial of Anne Boleyn 85, 210
Twain, Mark 153
Tynan, Kenneth 125

Unfaithfully Yours 64–72, 99, 208
Ustinov, Peter 86

Vallee, Rudy 68, 70
Van Druten, John 2, 15, 81, 89
Venus Observed 84–5, 86, 181
Verne, Karen 34
Vidal, Gore 103
VIPs, The 112
Volpone 132, 133
Voyage Round My Father 151

Wagner, Richard 67, 68
Wakefield, Hugh 46, 168
Walbrook, Anton 32, 33, 37

Walking Stick, The 79, 209
Wallach, Eli 140
Walsh, Kay 15
Wanger, Walter 109, 110, 111
Warner, Jack 87, 117, 118, 119
Warrender, Harold 16
Washbourne, Mona 121
Wayne, Naunton 38, 40
Wayne, Patricia 80
Weatherby, W. J. 163
Webb, Alan 33, 158
Weill, Kurt 79
Wicked Flee, The 17, 175
Wilcox, Herbert 48
Wilde, Cornel 154
Wilder, Thornton 111
Williams, Clifford 150, 151
Williams, Hugh 13
Wilson, Cecil 105
Windust, Bretaigne 77
Wodehouse, P. G. 103
Woman in the Window, The 80
Wood, Natalie 59
Wooland, Norman 64
Worsley, T. C. 147
Wright, Basil 25
Wynyard, Diana 13, 17, 32, 33, 37, 44, 45

Yellow Rolls Royce, The 129–30, 219
Yerby, Frank 60
Young, Roland 18
You of All People 38

Zanuck, Darryl F. 57, 61, 64, 65, 73, 112, 113, 140